Learn Japanese

2 manuscripts – Start Speaking Today. Absolute Beginner to Conversational Speaker Made Simple and Easy!

(Japanese Grammar 101
&
Japanese Vocabulary)

By

Languages World

Manuscript I

Japanese Grammar 101

No Boring Linguistic Jargon
No Overly Complex Explanations

The Easy To Digest, Simple Approach to Japanese

Contents

Introductionはじめに

Welcome to Japanese Grammar 101!
Grammar is the central pillar of language learning, however many students struggle learning it. New language structures, different tenses and conjugation can be intimidating.

We've heard lines like "grammar sucks", "I hate grammar" and we can understand why.
Most books out there teach grammar in a overly grammary way, that just flys over your head. There is nothing worse than being taught a new language only to be constantly stuck and confused. We don't want this!

Learning grammar shouldn't be a struggle, and a big reason why new students give up, is from being overwhelmed. When you don't understand something, making progress is near impossible.
If you've picked this book up, you're commited to improving your Japanaese grammar, so that's a great step in the right direction.

In this book we aim to overcome these problems, by teaching you grammar that focuses on giving you results – instead of getting you bored. We'll walk alongside you, so you don't get confused. No linguistic jargon that you will hardly ever use or overly complex explainations. Instead a practical approach to Japanese that will keep you wanting to learn, more and more.

So whether you are learning for business, travel or to make new friends. You can make Japanese grammar click.

About this book

This book is designed for beginner level speakers. No hard to digest sections that are difficult to understand, only bit size learning that you can manage – promise!
We aim to give you a solid grammar foundation that you can build upon. Therefore each section is based on a specific topic that builds on the previous. After each topic there will be a short exercise to test how well you have understood the section.

You may come across topics that you don't feel like skipping however stick to them, they'll become essential later in the book.

Follow these step by step and you'll be speaking Japanese in no time. And by the end of this series you'll be able to communicate with people in Japanese like never before. Trust me you'll be amazed at your results.

Grammar Learning Tips

1. Write in this book

This book is yours for life, feel free to scribble down notes and key points to remember – in fact we recommend it. Writing notes helps with long term memory and puts you in the zone, allowing everything to sink in better. Plus it's great for reference.

2. Patience equals Fluency

Many learners are so eager to learn. They rush through sections, hoping to absorb the language fast. Instead of learning quickly, they end up getting overwhelmed twice as fast. Don't fall in this trap, each section of this book is designed to build on top of the previous. Take it easy and make sure you fully understand each topic before moving on. There's no rush, learning a language takes time!

3. You don't have to know it all

We cover a lot of topics in this book, you don't need to know all of them to begin speaking Japanese. From the start you'll be learning useful phrases and structures. So we recommend, once you've studied a few sections, start putting them into practice. Don't wait until you've finished the book, learn as you go, bit by bit.

I think we've covered enough of the ground work, now let's begin learning Japanese!

Politeness Levels

敬語の使い分け（尊敬語/丁寧語/謙譲語）

One of the main parts of Japanese that's confusing as an English speaker, is politeness levels. In Japanese society politeness levels are very important to show respect and avoid being rude.

There are three types of politeness levels in Japanese:

- Informal speech
  Spoken with family and close friends

- Formal speech
  Spoken with strangers and colleagues

- Very fromal speech
  Spoken with teachers, bosses and customers

Using the incorrect politeness level is not the end of the world, however if possible, you should try and use the correct one.
Learning all three politeness levels can be very overwhelming. So we recommend to start with formal speech, as you can use this for most situations. Once you have the basics of formal speech down, using casual speech will become easier. Very formal speech is more advanced, so in this book we will be covering the informal and formal speech. These will be marked with the following:

Legend
(f) = formal speech
(inf) = informal speech

Pronunciation発音

Japanese pronunciation can be a tricky to understand, so we want to cover it in this first section.

A common mistake new learner's make is trying to pronounce Japanese characters the same was as in English. Although some character sounds remain the same, a lot are very different. So it's a good idea to get familiar with these pronunciations before you begin learning Japanese.

Vowels

Vowel in Japanese sound different to English. Have a look at the table below and practice speaking the listed words so you can get familiar with the sounds used.

Vowel	Sound	Example
a	ah as in art	akura
e	eh as in bed	eki
i	ee as in see	ichi
o	oh as in coat	odoru
u	oo as in moo	uma

Let's see the pronunciation break down

Akura = ah-koo-rah

Eki = eh-kee

Ichi = ee-chee

Odoru = oh-doh-roo

Uma = oo-mah

Double vowels

Double vowels lengthen the sound in Japanese, sometimes these are represented with a dash on top of the vowel.

Vowel	Sound	Example
aa	a as in father	okaasan
ee	e as in den	oneesan

ii	ee as in see	iiau
oo	oh as in coat	omou
uu	oo as in moo	fuun

Pronunciation breakdown:

okaasan = oh-kaa-sahn
oneesan = oh-nee-sahn
iiau = ee-ahoo
omou = oh-moou
fuun = f-oon

Keep an eye out for double vowels as meanings of words can change based on stress on the vowel:

ie = house
iie = no

Obasan = aunt
Obaasan = grandmother

Double Consonants

Whenever we have two consonants together, we need to put more stress on that character.

Gakko = school
Kitte = postal stamp
Rokku = six

Double constants meanings can also change depending on the stress applied. So make sure you look out for these aswell.

The Basics基本

Moving onto some basics, the first thing you will need to know in any language is how to greet someone.

Good morning (f)
= **Ohayo gozaimasuおはようございます**

Good afternoon
= **Konbanwaこんばんは**

Hello
= **konnichiwaこんにちは**

Goodbye (f)
= **Sayounaraさようなら**

How are you?
= **Ogenki desu ka? お元気ですか**

I'm fine
= **Genki desu元気です**

I'm not okay
= **Genki ja arimasen元気じゃありません**

So so
= **Maa maa desuまあまあです**

For informal speech, "Konnichiwaこんにちは" and "Konbanwaこんばんは" are not used, especially among friends. Instead, we call a person by their name, or simply say "Haiはい" similar to 'Hiこんにちは' in English.
Here are some examples for casual greetings.

Good Morning (inf)
= **Ohayoおはよう**

See you (inf)
= **Jyaa (ne) じゃあ（ね）/ Bai baiばいばい**

How are you? (inf)
= **Genki? 元気**

I'm fine (inf)
= **Genki元気**

I'm not fine (inf)
= **Genki janai元気じゃない**

So so (inf)
= **Maa maaまあまあ**

When talking with people you know, it's more common to ask them specific things rather than simply saying "How are you" (genki desu ka元気ですか)

To do this we can use the following pattern

Noun + wa+ do desu ka?
名詞 + は + どうですか
How is .... ?

Let's see some examples:

How is work?
= Shigoto wa do desu ka?
仕事はどうですか
(How is/are = do desu ka? どうですか)
(Work = Shigoto仕事)

How is school?
= Gakko wa do desu ka?
学校はどうですか
(How is/are = do desu ka? どうですか)
(School = Gakko学校)

In informal speech, we leave out "desu kaですか"

Example
How is work? (inf)
= Shigoto wa do?
仕事はどうですか
(How is/are = do? どう)
(Work = Shigoto仕事)

However this speech is used more with family and friends.

<u>Topic particle "waは"</u>
In the above sentence structure we use the topic particle "waは". Particles are used to modify a meaning of a word. As you learn more about Japanese, you will notice more and more particles.

This particle in placed right after the topic of the sentence. And tells the listener what the sentence is about.

We can translate this to "as for" "speaking of...."

Examples
I am tired
(as for me) I am tired
<u>Watashi wa</u> tsukare teru
私は 疲れてる
(watashi 私= I) (tired = tsukare teru疲れてる)

Where is your hometown?

(as for) your hometown where is it?
Shusshin wa doko desu ka?
出身はどこですか
(hometown = shusshin出身)
(where is it = doko desu ka? どこですか)

Waは is one of the most used particles when speaking japanese. Just remember it is used to mark a topic.

Basic Greeting

Now let's put what we have learnt together and go through a basic Japanese greeting.

Sato: Ohayo Gozaimasu

おはようございます

(Good morning)

Tanaka: Ohayo Gozaimasu

おはようございます

(Good morning)

Genki desu ka? げんきですか

(How are you?)

Sato: Hai, Genki desuはい、元気です

(I'm fine.)

Tanaka san, shigoto wa do desu ka?

田中さん、仕事はどうですか

(Mr. Tanaka, how is your work?)

Tanaka: Shigoto wa juncho desu

仕事は順調です

(Work goes well.)

Sato: Sayonaraさようなら

(Bye bye)

This is a formal greeting, if you want to make an informal greeting, simply use the casual words stated in the previous section.

Suffix "sanさん"

Something you may have noticed in the conversation is the use of the word "sanさん".

"sanさん" is used after a name to shows politeness or respect.

"sanさん" can be used for both men and women, to a family name or first name.

Mr. / Mrs. / Ms. Sato = **Sato san**

Yumi (girl's first name) = **Yumi san**

Takeshi (boy's first name) = **Takeshi san**

When talking to people who are the same age or younger we use different suffixes:

We use:
"chanちゃん" for girls
"kunくん" for boys

For example:
Yumi **chan**
Takeshi **kun**

Exercise

Highlight the topic of these sentences:

1) I am a student
2) Your dog is cute
3) I am going to the park this weekend
4) Suzuki watched tv at home

Answers

1) I am a student
Topic = I
(as for) I, am student

2) Your dog is cute
Topic = your dog
(as for) your dog, is cute

3) I am going to the park this weekend
Topic = weekend
(as for) weekend, I am going to the park

4) Suzuki watched tv at home
Topic = Suzuki
(as for) Suzuki, watched tv at home

Introductions紹介の仕方

Now let's cover some self-introductions.
When stating your name there are two ways to do this:

My name is ...
= **Watashi no namae wa + (name) + desu**
= **私の名前は+ (name) +です**

Or

I am ...
= **Watashi wa + (name) + desu**
= **私は + (name) + です**

(I = Watashi私)
(Name = Namae名前)

When using the phrase: **Watashi no namae私の名前:** "noの" is a particle to show possession. In this sentences it is used to state "the name belongs to me".
The use of particle "noの" will be explained in a later section. For now just remember "watashi no namae" as a set phrase and don't analyse it too much.

"**desuです**" is used in place of – is, am, are
We will also cover this in depth later.

Example
I am Toyota
Watashi no namae wa Toyota desu
私の名前は豊田です

Or

Watashi wa Toyota desu
私は豊田です

How to ask about someone's name

To ask someone what his/her name is, we use this phrase:

What is your name?

= Onamae wa nan desu ka?
お名前はなんですか

You can omit "nan desu kaなんですか" (what is?") and ask simply "onamae waお名前は" but this more informal.

Your name is? (inf)

= Onamae wa? お名前は

Now, to ask where he/she is from:

Where are you from?

= Susshin wa doko desu ka?
出身はどこですか

Or, informally:

Where are you from? (inf)

= Shusshin wa? 出身は

Shusshin actually translates to hometown. The literal translation is "where is your hometown?"

To answer we use this phrase:

I am from England

= Igirisu shusshin desu
イギリス出身です

(or simplified)

= **Igirisu desu**
イギリスです

(England = Igirisuイギリス)

Again, here the literal translation is "England is my hometown"
Next, to say "nice to meet you" in Japanese:

Nice to meet you / you too

= **Yoroshiku onegai shimasu**
よろしくお願いします

You too (alternative)

= **Kochira kosoこちらこそ**

"Yoroshiku onegai shimasuよろしくお願いします" can also be used in other situation because it also translates to "I am looking forward to working with you", however this is for business situations.

In the previous section we learnt "genki desu ka元気ですか?" is used to ask "how are you". But in Japanese you might find someone saying "hajimemashiteはじめまして" when they first meet you.

How do you do?

= **Hajimemashite**
はじめまして

The phrase "Hajimemashiteはじめまして" is often translated as "Nice to meet you" or "How do you do" in English.

This phrase is only used with people you have never met before. Therefore it is a first time greeting with strangers. After you have met the person and cannot say "hajimemashiteはじめまして", instead you would say "genki desu ka元気ですか".

Basic Conversation - part II

Now, let's put these phrases together and go through a basic introduction in Japanese.

Yoshida: Hajimemashiteはじめまして
(How do you do?)

Toyota: Konnichiwa, Hajimemashite
にちは、はじめまして
(Hello, how do you do?)

Yoshida: Watashi no namae wa Yoshida desu. Onamae wa?
私の名前は吉田です。お名前は
(My name is Yoshida. And your name?)

Toyota: Toyota desu. 豊田です
(I am Toyota.)

Yoshida: Shusshin wa doko desu ka?
出身はどこですか
(Where are you from?)

Toyota: Tokyo shusshin desu. Yoshida san wa?
東京出身です。吉田さんは
(I'm from Tokyo. What about you, Mr. Yoshida?)

Yoshida: Osaka shusshin desu.
大阪出身です
(I'm from Osaka.)

Toyota: So desu ka. Yorosiku onegai shimasu
そうですか。よろしくお願いします
(I see. Nice to meet you.)
[I see = so desu kaそうですか]

Yoshida: Kochirakoso yoroshiku onegai shimau

こちらこそよろしくお願いします

(You too.)

Pronouns代名詞

Now that we understand basic introductions, let's move onto covering personal subject pronouns. Simply put, it refers to words like: I, you, he etc.

I	=	Watashi私
	=	Boku/Ore 僕/俺 (masculine, inf)
You	=	Anataあなた
You (plural)	=	Anatagata あなた方 (f) Anata tachi あなた達 (inf)
He	=	Kare彼
She	=	Kanojo彼女
We	=	Watashi tachi私達
They	=	Karera彼ら

The pronouns for "he" and "she" are also used to mean "boyfriend" and "girlfriend" in Japanese, so keep an eye out for these.

In Japanese personal pronouns are rarely used when speaking. Instead we use the person's name:

~~She~~ is cute
~~Kanojo~~ wa kawaii
~~彼女~~はかわいい

=
Kim is cute
Kim san wa kawaii desu
キムさんはかわいいです

~~You~~ are tall
Miko (you) are tall
Miko san wa segatakai desu
みこさんは背が高いです

If we don't know the person's name, then we have to use these pronouns. However if you do know, it should be avoided.

<u>Common beginner mistake</u>
Many beginners, over use the word "watashi私". Japanese speakers find this very annoying.
In English we use 'I' pronoun a lot. However in Japanese "watashi" is dropped when it is clear we are talking about ourselves.

For example, if you have already said "watashi wa私は" and the conversation topic is still on you. You no longer need to use "watashi wa私は".

Examples
Watashi wa John desu私はジョンです
~~Watashi wa~~ Isha desu
~~私は~~医者です
(doctor = isha医者)

In this example we can just say "isha desu医者です" as it's already clear we are still talking about ourselves.

Once the topic changes, then we can use "watashi wa私は" again to bring the topic back to ourselves.

This can be applied to any topic we are talking about, if the topic of the conversation is still the same.

Examples

Japanese food is cheap

Nipponshoku wa yasui

日本食は安い

Japanese food is healthy

~~Nipponshoku wa~~ oishī desu

~~日本食は~~おいしいです

Demonstratives (ko-so-a-do)

指示語-（こ・そ・あ・ど）

Demonstratives refers to words, such as "this", "that", "here", "there", etc

Japanese demonstratives are very different to English. They follow the pattern ko-so-a-do. However for each case the final letters change depending on what you want to express.
Let's go through them one by one.

Unspecific demonstratives

Japanese unspecific demonstratives are followed by the letters "re" after each ko-so-a-do. The reason they're unspecific is because they do not refer to any particular noun.
The forms are:

"koreこれ", "soreそれ", "areあれ", "doreどれ"

Each of these demonstratives are used according to the distance of an object from both the speaker and listener.

Koreこれ (this)	Close to the speaker Far from the listener
Sore それ(that)	Far from the speaker Close to the listener
Areあれ (that)	Far from both speaker and listener
Dore? どれ	(Which one?)

Therefore when using unspecific demonstratives you have to judge how close an object is to you.

Let's see how this would work in a real life situation.

At a restaurant:
I want to talk about the food I've been served. In this case we would use "koreこれ" because the food I'm talking about is closer to me than the listener.

I want to talk about food my friend's been served, I would use "soreそれ" because it's closer to my friend than me.

I want to talk about something that is far from both of us, for example the outside of the restaurant, I would use "areあれ".

I want to ask, "which one is tasty" I would use "doreどれ":

For example
What is this?
Kore wa nan desu ka?
これはなんですか
(what = nanなん)

That is a sushi
Sore wa sushi desu
それは寿司です

Specific demonstratives

If we want to be specific about an item, we use the ending "no" after each ko-so-a-do word.

These word follow the same distance pattern as "koreこれ", "soreそれ", "areあれ" "doreどれ".

Konoこの (this + noun) Close to the speaker

	Far from the listener
Sonoその (that + noun)	Far from the speaker Close to the listener
Anoあの (that + noun)	Far from both speaker and listener
Dono? どの	Which (noun)

Examples

Kono Pasokon

このパソコン

= **This PC**

(pasokon = pc)

Sono Pasokon

そのパソコン

= **That PC**

(close to the listener, far from the speaker)

Ano Pasokon

あのパソコン

= **That PC**

(far from both listener and speaker)

Dono Pasokon?

どのパソコン

= **Which PC?**

From the examples you can see all demonstratives refer to a specific noun, therefore we have to use "konoこの, sonoその, anoあの, donoどの" and not "koreこれ, soreそれ, areあれ, doreどれ"

Location Demonstratives

If we want to talk about location, we can use demonstratives with the ending "ko"
These words follow the same distance pattern as "koreこれ", "soreそれ", "areあれ" "doreどれ".

Kokoここ (here)	Close to the speaker Far from the listener
Sokoそこ (there)	Close to the listener Far from the speaker
Asokoあそこ (there)	Far from both speaker and listener
Dokoどこ (where)	Location unknown

Examples

The cat is here
Neko wa **koko** ni imasu
猫はここにいます
(cat = neko猫)

The cat is there
Neko wa **soko** ni imasu
猫はそこにいます
(close to the listener, far from the speaker)

The cat is there
Neko wa **asoko** ni imasu
猫はあそこにいます
(far from both speaker and listener)

Where is the cat?
Neko wa **doko** desu ka?

猫は<u>どこ</u>ですか

The way we use these demonstratives in sentences will become clear once we reach the existence section.

<u>Direction Demonstratives</u>

When talking about directions, we can use demonstratives with the ending "chira"
These words follow the same distance pattern as "koreこれ", "soreそれ", "areあれ" "doreどれ".

Kochiraこちら (this way)	Close to the speaker Far from the listener
Sochiraそちら (that way)	Close to the listener Far from the speaker
Achiraあちら (that way over there)	Far from both speaker and listener
Dochiraどちら	Which way?

In Japanese we normally use this pattern when introducing people.
Referring to people as "this" or "that" is seen as being rude. Instead we use "this way" and "that way" which is more polite:

This is Akira
<u>Kochira</u> wa Akira desu
<u>こちら</u>は明です。
This way is Akira

Who is that person? (over there)
<u>Achira</u> wa donata desu ka?
明はどなたですか

There are more forms of ko-so-a-do words in Japanese but they are more advanced. These are the most common you will come across.

Exercise

Use the correct Demonstratives for these situations

1) "that" referring to something that is far from the speaker but close to the listener.

2) this tv
(tv = terebiテレビ)

3) here

4) "there" referring to something that is far from the listener and speaker

5) "that way" referring to something that is far from the listener but close to the speaker

Answers

1) soreそれ
2) kono terebiこのテレビ
3) kokoここ
4) asokoあそこ
5) sochiraそちら

Super Simple Structure
とても基本的な文章構造

Now that we have a basic understanding of Japanese, let's go through a very useful sentence structure.

A wa B desu
(A is B)

This expression can be used in a variety of situations, making it extremely useful for beginners. A is always a noun, while B can be a noun or an adjective.

Desu and its uses

Desu is known as "verb to be" and refers to "is" "am" "are".

Example sentence:
Watashi wa John desu
私はジョンです
(Watashi 私= I)
I am John

If we were going to translate this literally it would be:
(as for me, John am)

However when we translate this, it becomes "I am john"

Once thing to remember, desu is a polite copula and is only used in formal speech. For informal speech we would omit "desu".

Now let's look at some examples using A is B structure.

She is a university student
Kanojo wa daigakusei desu
彼女は大学生です

(Kanojo彼女 = she) (Daigakusei大学生 = university student)
As for her, university student is.

A = she
B = univeristy student

The library is quiet
Toshokan wa shizuka desu
図書館は静かです
(Toshokan 図書館= library) (Shizuka 静か= quiet)
As for the library, quiet is

A = library
B = quiet

The coffee is tasty
Koohii wa oishi desu
コーヒーはおいしいです
(Koohiiコーヒー = coffee) (Oishiiおいしい = tasty)
As for coffee, tasty is.

A = coffee
B = oishi

We can use this structure with the previous demonstratives we have learnt to form more sentences.

This is cold
Kore wa samui desu
これは寒いです
(this = koreこれ) (cold = samui寒い)

That house is big
Ano ie wa ōkī desu
あの家は大きいです
(house = ie家) (big = oki大きい)

The structure A is B desu, can also be used when saying (A am B) or (A are B).

Examples
I am a teacher
Watashi wa sensei desu
私は先生です
(I = watashi私) (teacher = sensei先生)
As for me, teacher am

*Note
In Japanese there is no indefinite article "a/an" so we just omit this.

They are fast
Karera wa hayai desu
彼らは速いです
(fast = hayai速い)

Like previously stated we can omit the subject if it is clear who we are talking about:

Examples
I am john
Watashi wa John desu
私はジョンです

I am a student
~~Watashi wa~~ gakusei desu
~~私は~~学生です
= gakusei desu 学生です

This way is Jaden
Kochira wa Jaden desu
こちらはジェーデンです

He is a doctor.
~~Kare wa~~ isha desu

~~彼は~~医者です
= isha desu医者です

If it is confusing and we want to clarify, then we can add the subject.

<u>Exercise</u>:
Translate these sentences:

1. I am American
(American = amerikajinアメリカ人)(I = watashi私)

Answer:
Watashi wa amerikajin desu
私はアメリカ人です

2. This is a library
(library = toshokan図書館)

Answer:
Sore wa toshokan desu
それは図書館です

3. Mr. Sato is a teacher
(Sato san佐藤さん = Mr. Sato) (Sensei 先生= teacher)

Answer:
Sato san wa sensei desu
佐藤さんは先生です

4. I am an office worker
(Kaishain会社員 = office worker)

Answer:
Watashi wa kaishain desu
私は会社員です

Desu Conjugationです活用形

Conjugation is when we change a verb/adjective to create a new meaning. In this section we will be conjugating the verb "desuです" to form even more sentences.

When we conjugate desu, we can make statements like:

Positive Present = A is B

Negative Present = A is not B

Positive Past = A was B

Negative Past = A was not B

Let's look at the four types of conjugation for desu

1. Positive Present = desuです
2. Negative Present
= ja nai desuじゃないです
= ja arimasenじゃありません
3. Positive Past = deshitaでした
4. Negative Past
= ja nakatta desu じゃなかったです
= ja arimasen deshitaじゃありませんでした

Let's look at examples of "desu" conjugation, to make better sense of them.

Example
1. I am a student
= watashi wa gakusei desu私は学生です

2. I am not a student
= watashi wa gakusei ja nai
私は学生じゃない (inf)

= watashi wa ja arimasen
私はじゃありません (f)

3. I was a student
= watashi wa gakusei deshita私は学生でした

4. I was not a student
= watashi wa gakusei ja nakatta
私は学生じゃなかった (inf)
= watashi wa gakusei ja arimasen deshita
私は学生じゃありませんでした (f)

We will go into all of these conjugations in detail below. We have already covered desu so let's begin with the present negative:

Present Negative (A is not B):
We use "ja naiじゃない" and "ja arimasenじゃありません" to make negative present tense sentences. For a more casual tone, we add **janai**じゃない before **desu**です and for a more formal tone we use **ja arimasen**じゃありません.

A is not B:

A wa B desu → **A wa B** ja nai
or
A wa B desu → **A wa B** ja arimasen

Examples:
Sensei desu
先生です
= I am a teacher

Sensei ja arimasen (f)
先生じゃありません
= I am not **a teacher**

Isha desu

医者です
= I am a doctor

Isha ja arimasen (f)
医者じゃありません
= I am not **a doctor**
(doctor = isha医者)

Bengoshi desu
弁護士です
= I am a laywer

Bengoshi ja arimasen (f)
弁護士じゃありません
(laywer = bengoshi弁護士)
= I am not **a laywer**

Kanojo wa daigakusei ja nai (inf)
彼女は大学生じゃない
(Kanojo 彼女= she)
(Daigakusei 大学生= university student)
She is not a university student

Senkou wa nihongo ja arimasen (f)
専攻は日本語じゃありません
(Senkou専攻 = major)
(Nihongo日本語 = Japanese)
My major is not Japanese language

Past Positive (A was B):
Now let's look at using **desu** in the past positive tense.

A was B

A wa B desu **→** **A wa B** deshita **(A was B)**

Example sentences:

Senkou wa bijinesu deshita

専攻はビジネスでした

(Senkou専攻 = major)

(Bijinesu ビジネス = business)

My major was business

Tanaka san wa isha deshita

田中さんは医者でした

(Tanaka san = Mr. Tanaka) (Isha医者 = doctor)

Tanaka san was a doctor

Past Negative (A was not B):

When expressing 'A was not B', we use **ja nakatta desu** じゃなかったです for a more casual tone, and formally we use **ja arimasen deshita** じゃありませんでした.

A was not B

A wa B janai → **A wa B** ja nakatta (inf)

A wa B ja arimasen + deshita → **A wa B** ja arimasen deshita (f)

Example sentences:

Senkou wa bijinesu ja nakatta (inf)

専攻はビジネスじゃなかった

(Senkou専攻 = major)

(Bijinesu ビジネス = business)

My major was not business

Tanaka san wa isha ja arimasen deshita (f)

田中さんは医者じゃありませんでした

(Tanaka san = Mr. Tanaka) (Isha 医者= doctor)

Tanaka san was a not doctor

Exercise:

Translate the sentences into Japanese.

1. The girl is 8 years old
(Girl = onna no ko女の子)
(8 years old = hassai八才)

Answer:
Onna no ko wa hassai desu.
女の子は八才です

2. The boy is not an elementary school student (Casual)
(Boy = otoko no ko男の子) (Elementary school student = shougakusei小学生)

Answer:
Otoko no ko wa shougakusei janai
男の子は小学生じゃない

3. He was a politician
(He = kare) (Politician = seijika)

Answer:
Kare wa seijika deshita.
彼は政治家でした

4. Kim was not an actress (Formal)
(Friend = tomodachi友達)
(Actress = joyuu女優)

Answer:
Kim wa joyuu ja arimasen deshita.
キムは女優じゃありませんでした

Possessive Pronouns所有代名詞

Possessive pronouns refer to words like "my" "your" "his" etc. In Japanese we have to use the particle "noの" to make these words. The particle "noの" is used to show possession.

Here is a list of possessive pronouns

My = **Watashi no私の**
Yours = **Anata noあなたの**
Your (plural) = **Anata tachi noあなた達の**
His = **Kare no彼の**
Hers = **Kanojo no彼女の**
Ours = **Watashi tachi no私達の**
Theirs = **Karera no彼らの**
Its = **Sore no, Kore no, Are no**
それの、これの、あれの

As we have seen in the "Introduction" we use the particle 'noの' to say 'my name':

"My name"
Watashi no namae
私の名前"

By simply adding a noun after the possessive pronoun with the particle "no", we can make a possessive sentence.

Language pattern

Pronoun + "no" + Noun

Examples

My teacher
= Watashi no Sensei
私の先生
(Teacher = Sensei先生)

His girlfriend
= Kare no Kanojo
彼の彼女
(Girlfriend = Kanojo彼女)

Your notebook
= Anata no nooto
あなたのノート
(Notebook = Nootoノート)

Their school
= Karera no gakko
彼の学校
(School = Gakko学校)

Remember as stated before, in Japanese we avoid using, "you / your". Instead when we want to say 'you' or 'your' we use the name of the person instead.

Example:
~~Your~~ notebook
= ~~Anata~~ no nooto
~~あなた~~のノート
John's notebook
= John san no nooto
ジョンさんのノート
(Notebook = Nootoノート)

~~His~~ friend
= ~~Kare~~ no tomodachi
彼の友達

Yoshida's friend
= Yoshida san no tomodachi
吉田さんの友達
(Friend = tomodachi友達)

Whenusing the particle "noの", it also refers to the **'s** in English.
Therefore when we say things like sam's shoe**'s** or the man**'s** hat, we have to use "noの":

Examples
The dog's leg
Inu no ashi
犬の足
(dog = inu犬) (leg = ashi足)

Canadian winter
Translates to Canada's winter
Kanada no fuyu
カナダの冬
(winter = fuyu冬)

Suzuki's bag
Suzuki no kaban
鈴木のカバン
(bag = kabanカバン)

Let's see some examples of "no" in sentences

This is his book
Kore wa kare no hon desu
これは彼の本です
(book = hon本)

That is not my car
Sore wa watashi no kuruma ja arimasen
それは私の車じゃありません

(car = kuruma車)

That is Yumi's dog
Sore wa Yumi san no inu desu
それは由美さんの犬です
(dog = inu犬)

Exercise
Translate the following phrase

1) His dog
(dog = inu犬)

2) Jake's bike
(bike = jitensha自転車)

3) The cat's food
(food = tabemono食べ物) (cat = neko猫)

4) My car
(car = kuruma車)

Answers
1) Kare no inu彼の犬
2) Jake no jitenshaジェイクの自転車
3) Neko no tabemono猫の食べ物
4) Watashi no kuruma私の車

Like / Dislike好き/好きじゃない

To state things that we like or dislike in Japanese, we use two phrases:

These are "suki na好きな" (to like) and "kirai na嫌いな" (to hate).

These are both "na" adjectives, we will go through "na" adjectives in a later section, but first let's get familiar with this language pattern:

Sentence structure:

X wa Y ga Suki desu	=	**X likes Y.**
X wa Y ga Kirai desu	=	**X hates Y.**

In this structure we have a new particle "gaが". Ga can be confusing to understand until you know more Japanese. So we will leave this out until we reach the particle section. In this section we really want you to focus on this language pattern instead.

Let's see some examples in use:

I like fish.
Watashi wa Sakana ga suki desu
私は魚が好きです
(sakana魚 = fish)

Yuko hates mathematics.
Yuko san wa sugaku ga kirai desu
ゆこさんは数学が嫌いです
(suuaku数学 = mathematics)

Like with other parts of Japanese we can omit the subject if it is clear:

I like Japan

~~Watashi wa~~ Nihon ga suki desu
~~私は~~日本が好きです
= Nihon ga suki desu
日本が好きです
(Japan = Nihon日本)

When stating things that you don't like, it is better to use the negative form of suki (suki ja arimasen/ja nai). This is because the word "kirai嫌い" is very strong and expresses an extreme dislike/hate.

I don't like sushi
(Watashi wa) sushi ga suki ja arimasen
(私は）寿司が好きじゃありません

I don't like cats (inf)
(Watashi wa) neko ga suki ja nai
(私は）猫は好きじゃない

Now if you are neutral, and neither like or dislike something, you can use this phrase:

X wa Y ga suki demo kirai demo arimasen
(neither like or dislike)

Example:
I neither like nor dislike fish
Watashi wa sakana ga suki demo kirai demo arimasen
私は魚が好きでも嫌いでもありません
(Sakana魚 = fish)

I neither like nor dislike school
Watashi wa gakko ga suki demo kirai demo arimasen
私は学校が好きでも嫌いでもありません
(gakko学校= school)

<u>**Exercise**</u>

Now it's your turn, translate these phrases

1) I like Japanese food
(Japanese food = nipponshoku日本食)

2) I don't like Monday
(Monday = getsuyobi月曜日)

3) I neither like or dislike cake
(cake = kekiケーキ)

<u>Answers</u>
1) Watshi wa nipponshoku ga suki desu
私は日本食が好きです

2) Watashi wa getsuyobi ga suki ja arimasen
私は月曜日が好きじゃありません

3) Watashi wa keki ga suki demo kirai demo arimasen
私はケーキが好きでも嫌いでもありません

Question Marker "ka"

クエスチョンマーク"か"

"ka" is a question marking particle and used to make questions in Japanese. To make a sentence into a question, we add "ka" to the end.

Sentence structure

Sentence + ka?

Examples:

Sentence 1

Anata wa Sushi ga suki desu

あなたは寿司が好きです

= You like Sushi

Anata wa Sushi ga suki desu ka?

あなたは寿司が好きですか

= Do you like Sushi?

Sentence 2

Tokyo wa kirei desu

東京は綺麗です

= Tokyo is clean.

Tokyo wa kirei desu ka?

東京は綺麗ですか

= Is Tokyo clean?

(Kirei綺麗 = clean)

Sentence 3

Kore wa anata no inu desu

これはあなたの犬です

= This is your dog

(dog = inu犬)

Kore wa anata no inu desu ka?
これはあなたの犬ですか
= Is this your dog?

We can answer these question, with the same A is B pattern. Let's look at some questions and answers together:

Anata wa Sushi ga suki desu ka?
あなたは寿司が好きですか
= Do you like Sushi?

Hai, (watashi wa) sushi ga suki desu
はい、（私は）寿司が好きです
= Yes, I like Sushi.
(yes = haiはい)

Iie, (watashi wa) sushi ga suki ja arimasen
(いいえ、私は）寿司が好きじゃありません
= No, I don't like sushi.
(no = iieいいえ)

Tokyo wa kirei desu ka?
東京は綺麗ですか？
= Is Tokyo clean?
(clean = kirei綺麗)

Hai, Tokyo wa kirei desu
はい、東京は綺麗です
= Yes, Tokyo is clean.

Iie, Tokyo wa kirei ja arimasen
いいえ、東京は綺麗じゃありません
= No, Tokyo isn't clean.

We can even simply say yes or no:

Kore wa anata no inu desu ka?
これはあなたの犬ですか
= Is this your dog?

Haiはい
= Yes

Iieいいえ
= No

For informal speech we don't use "ka", instead we use a rising tone to ask questions:

Tokyo wa kirei?
東京は綺麗 (inf)
= Is Tokyo clean?

Kore wa anata no inu?
これはあなたの犬
= Is this your dog?

Remember in informal speech we omit desu. There is another way to make questions in informal speech, this is by adding the particle "noの" at the end.

Exercises:
Change these statements into sentences

1) This food is hot
Kono tabemono atsui desu
この食べ物熱いです
(food = tabemono食べ物)

2) Yuri is his younger sister (casual)
Kare no imoto wa Yuri
彼の妹はゆり

(younger sister = imoto妹)

3) This phone is expensive
Kono denwa takai desu
この電話高いです
(phone = denwa電話) (expensive = takai高い)

Answers

1) Is this food is hot?
Kono tabemono atsui desu ka?
この食べ物熱いですか

2) Is Yuri is his younger sister? (casual)
Kare no imoto wa Yuri
彼の妹はゆり(rising tone)

3) Is this phone is expensive?
Kono denwa takai desu ka?
この電話は高いですか

Question Word: Whose? 疑問形:誰の

Let's go through the question word "whose" which is "dare no誰の".

One thing to keep in mind, when using question words you also need to use the question particle "kaか" at the end of the sentence.

Whose = **Dare no誰の**

Example

Whose Umbrella is this? = **Dare no kasa desu ka? 誰の傘ですか**

It is my umbrella = **Watashi no kasa desu私の傘です**
(Umbrella = kasa傘)

This question word is often used in combination with "koreこれ, soreそれ, areあれ" words

Whose book is this?
= Kore wa dare no hon desu ka?
これは誰の本ですか

That is my book
= Sore wa watashi no hon desu
それは私の本です
(Book = Hon本)

Whose bag is that?
= Are wa dare no kaban desu ka?
あれは誰のカバンですか

That is Honda's bag
= Are wa Honda san no kaban desu
あれは本田さんのカバンです

(Bag = Kabanカバン)

Adjectives形容詞

Moving onto adjectives, in Japanese we have two types of adjectives.

They are called, "i adjectives" and "na adjectives".

i adjectives: end with "i" sound
Examples:

Kawaiiかわいい	**cute**
Wakai若い	**young**
Ookii大きい	**big**
Chiisai小さい	**small**
Omoshiroi面白い	**interesting**
Isogashii忙しい	**busy**
Kowaii怖い	**scary**
Oishiiおいしい	**tasty/delicious**

Na- adjectives: end with "na" sound
Examples:

Kirei na綺麗な	**clean**
Shizuka na静かな	**quiet**
Genki na元気な	**cheerful**
Taikutsu na退屈な	**boring**
Hima na暇な	**free time**
Nigiyaka naにぎやかな	**lively**

We can use these adjectives in the same basic sturucture pattern, A is B

Yoko is cute
Yoko san wa kawaii desu
洋子さんはかわいいです

Winter in Canada is cold

Kanada no fuyu wa samui desu
カナダの冬は寒いです

(remember no particle is needed because you are referring to Canada's winter)

When using these adjectives, we use them in different ways

'I adjectives' remain the same and do not change:

Examples
She is young
= (Kanojo wa) wakai desu
= (彼女は）若いです
(young = wakai若い)

I am busy
= (Watashi wa) isogashī desu
= (私は）忙しいです
(busy = isogashi忙しい)

With "Na- adjective", when the pattern is "Subject is adjective", the last "na" is dropped.

Kirei na綺麗な
(beautiful/clean)

1. Drop "Na" Kirei ~~na~~ → Kirei
2. Add "desu" Kirei → Kirei + desu

Example
Subject is adjective
Yumi is beautiful
Yumi san wa kirei desu.
由美さんは綺麗です

I am free

(Watashi wa) hima desu.
(私は）暇です

Another way to think of it:
“na” depends on the position of the adjective:

If the na adjective is before the noun, we add “na”.

If the na adjective is after the noun we remove “na”.

Adjective before the noun:
Yūmei**na** gakkō desu.
有名な学校です
It is a famous school.

Adjective after the noun:
Kono gakkō wa yūmei desu.
この学校は有名です
This school is famous.

So when it comes to adjectives, it’s good practice to remembering what type each adjective is, aswell as its meaning.

Even though some na adjectives maybe tricky to determine. You can always find out the type of an adjective by the sound they end in.

Exercise
Translate these sentences into Japanese

1) This textbook is interesting.
(textbook = kyokasyo教科書)

2) It is my pretty sister.
(sister = imoto妹)

3) I like this quiet café.
(café = kafeカフェ)

Answers

1) This textbook is interesting.
Kono kyoukasyo wa omosiroi desu.
この教科書は面白いです

2) It is my pretty sister.
Kore wa watashi no kawaii imoto desu.
これは私のかわいい妹です

3) I like this quiet café.
Watashi wa kono shizuka na kafe ga suki desu.
私はこの静かなカフェが好きです

I Adjective Conjugation

い形容詞活用形

Now that we know the basics of *i* – adjectives, we going to learn how to conjugate them to make more forms and tenses.

Let's look at the conjugations with the example i-adjective "kawaiiかわいい":

There are four types of conjugation for 'i' adjectives
1. Positive Present = kawaiiかわいい
2. Negative Present
= kawaikunaiかわいくない
= kawaiku arimasenかわいくありません
3. Positive Past = kawaikattaかわいかった
4. Negative Past
= kawaikunakatta
= kawaiku arimasen deshitaかわいくありませんでした

Example
1. I am cute = watashi wa kawaii desu私はかわいいです
2. I am not cute
= watashi wa kawaikunai desu私はかわいくないです
= kawaiku arimasenかわいくありません
3. I was cute = watashi wa kawaikatta私はかわいかった
4. I was not cute
= watashi wa kawaikunakatta私はかわいくなかった
= kawaiku arimasen deshitaかわいくありませんでした

Negative Present (not cute):
To make negative present, you simply remove the last 'i' from the adjective and replace it with **kunai**くない or a more formal **ku arimasen**くありません.

Kawaii (cute) → **kawai + kunai →**

kawaikunai **(not cute)**

Kawaii (cute) → kawai + ku arimasen → kawaiku arimasen (not cute)

Examples:
Ooki i 大きい(big)
→ ookikunai 大きくない(not big)

Chiisai 小さい(small)
→ chiisaku arimasen小さくありません (not small)

Isogashii忙しい (busy)
→ isogashikunai忙しくない (not busy)

Omoshiroi 面白い(interesting)
→ omoshiroku arimasen面白くありません (not interesting)

There are some adjectives that are irregular that dont follow this pattern. But luckily it's only two:

! (Irregular adjective)
Iiいい (good)
→ yokunaiよくない (not good)

! (Irregular adjective)
Kakkoiiかっこいい (handsome)
→ kakkoyoku arimasen かっこよくありません(not handsome)

Positive Past (was cute):
To make positive past tense 'i' adjectives, the last 'i' of the adjective is removed and replaced by **kattaかった**.
Kawaii (cute) → kawai + katta → kawaikatta (was cute)

Examples:

Ookii大きい (big)
→ ookikatta大きかった (was big)

Chiisai小さい (small)
→ chiisakatta小さかった (was small)

Isogashii忙しい (busy)
→ isogashikatta忙しかった (was busy)

Omoshiroi面白い (interesting)
→ omoshirokatta面白かった (was interesting)

! (Irregular adjective)
Ii いい(good)
→ yokattaよかった (was good)

! (Irregular adjective)
Kakkoiiかっこいい (handsome)
→ kakkoyokattaかっこよかった (was handsome)

Negative Past (was not cute):
To make a negative past tense adjective, the last 'i' of the negative form adjective is removed and replaced by **kunakatta**くなかった, or using a more formal tone is **ku arimasen deshita**くありませんでした.

Kawaikunai → kawaikunakatta (was not cute)
Kawaikuarimasen + deshita →kawaiku arimasen deshita (was not cute)

Examples:
Ookikunai大きくない (not big)
→ ookikunakatta大きくなかった (was not big)

Chiisakuarimasen小さくありません (not small)
→ chiisaku arimasen deshita小さくありませんでした (was not small)

Isogashikunai 忙しくない(not busy)
→ isogashikunakatta忙しくなかった (was not busy)

Omoshirokuarimasen面白くありません (not interesting)
→ omoshiroku arimasen deshita面白くありませんでした (was not interesting)

! (Irregular adjective)
Yokunaiよくない (not good)
→ yokunakattaよくなかった (was not good)

! (Irregular adjective)
Kakkoyoku arimasenかっこよくありません (not handsome)
→ Kakkoyoku arimasen deshitaかっこよくありませんでした (was not handsome)

Exercise:
Translate the sentences into Japanese.
1. The car is expensive.
(Car = kuruma車) (Expensive = takai高い)

Answer:
Kuruma wa takai desu.
車は高いです

2. The movie is not scary.
(Movie = eiga映画) (Scary = kowai怖い)

Answer:
Eiga wa kowaikunai desu.
映画は怖いです

3. The newspaper was interesting.
(Newspaper = shinbun新聞) (Interesting = omoshiroi面白い)

Answer:

Shinbun wa omoshirokatta desu.
新聞は面白かったです

4. The dinner was not tasty.
(Dinner = bangohan晩御飯) (Tasty = Oishiiおいしい)

Answer:
Bangohan wa oishikunakatta desu.
晩御飯はおいしいです

5. The house was not big. (Polite)
(House = ie家) (Big = Ookii大きい)

Answer:
Ie wa ookikuarimasen deshita.
家は大きくありませんでした

Na Adjective Conjugation

な形容詞活用形

Luckily you don't have to remember another conjugation because na – adjective conjugation is the same as **desu** conjugation.

There are four types of conjugation for na adjectives
1. Positive Present = (naな)
2. Negative Present
 = ja nai desuじゃないです
 = ja arimasenじゃありません
3. Positive Past = deshitaでした
4. Negative Past
= ja nakatta desuじゃなかったです
= ja arimasen deshitaじゃありませんでした

Example
1. I am beautiful = watashi wa kirei (~~na~~) desu私は綺麗（~~な~~）です
2. I am not beautiful
= watashi wa kirei ja nai (desu)私は綺麗じゃない（です）
= /ja arimasenじゃありません
3. I was beautiful = watashi wa kirei deshita私は綺麗でした
4. I was not beautiful
= watashi wa kirei ja nakatta desu私は綺麗じゃなかったです
= /ja arimasen deshitaじゃありませんでした

Negative Present (not beautiful):

Kirei ~~na~~ (beautiful) Kirei desu kirei janai desu (inf)
Kirei ~~na~~ (beautiful) Kirei ~~desu~~ kirei ja arimasen (f)

Examples:
Shizuka na (quiet) 静かな
shizuka janai desu (not quiet) 静かじゃないです

Genki na (cheerful) 元気な
genki ja arimasen (not cheerful) 元気じゃありません

Taikutsu na (boring) 退屈な
taikutsu janai desu (not boring) 退屈じゃないです

Hima na (free, spare time) 暇な
hima ja arimasen (not free) 暇じゃありません

Nigiyaka na (lively) にぎやかな
nigiyaka janai desu (not lively) にぎやかじゃないです

Yuumei na (famous) 有名な
yuumei ja arimasen (not famous) 有名じゃありません

Positive Past (was beautiful):
Kirei na (beautiful) Kirei desu kirei deshita

Examples:
Shizuka na (quiet) 静かな
shizuka deshita (was quiet) 静かでした

Genki na (cheerful) 元気な
genki deshita (was cheerful) 元気でした

Taikutsu na (boring) 退屈な
taikutsu deshita (was boring) 退屈でした

Hima na (spare time) 暇な
hima deshita (was free) 暇でした

Nigiyaka na (lively) にぎやかな
nigiyaka deshita (was lively) にぎやかでした

Yuumei na (famous) 有名な
yuumei deshita (was famous) 有名でした

Negative Past (was not beautiful):

Kirei janai (not beautiful) → kirei ja nakatta desu (inf)

Kirei ja arimasen (not beautiful) Kirei ja arimasen + deshita →Kirei ja arimasen deshita (f)

Examples:

Shizuka janai desu (not quiet)

静かじゃないです

shizuka ja nakatta desu (was not quiet)

静かじゃなかったです

Genki ja arimasen (not cheerful)

元気じゃありません

genki ja arimasen deshita (was not cheerful)

元気じゃありませんでした

Taikutsu janai desu (not boring) 退屈じゃないです

taikutsu ja nakatta desu (was not boring)

退屈じゃなかったです

Hima ja arimasen (not free)

暇じゃありません

hima ja arimasen deshita (was not free)

暇じゃありませんでした

Nigiyaka janai desu (not lively)

にぎやかじゃないです

nigiyaka ja nakatta desu (was not lively)

にぎやかじゃなかったです

Yuumei ja arimasen (not famous)

有名じゃありません

yuumei ja arimasen deshita (was not famous)

有名じゃありませんでした

Exercise:

Translate the given sentences:

1. The town is quiet
(town = machi町) (quiet = shizuka na静かな)

Answer:
Machi wa shizuka desu.
町は静かです

2. My friend is not cheerful (Casual)
(friend = tomodachi友達)
(cheerful = genki na元気な)

Answer:
Tomodachi wa genki janai desu.
友達は元気じゃないです

3. The move was boring
(movie = eiga映画)
(boring = taikutsu na退屈な)

Answer:
Eiga wa taikutsu deshita.
映画は退屈でした

4. The actress was not famous
(Actress = joyuu女優)
(Famous = yumei na有名な)

Answer:
Joyuu wa yumei ja arimasen deshita.
女優は有名じゃありませんでした

Number in Japanese日本語の数字

Japanese number system is very easy to learn. Once you can count from 1 to 10, you can combine these numbers to count up to 99. Some numbers have two forms and using them depends on the function of the number e.g. time (hour and minute), counter word, etc...

Below is a list of the first 10 numbers:

1 Ichi一
2 Ni二
3 San三
4 Yon/shi四
5 Go五
6 Roku六
7 Nana/Shichi七
8 Hachi八
9 Kyu/ku九
10 Juu十

When you want to make numbers larger than 10, we combine the separate parts of these numbers together:

e.g. 11
10 + 1 Juu + ichi → Juu ichi十一

e.g. 34
3 + 10 + 4 **San + Juu + Yon** → San ju yon三十四

There are two ways to say numbers 4, 7 and 9. However, when you make 40, 70, and 90, the following phrases are always applied:

40 = Yon juu四十 **70 =** Nana juu七十 **90 =** Kyuu juu九十

Bigger numbers are as follows:

100 = Hyaku百
1,000 = Sen 千
10,000 = Man万

There are some exceptions.
The following numbers have different pronunciation:

300 San Byak三百
3,000 San Zen三千
600 Roppyaku六百
800 Happyaku八百

In Japanese it is a good idea to get familiar with larger number because Japanese currency get big very quickly.

<u>Exercise</u>:
Translate the list of number below.

18 = ...
35 = ...
97 = ...
138 = ...
824 = ...
200 = ...
5000 = ...
1630 = ...

Answer:
18
Jyuu + hachi
= Jyuuhachi
十八

35
San + jyuu + go
= Sanjyuugo

三十五

97
Kyuu + jyuu + nana
= Kyuujyuunana
九十七

138
Hyaku + san + jyuu+ hachi
= Hyakusanjyuuhachi
百三十八

824
Hachi + hyaku + ni + jyuu + yon
= Happyaku nijyuuyon
八百二十四

200
Ni + hyaku
= Ni hyaku
二百

5000
Go + sen
= Go sen
五千

1630
Sen + roku + hyaku + san + jyuu
= Senroppyaku sanjyuu
千六百三十

Question Word: How Much?

質問形:どれくらい

Now that we have a better understanding of numbers, we can learn how to ask for price in Japanese:

To ask for the price of an item we use the following phrase:

How much is it? = **Ikura desu ka? (f)** いくらですか
= **Ikura (inf)** いくら

It's .... yen. = **.... en desu (f)** 円です
= **... en (inf)** 円

Japanese currency is "yen" and is pronounced as "en".

Examples:

300 yen = **San byaku en** 三百円
7600 yen = **Nana sen roppyaku en**
七千六百円

15000 yen = **Ichi man go sen en**
一万五千円

823 yen = **Happyaku nijuu san en**
八百二十三円

We can also combine this with the ko-so-do-a words to be more specific about items:

Examples:
Sore wa ikura desu ka?
それはいくらですか

= How much is that?

Kono hon wa ikura desu ka?
この本はいくらですか
= How much is this book?
(Book = hon本)

Ano kaban wa ikura desu ka?
あのかばんはいくらですか
= How much is that bag?
(Bag = Kabanカバン)

Remember, kono/sono/ano is used when talk about a specific noun.

<u>**Exercise**</u>
Translate the given sentences:

1. How much is this ticket? It's 3,000 yen.
(ticket = chiketto チケット)

Answer:
Kono chiketto wa ikura desu ka? Sanzen en desu.
このチケットはいくらですか？三千円です

2. How much is that bouquet? It's 1200 yen.
(bouquet = hanataba花束)

Answer:
Ano hanataba wa ikura desu ka? Sen nihyaku en desu.
あの花束はいくらですか？千二百円です

3. How much is the rice? It's 1800 yen.
(rice = okomeお米)

Answer:
Sono okome wa ikura desu ka? Sen happyaku en desu.
そのお米はいくらですか？千八百円です。

Japanese Verbs日本語の動詞

Like adjectives, there are two types of verbs in Japanese. These are "u-verbs" and "ru-verbs".

Ru verbs end in the letters "iru" or "eru"
U verb end in 'u'

There are some exception to this rule, as some verbs ending in "iru" and "eru" are u verbs. So try to remember these exceptions when you come across them, to avoid getting confused.

Ru-verbs

Taberu食べる	=	to eat
Neru寝る	=	to sleep
Miru見る	=	to see, to watch
Okiru起きる	=	to wake up

U-verbs

Nomu飲む	=	to drink
Kaku書く	=	to write
Iku行く	=	to go
Hanasu話す	=	to speak
Hashiru走る	=	to run (exception)
Kiku聞く	=	to listen, to hear

Japanese also consists of two irregular verbs, since these verbs are irregular they do not fall into the catergories above.

Irr verbs

Kuru来る = to come
Suruする = to do

Using "suruする"

Adding "-suru" to a noun can transform it into a verb.

For example,

Benkyo (Study) + Suru (to do)
= to study

Sentaku (laundry) + Suru (to do)
= to do laundry

The word "suru" can also be added to the name of a sport to state that you play that sport:

Examples:

Sakkaa suruサッカーする= to play soccer
Yakyuu suru野球する = to play baseball
Tenisu suruテニスする = to play tennis

All the verbs listed above are in their informal forms, we will cover formal forms in the next section.

Particle 'o/woを(お)'

When using verbs we need to use the particle 'o', this particle is also written as 'wo' but always pronounced as 'o'. A lot of beginners get confused by this.

The 'o' particle is used after an object. Without using the 'o' particle, it can be difficult to determine the object in the sentence.

Lets see some example of how to use the 'o' particle:

I eat sushi
(Watashi wa) sushi o taberu
私は寿司を（お）食べる
(eat = taberu食べる)

Here sushi is the object we are talking about, therefore we need to mark this with the particle 'o' right after the word.

I drink water

Watashi wa mizu o nomu
私は水を（お）飲む
(water = mizu水) (drink = nomu飲む)

I listen to music
(Watashi wa私は) ongaku o hiku
音楽を（お）聴く
(music = ongaku音楽) (listen = kiku聴く)

<u>**Exercise**</u>
Translate the given sentences:

1. I do my homework.
(homework = syukudai宿題)

Answer:
Watashi wa syukudai o suru.
私は宿題を（お）する

2. His girlfriend goes to university.
(university = daigaku大学)

Answer:
Kare no kanojyo wa daigaku ni iku.
彼の彼女は大学に行く

3. My big brother works at that company.
(big brother = ani 兄) (work = hataraku 働く) (company = kaisya会社)

Answer:
Watashi no ani wa ano kaisya de hataraku.
私の兄はあの会社で働く

4. My frind eats wasabi.
(friend = tomodachi友達)

Answer:

Watashi no tomodachi wa wasabi o taberu.

私の友達はわさびを（お）食べる

Masu Verb Conjugation

ます動詞活用形

In the previous topic we have learnt the basic verbs in informal speech. If we want to use verbs in formal speech we need to conjugate into “masu” form.

It’s handy to know masu form as it can be used in many situations.

There are four types of conjugation for masu
1. Positive Present = masuます
2. Negative Present = masenません
3. Positive Past = mashitaました
4. Negative Past = masen deshitaませんでした

We conjugate slightly differently depending on the type of verb we are using:

Positive Present (masu)

Ru-verbs:
1. Drop the final “ru”
2. Add “masu”

e.g. Tabe~~ru~~ (to eat) → Tabe + masu → Tabemasu

U-verbs:
1. Drop the final “u”
2. Add “-imasu”

e.g. Kak~~u~~ (to write) → Kak + imasu → Kakimasu
Yom~~u~~ (to read) → Yom + imasu → Yomimasu

Irregular verbs:
Kuru
1. Drop the final “uru”
2. Add “-imasu”

e.g. K~~uru~~ (to come) → K + imasu → Kimasu

Suru
1. Drop the final "uru"
2. Add "-himasu"

e.g. S~~uru~~ (to do) → S + himasu → Shimasu

Examples
I eat sushi
Sushi o tabemasu
寿司を（お）食べます

I solve the problem
(to solve = toku解く) (problem = mondai問題)
Mondai o tokimasu
問題を（お）解きます

I ride a bike
(ride = noru乗る)
Jitensya ni norimasu
自転車に乗ります

I study Japanese
Nihonngo o benkyou shimasu
日本語の勉強します

Negative Present:
The **masu** ending is replaced with **masen.**

Taberu (to eat) **tabe**masu **tabe**masen
(*ru*-verb)

Examples:

Neru (to sleep) nemasu nemasen
(*ru*-verb)

Yomu (to read) yomimasu
yomimasen
(*u*-verb)

Suru (to do) shimasu
shimasen
(irregular verb)

Sentence examples
I do not wake up
Okimasen
起きません

I do not buy it
Sore o kaimasen
それを（お）買いません

I do not go there
(there = asokoあそこ)
Asoko ni ikimasen
あそこに行きません

I do not drink juice
(juice = jyuusuジュース)
Jyuusu o nomimasen
ジュースを（お）飲みません

Positive Past:
The **masu** ending is replaced with **mashita.**

Taberu (to eat) **tabe**masu
tabemashita
(r*u*-verb)

Examples:

Neru (to sleep) nemasu
nemashita
(*ru*-verb)

Yomu (to read) yomimasu
yomimashita

(*u*-verb)
Suru (to do) shimasu
shimashita
(irregular verb)

Sentence examples
I ate dinner
Bangohan o tabemashita
晩御飯を（お）食べました

I saw the sky
(sky = sora空)
Sono sora o mimashita
その空を（お）見ました

I played soccer
Sakkaa o shimashita
サッカーを（お）しました

I watched a movie
(to watch = miru観る)
Eiga o mimashita
映画を（お）観ました

Negative Past:
The **masu** ending is replaced with **masen deshita.**
Taberu (to eat) **tabe**masu
tabemasen deshita
(r*u*-verb)

Examples:
Neru (to sleep) nemasu

nemasen deshita
(*ru*-verb)

Yomu (to read) yomimasu
yomimasen deshita
(*u*-verb)

Suru (to do) shimasu
shimasen deshita
(irregular verb)

Sentence examples

I did not write a letter
(letter = tegami 手紙)
Tegami o kakimasen deshita
手紙を（お）書きませんでした

I did not visit my friend
(visit = otozureru 訪れる)
Tomodachi o otozuremasen deshita
友達を訪れませんでした

I did not talk with my mother
(mother = haha母)
Haha to hanashimasen deshita
母と話しませんでした

I did not read the newspaper
(newspaper = shinbun新聞)
Shinnbunn o yomimasen deshita
新聞を（お）読みませんでした

Now let's see these in longer sentences:

1. I do not go to school.
(I = watashi私) (To go = iku行く)
(School = gakko学校)

Watashi wa gakko ni ikimasen.
私は学校に行きません

2. I do not watch scary movies.
(I = watashi私) (To watch = miru観る)
(Scary = kowai怖い) (Movie = eiga映画)
Watashi wa kowai eiga wo mimasen.
私は怖い映画を（お）観ません

3. I did the laundry.
(I = watashi私) (To do laundry = sentaku suru洗濯する)
Watashi wa sentaku shimashita.
私は洗濯しました

4. I did not do my homework.
(I = watashi私) (Homework = shukudai宿題)
(To do = suruする)
Watashi wa shukudai o shimasen deshita.
私は宿題を（お）しませんでした

5. I don’t watch television
(tv = terebiテレビ) (watch = mimasu見ます)
Watashi wa terebi o mimasen.
私はテレビを（お）見ません

6. I ate breakfast.
(breakfast = asagohan朝御飯)
(eat = tabemasu食べます)
Asagohan o tabemashita.
朝ごはんを（お）食べました

7. I don’t eat breakfast.
(breakfast = asagohan朝御飯) (eat = tabemasu食べます)
Asagohan o tabemasen.
朝御飯を（お）食べません

If you are unsure of some of the particles used don't worry, they will become clear once we reach the particle section.

Exercise:
Write the following words in masu-form

Change to masu present positive:
Iku行く (to go)
Nomu飲む (to drink)
Taberu食べる (to eat)

Change to masu present negative:
Tetsudau手伝う (to help)
Okuru送る (to send, u-verb)
Kau買う (to buy)

Change to masu past positive:
Kariru借りる (to borrow)
Tsukuru作る (to make, u-verb)
Tsukau使う (to use)

Change to masu past negative:
Naosu直す (to fix/ to correct)
Oshieru教える (to tell, to teach)

Answers:
Iku行く = Ikimasu行きます

Nomu 飲む = Nomimasu飲みます
Taberu食べる = Tabemasu食べます

Tetsudau手伝う = Tetsudaimasen 手伝いません

Okuru送る = Okurimasen

送りません

Kau買う	=	Kaimasen 買いません
Kariru借りる=	Karimashita 借りました	
Tsukuru作る	=	Tsukurimashita 作りました
Tsukau使う	=	Tsukaimashita 使いました
Naosu直す	=	Naoshimasen deshita 直しませんでした
Oshieru教える	=	Oshiemasen deshita 教えませんでした

Informal Verb Conjugation
敬語でない動詞の活用形

We can conjugation verbs in informal tense to create to meanings to sentences. Conjugation into informal tense is also based on the type of verb used.

Let's go through each conjugation, starting with present negative

Present Negative
Ru verbs
Verbs ending in iru and eru, we change the last ru to nai

Example
Taberu食べる = tabenai食べない

U verbs
For u verbs we change the u to anai
Nomu飲む = Nomanai飲まない

If the u verb ends in a (vowel + u), we replace u with wanai.

Example
Au会う = awanai会わない

Irregular verbs
The two irregular verbs are conjugated in the following way:
Kuru来る = konai来ない
Suruする = shinaiしない

Past Positive
Ru verbs
Verbs ending in iru and eru, we change the last ru to ta

Example
Taberu食べる = tabeta食べた

U verbs

U verbs are a little bit more complicated and change depending on the specific ending:

Ku く = itaいた
Gu ぐ = idaいだ
U tsu ru う つ る = ttaった
Nu bu mu の ぶ む = ndaんだ
Suす = shita した

Past Negative

To make the past negative of informal speech we change nai (from negative speech) to nakatta:

Examples

Nomanai飲まない
= nomanakatta飲まなかった

Tabenai食べない
= tabenakatta食べなかった

Examples in sentences

I don't watch tv
Terebi o minaiテレビを（お）見ない

I don't write letters
Tegami o kakanai手紙を（お）書かない

Exercise:

Translate the given sentences in informal form:

1. I do not drink beer.
(beer = biiru ビール)

Answer:

Watashi wa biiru o nomanai.
私はビールを（お）飲まない

2. Her father did not come here.
(father = chichi父) (here = kokoここ)

Answer:
Kanojyo no chichi wa koko ni konakatta.
彼女の父はここに来なかった

3. My big sister met my boyfriend.
(big sister = ane 姉) (to meet = au会う)

Answer:
Watashi no ane wa watashino kareshi ni atta.
私の姉は私の彼氏に会った

4. She flew to London.
(to fly = tobu 飛ぶ) (London = rondon ロンドン)

Answer:
Kanojyo wa rondon ni tonda.
彼女はロンドンに飛んだ

Future Tense & Time Expression
未来形と時間表現

Japanese does not have the future tense word "will", like in English. Instead the present form is used to state actions that hapeen in the present or in the future.

Examples:
I eat sushi
= sushi o tabemasu
寿司を（お）食べます
I will eat sushi
= sushi o tabemasu
寿司を（お）食べます

He sleeps = kare wa nemasu彼は寝ます
He will sleep = kare wa nemasu彼は寝ます

As you see it can get confusing to tell the difference in tenses, because both phrases are the same.

So to make it clear we use time expressions to emphasize that something will happen in the future.

> **Ashita watashi wa yomimasu**
> **明日私は読みます**
> **= I will read tomorrow.**
> (Tomorrow = Ashita明日)

Now the sentence is clearly talking about something that will happen in the future.

There are two types of time expressions, with particle "ni" and without.

'Niに' particle
The particle 'ni' has many uses and one of them is to express time.

For non specific we don't use 'ni'
For specific time we use 'ni' after the time phrase

<u>Time expressions without particle "ni"</u>

Yesterday	**=**	**Kinou昨日**
Today	**=**	**Kyou今日**
Tomorrow	**=**	**Ashita明日**
Morning	**=**	**Asa朝**
Daytime	**=**	**Hiru昼**
Evening	**=**	**Yuugataタ方**
Night	**=**	**Yoru 夜**
This morning	**=**	**Kesa今朝**
This evening	**=**	**Konban今晩**
This night	**=**	**Konya今夜**
This week	**=**	**Konshu今週**
This weekend	**=**	**Konshuu matsu今週末**
This month	**=**	**Kongetsu今月**
This year	**=**	**Kotoshi今年**
Next week	**=**	**Raishuu来週**
Next weekend	**=**	**Raishuumatsu 来週末**
Next month	**=**	**Raigetsu来月**
Next year	**=**	**Rainen来年**
Last week	**=**	**Senshuu先週**
Last weekend	**=**	**Senshumatsu 先週末**
Last month	**=**	**Sengetsu先月**
Last year	**=**	**Kyonen去年**

These time expressions do not require the particle "ni" because they are not specific times.

Time expression with particle "ni"

The time expressions that require the particle "ni" are numerical time expressions such as "at 7:00 AM" and specific days.

Examples:

1. Specific time

I eat breakfast at 7:00 am.
= shichiji ni asagohan o tabemasu.
七時に朝御飯を（お）食べます
(breakfast = asagohan朝御飯)

2. Specific Day

I will watch this movie on Saturday.
= Doyobi ni kono eiga o mimasu.
土曜日にこの映画を（お）観ます

I will go next Tuesday.
= Raishu no kayobi ni ikimasu.
来週の火曜日に行きます
(raishuu来週 = next week)
Literally means "next week Tuesday I will go"

Here is the list of days of the week in Japanese, for reference:
Days of the week

Monday	**=**	**Getsuyobi月曜日**
Tuesday	**=**	**Kayobi火曜日**
Wednesday	**=**	**Suiyobi水曜日**
Thursday	**=**	**Mokuyobi木曜日**
Friday	**=**	**Kinyobi金曜日**
Saturday	**=**	**Doyobi土曜日**
Sunday	**=**	**Nichiyobi日曜日**

Exercise

Translate the given sentences:

1. I will meet my boyfriend tomorrow.

Answer:
Watashi wa watashi no kareshi ni ashita au.
私は私の彼氏に明日会う

2. I will go to Japan next month.

Answer:
Watashi wa raigetu nihon ni iku.
私は来月日本に行く

3. I will go to countryside on Wednesday
(countryside = inaka田舎)

Answer:
Watashi wa suiyoubi inaka ni iku.
私は水曜日に田舎に行く

4. She will watch a movie with her mother this evening.

Answer:
Kanojyo wa kanojyo no haha to konban eiga o miru.
彼女は彼女の母と今晩映画を（お）観る

Particles助詞

Particles play an essential part in Japanese and are used to modify the meaning of words. Therefore it is important to understand particles, as the meaning of sentences can change based on the particle used.

One thing to remember is particles can have more than one function. So don't be alarmed if you see them used in different situations.

Let's cover most important particles first:

Waは particle

As covered before waは is a topic marking particle and used to mark the topic of a sentence.

Waは particle function II

Waは can also be used to mark contrast between two sentences. In this case we mark the contrasting sentences with "waは" and use the word "demoでも" (but).

Examples

I eat fish but don't eat meat

Sakana wa tabemasu demo niku wa tabemasen

魚は食べます、でも肉は食べません

Normally we would say "sakana o tabemasu魚を（お）食べます" to say "I eat fish", however since we are contrasting this sentence with "I don't eat meat", we need to use "waは".

So when we use "waは" here, we put a lot of contrast between the two sentences.

More examples

I like dogs but not cats

Inu wa suki desu demo neko wa kirai desu

犬は好きです、でも猫は嫌いです

Again, here we would use "gaが" however we need to use "waは" as we are contrasting both sentences.

Gaが particle

Gaが is commonly used to add emphasis.

Examples

Kore wa pen desu

これはペンです

= this is a pen

If I want to emphasis this statement, you replace waは with gaが:

Kore ga pen desu

これがペンです

= THIS is a pen

A situation you could use this is, if you are talking to a baby and they don't know what this item is. You can use ga to say that "THIS" item is a pen. Or if you are in an argument and you want to empahisis something, such as "MOVIE A" is better, here you would use "gaが".

Gaが particle function II

Gaが particle is also used in set statements such as about existence and desires. We will cover these later in the book, so keep an eye out for these.

Niに particle

As stated previously "niに" is used as a time marking particle for specific time expressions. Such as specific days or times with numbers.

Niに particle function II

"niに" is also used to show movement, therefore it is used with words like "iku行く" and "kuru来る"

Examples

I go to the cinema

Eigakan ni ikimasu
映画館に行きます

The cat come to my house everyday
Neko wa mainichi uchi ni kimasu
猫は毎日うちに来ます

Here the use of niに is showing the direction of movement, in this case "to the cinema" or "to my house".

Since particle "niに" has many usages, it can be seen more than once in a sentence.

On Monday I go to the library
Getsuyobi ni toshokan ni ikimasu
月曜日に図書館に行きます

In this sentence the first "niに" marks the time and the other marks the direction of movement.

<u>Deで particle</u>
De is used to express where an action is taking place. It can be thought of as the word "at" or "in".

Example
Ill see a movie in the cinema
Eigakan de映画館で
= in the cinema
I see a movie
= Eiga o mimasu映画を（お）観ます

I see a movie in the cinema
= Eigakan de eiga o mimasu
映画館で映画を（お）観ます

At the resturant
= Restaurant deレストランで

Eat dinner
= bangohan o taberu晩御飯を（お）食べる

I eat dinner at the restaurant (inf)
= Restaurant de bangohan o taberu
レストランで晩御飯を（お）食べる

So when you are stating where an action is happening, use the "de" particle

De で particle function II

The second function of "deで" is to state "by using" or "means of"

Example
I draw a picture with a pen
With a pen = actually means by using a pen
Pen de ei o kakimasu
ペンで絵を（お）描きます

I go to work by bus.
Basu de shigoto ni ikimasu
バスで仕事に行きます
(by using bus ...)

I write my name by pen
Pen de namae o kakimasu
ペンで名前を（お）書きます
(by using pen ...)

To と particle

This particle is used to connect two or more nouns, it refers to the word "and". Such as "A and B and C"

Example
Handburger potatoe and coke please
Hanbaga to potatoe to coke o kudasi
ハンバーガーとポテトとコークを（お）ください

I like cake and fish
Keki to sakana ga suki desu
ケーキと魚が好きです

To particle function II
To can also be used to say "with"

John saw a movie with yoko
John wa yoko to eigo o mimashita
ジョンは洋子と映画を（お）観ました

Tomorrow I go on a date with minami
Ashita, miniami san to detto o shimasu
明日、みなみさんとデートを（お）します

Moも particle
This particle is used to mean also, when we use this particle it takes the postion of the previous particle waわ, gaが, oお

Ken is also Canadian
Ken san mo kanada jin desu
ケンさんのカナダ人です

That is also mine
Sore mo watashi no desu
それも私のです

O おparticle
Oお shows a direct object, a thing that is directly involved or affected by the event.

In the following sentences, "I drink coffee", "I watch a movie", "coffee" and "a movie" are direct objects. The particle "oお" comes after the direct object.

I drink coffee. **Coffee + o**
in Japanese: Koohii o nomimasu.
日本語:コーヒーお 飲みます
(koohii コーヒー= coffee)

I watch a movie **Movie + o**
In Japanese: Eiga o mimasu.
日本語:映画を お 観ます
(eiga映画= movie)

This particle can also be referred to as "woを" but is always pronounced as 'oお'

<u>**Exercise**</u>
Translate the given sentences:

1. I study Japanese but do not study English
(English = Eigo英語)

Answer:
Watashi wa nihongo wa benkyou shimasu, demo eigo wa benkyou shimasen.
私は日本語は勉強します、でも英語は勉強しません

2. He goes to university on Friday.

Answer:
Kare wa kinyoubi ni daigaku ni ikimasu.
彼は金曜日に大学に行きます

3. I ordered coffee and cake at the café.
(order = tanomu頼む)

Answer:
Watashi wa kafe de koohii to keki o tanonda
私はカフェでコーヒーとケーキを（お）頼んだ

4. She wrote a letter with the pen.

Answer:
Kanojyo wa pen de tegami wo kaita.
彼女はペンで手紙を書いた

Wh- Questions質問形

At the start of this book we covered closed questions and question word "whose誰の". Now let's look into making complex questions:

What	=	Nani何
When	=	Itsuいつ
Where	=	Dokoどこ
Who	=	Dareだれ
Which	=	Donoどの
How	=	Do yatteどうやって

Examples:

A: What do you do on weekend?
= Shuumatsu nani o shimasu ka?
週末は何をしますか

In this example weekend is the topic therefore in comes before the question word. Particle "waは" is also omitted as weekend is a unspecfic time expression. Unspecific time expressions don't use particles.

A: When will you go to the United States?
= Itsu Amerika ni ikimasuka?
いつアメリカに行きますか

B: I will go next month.
= Raigetsu ikimasu.
来月行きます

A: Where do you often study?
=Doko de yoku benkyo shimasu ka?
どこでよく勉強しますか

B: I often study in the library.

= Yoku Toshokan de benkyo shimasu.
よく図書館で勉強します

A: Who cleans on Saturday?
= Doyobi ni dare ga soji shimasu ka?
土曜日に誰が掃除しますか

B: My older brother cleans.
= Ani ga soji shimasu.
兄が掃除します
(Ani = older brother)

A: How will you come to the concert?
= Do yatte konsaato ni kimasu ka?
どうやってコンサートに来ますか

B: I will got by train
= Densha de ikimasu.
電車で行きます

Exercise

Translate the given sentences:

1. When will you come to my house? I will go on Sunday.
(house = ie家)

Answer:
Itsu watashi no ie ni kimasuka? Nichiyoubi ni ikimasu.
いつ私の家に来ますか？日曜日に行きます

2. Where do you work? I work in Tokyo.

Answer:
Doko de hatarakimasuka? Tokyo de hatarakimasu.
どこで働きますか？東京で働きます

3. Who teaches you math? My mother teaches me math.

(math = sugaku数学)

Answer:
Dare ga anata ni sugaku o oshiemasuka? Watashi no haha ga oshiemasu.
誰があなたに数学を（お）教えますか？私の母が教えます

4. How did you go back to your dorm? I came back by train.
(to go back = kaeru 帰る) (dorm = ryo 寮)

Answer:
Do yatte ryo ni kaerimashitaka? Densya de kaerimashita.
どうやって寮に帰りましたか？電車で帰りました

5. **What will you do this weekend? I will go to gym.**
(gym = jimuジム)

Answer:
Konsyumatu wa nani o shimasuka?
今週末は何を（お）しますか？ジムに行きます

Japanese Sentence Structure
日本語の文章構造

So for we have covered a lot of the elements of Japanese. Now let's see where they are placed in a sentence.

Sentence structure:

Topic + Time + Location + Object + Verb

Remember each part of this structure will require a particle.
Let's look at an example:

e.g.

Watashi wa nichiyobi ni toshokan de eigo o benkyoshimasu.
私は日曜日に図書館で英語の勉強をします
I study English at the library on Sunday

Topic = Watashi 私(I)
Time = Nichiyobi 日曜日(Sunday)
Location = Toshokan図書館 (library)
Object = Eigo英語 (English)
Verb = benkyoshimasu勉強します (study)

If a sentence does not contain any of the listed topics you can omit these.

e.g.

1. Watashi wa doyoubi ni tenisu o shimasu.
私は土曜日にテニスを（お） します
(Tenisuテニス = tennis),
(Saturday = doyoubi土曜日)
= I play tennis on Saturday.

2. Watashi no chichi wa mainichi 10:00 ji ni ie ni kaeri masu.
私の父は毎日十時に家に帰ります
(Chichi父 = father), (ie家 = to home), (kaerimasu帰ります = to come back)

= My father comes home at 10:00 PM every day.

3. Yoshida san wa toshokan de shinbun o yomimasu.
吉田さんは図書館で新聞を読みます
(shinbun新聞 = newspaper)
(yomimasu読みます = to read)
= Ms. Yoshida reads newspaper in the library.

Exercise
Now it's your turn:
Arrange the selection of words to form the outlined sentence:

1. I study English at the library on Sunday = ?

Watashi私 = I
Nichiyobi日曜日 = Sunday
Toshokan図書館 = Library
Eigo英語 = English
Benkyoshimasu勉強します = to study
Waは, niに, deで, oを（お）

Answer:
Watashi wa nichiyobi ni toshokan de eigo o benkyo shimasu.
私は日曜日に図書館で英語を勉強します

2. He eats breakfast at 7:00 am at the café.
Kare彼 = He
Tabemasu食べます = to eat
Asagohan朝御飯 = breakfast
Nana ji七時 = 7:00 am
Kissaten喫茶店 = Café
Waは, deで, niに, oを

Answer:
Kare wa nana ji ni kissaten de asagohan o tabemasu.

彼は七時に喫茶店で朝御飯を食べます

3. I eat sushi at a restaurant at night.
Watashi私 = I
Tabemasu食べます = to eat
Sushi寿司 = Sushi
Resutoranレストラン = Restaurant
Night夜 = Yoru
Waは, deで, oを（お）

Answer:
Watashi wa yoru resutoran de sushi o tabemasu.
私は夜レストランで寿司を食べます

4. I go to school
Watashi私 = I
Gakko学校 = School
Iku行く= Go
Waは, niに

Answer
watashi wa gakko ni ikimasu
私は学校に行きます
or
gakko ni ikimasu
学校に行きます
Remember in Japanese certain topics can be omitted if not necessary

5. I studied English at the library on Sunday
Watashi私 = I
Nichiyobi日曜日 = Sunday
Toshokan図書館 = Library
Eigo英語 = English
Benkyoshimashita勉強しました = to study
Haは, niに, deで, oを（お）

Answer:
Watashi wa nichiyoubi ni toshokan de eigo o benkyo shimashita.
私は日曜日に図書館で英語を（お）勉強しました

6. She ate breakfast at 8:00 am at home.
Kanojo彼女 = She
Tabemashita食べました = ate
Asagohan朝御飯 = breakfast
Hachi ji八時 = 8:00 am
Uchiうち = Home
Waは, deで, niに, oを（お）

Answer:
Kanojo wa hachi ji ni uchi de asagohan o tabemashita.
彼女は八時にうちで朝御飯を（お）食べました

7. I went to America last year.
Watashi私 = I
Ikimashita行きました = Went
Amerikaアメリカ = America
Kyonen去年 = Last year
Waは, niに

Answer:
Watashi wa kyonen amerika ni ikimashita.
私は去年アメリカに行きました

Expressing Desire欲求表現

Knowing how to express what you want is extremely helpful in Japanese.

Nouns are used together with **hoshii欲しい** when expressing that you want a certain object.

(Watashi wa) noun + ga hoshii desu
(I want… object)

We use ga particle anytime we are stating desires. In this case, it does not state emphasis, it is just one of those patterns we have to accept and shouldn't analyse.

Example sentences:
(Watashi wa) atarashii pasokon ga hoshii desu
私は）新しいパソコンが欲しいです
(Atarashii 新しい= new)
(Pasokonパソコン = PC)
I want a new PC

Kakkoii kareshi ga hoshii desu
かっこいい彼氏が欲しいです
(Kakkoiiかっこいい = handsome)
(Kareshi彼氏 = boyfriend)
I want a handsome boyfriend

Changing **hoshii欲しい** into its negative form allows is to express that we do not want something.

In Japanese **hoshii欲しい** is an adjective not a verb. Therefore its conjugation is the same as any i – adjective.

(Watashi wa) noun + ga hoshikunai desu
(I do not want...)

Example sentences:
Takai purezento ga hoshikunai desu
高いプレゼントが欲しいです
(Takai高い = expensive)
(Purezentoプレゼント = present)
I do not want expensive presents

Shukudai ga hoshikunai desu
宿題が欲しくないです
(Shukudai宿題 = homework)
I do not want homework

Exercise:
Translate the following sentences to Japanese.

1. I want kind friends
(Kind = yasashii優しい)
(Friends = tomodachi友達)

Answer:
Yasahii tomodachi ga hoshii desu
優しい友達が欲しいです

2. I want a beautiful haircut
(Beautiful = kirei綺麗)
(Haircut = kaminoke髪の毛)

Answer:
Kirei na kaminoke ga hoshii desu
綺麗な髪の毛が欲しいです

3. I do not want noisy neighbors
(Noisy = urusaiうるさい)
(Neighbor = rinjin隣人)

Answer:
Urusai rinjin ga hoshikunai desu.
うるさい隣人が欲しくないです

4. I do not want a slow car
(Slow = osoi遅い) (Car = kuruma車)

Answer:
Osoi kuruma ga hoshikunai desu
遅い車が欲しくないです

Want to – Tai Formたい活用形

In the previous section we learnt how to say we want something with "hoshii欲しい".

If we "want to do something" we cannot use "hoshii欲しい". Instead we have to use a different form of conjugation, which is taiたい form. Remember "hoshii欲しい" can only be used with nouns.

hoshii欲しい = want (for nouns)
taiたい form = want to (verbs)

The easiest way to conjugate into tai form is to start from the masu conjugation. From here the first step is to take off the masu part of the verb.

Example:

Taberu	**→**	**Tabe~~masu~~**	**→Tabe**
Nomu	**→**	**Nomi~~masu~~**	**→Nomi**
Kau	**→**	**Kai~~masu~~**	**→Kai**
Kaku	**→**	**Kaki~~masu~~**	**→Kaki**
Hanasu	**→**	**Hanashi~~masu~~**	**→Hanashi**
Iku	**→**	**Iki~~masu~~**	**→Iki**
Suru	**→**	**Shi~~masu~~**	**→Shi**
Kuru	**→**	**Ki~~masu~~**	**→Ki**

Once we have this we add "tai" to the verb.

Example:

Taberu **→** **Tabe** **→** **Tabetai**
(*ru*-verb)

Nomu **→** **Nomi** **→** **Nomitai**
(*u*-verb)

Kau **→** **Kai** **→** **Kaitai**
(*u*-verb)

Kaku → **Kaki** → **Kakitai**
(*u*-verb)

Hanasu → **Hanashi**→ **Hanashitai**
(*u*-verb)

Iku → **Iki** → **Ikitai**
(*u*-verb)

Suru → **Shi** → **Shitai** (irregular verb)

Kuru → **Ki** → **Kitai** (irregular verb)

When using tai form in polite level speech we need to include desu at the end. Without desu the statement sounds very casual.

When using tai form we can also use particles ga or o. Both are interchangeable.

... + ga/o + verb (tai form) + desu
(I want to do...)

Example sentences:
I want to drink tea
(watashi wa) o-cha ga nomitai desu
(私は）お茶が欲しいです
(tea = o-chaお茶) (drink = nomu)

I want to eat fish
(watashi wa) sakana o tabetai desu
(私は）魚を（お）食べたいです
(fish = sakana魚) (eat = taberu食べる)

One thing that confuses many students when we use tai form is the ending. Since tai ends in "I", the verb actually becomes an "I" adjective.

Therefore when we want to make a negative form of this phrase, we have to use i adjective conjugation.
So to conjugation *i*- adjectives into past present, we use kunai.

Example:
Tabetai → Tabetai
→Tabetakunai

Nomitai → Nomitai
→Nomitakunai

Kaitai → Kaitai
→Kaitakunai

Kakitai → Kakitai
→Kakitakunai

Hanashitai → Hanashitai
→Hanashitakunai

Ikitai → Ikitai
→Ikitakunai

Shitai → Shitai
→Shitakunai

Kitai → Kitai
→Kitakunai

Example sentences:
I don't want to watch that movie
Sono eiga o mitakunai desu
その映画を（お）観たくないです
(movie = eiga映画) (watch = miru観る)

I don't want to go to school
Watashi wa gakko ni ikitakunai desu

私は学校に行きたくないです
(school = gakko学校) (go = iku行く)
We have to use “niに” as we are stating direction of movement

Exercise:

Express the desire to do/ to not do something by forming sentences with given words.

1. Shuumatsu + eiga + miru (Positive)
(Shuumatsu = weekend) (Eiga = movie)
(Miru = to see, to watch)

Answer:
Shuumatsu ni eiga o/ ga mitai desu
週末に映画を（お）/が観たいです

2. Heya + soji suru (Negative)
(Heya = room) (Soji suru = to clean)

Answer:
Heya o/ ga soji shitakunai desu
部屋を（お）/が掃除したくないです

3. Rainen + Nihon + iku (Positive)
(Rainen = next year) (Nihon = Japan) (Iku = to go)

Answer:
Rainen Nihon ni ikitai desu
来年日本に行きたいです

4. Kono + mise + fuku + kau (Negative)
(Mise = store) (Fuku = clothes) (Kau = to buy)

Answer:
Kono mise de fuku o/ ga kaitakunai desu
この店で服を（お）/が買いたくないです

Frequency Words頻度を表す単語

Frequency words are very helpful in Japanese, they are used to state how often you do something.
Below are a list of common frequency words:

Always = Itsumoいつも
Often = Yokuよく
Usually = Taiteiたいてい
Sometimes = Tokidokiときどき
Not much = Amari あまり+ negative
Rarely = Mettani滅多に + negative
Never = Zenzen全然 + negative

Every day = Mainichi毎日
Every week = Maishuu毎週
Every weekend = Maishuu matsu毎週末

These frequency words are usually placed after the topic of the sentence.

Examples:
I often watch a movie
= (Watashi wa) Yoku eiga o mimasu.
(私は）よく映画を（お）観ます
(movie = eiga映画)

I go to a bar every weekend
= Maishumatsu Baa ni ikimasu
毎週末バーに行きます
(bar = baaバー)

When we use words like "not much", "rarely" "not at all" double negations apply. Therefore they have to be followed by a negative form.

Example:

I do not eat fish at all

= Zenzen **sakana o** tabemasen

全然**魚を（お）**食べません

(fish = sakana魚)

I rarely drink coffee

= Mettani **kohi o** nomimasen

滅多に**コーヒーを（お）**飲みません

(coffee = kohiコーヒー)

Invitingお誘い

In this chapter we will cover how to invite someone to do something.

Invitation expressions go as follows:

Why don't we~? /Won't you~?
Verb + present negative masu form + ka?

This pattern is normally used with the word "issho ni一緒に" which means together.

Examples:
Issho ni ohirugohan o tabemasen ka?
一緒にお昼ご飯を（お）食べませんか
= Why don't we have lunch together?
(isshoni一緒に = together)
(ohirugohanお昼ご飯 = lunch)

Issho ni eiga o mimasen ka?
一緒に映画を（お）観ませんか
= Why don't we watch a movie together?
(movie = eiga映画) (watch = miru観る)

You can answer in the follow way:
Yes: Hai, ii desu ne.
はい、いいですね

No: Sumimasen, chotto...
すみません、ちょっと...
(sumimasenすみません = sorry)

Japanese people usually don't say "no" when refusing, instead they use "chottoちょっと". "Chottoちょっと" literally means "a bit", but it shows your hesitation. The person will understand that you are not able to or you simply don't want to.

Exercise

There are three situations. Read carefully and think about how to invite someone using the given words.

1. You have two movie tickets and want to ask your friend if he/she wants to watch a movie tomorrow.

Movie = Eiga映画
Watch = Miru観る
Tommorrow = Ashita明日

Invite:

Answer:
Ashita eiga o (issho ni) mimasen ka?
明日映画を（お）観ませんか

2. You are going to study Japanese in the library at 5pm today. You want to invite your friends as well.

Study = Benkyosuru勉強する
Japanese = Nihongo日本語
Library = Toshokan図書館

Invite:

Answer:
Kyou, Goji ni toshokan de benkyo shimasen ka?
今日、五時に図書館で勉強しませんか

3. It's lunch time now, but you have no one to eat with you today. Invite someone to your lunch.

Eat = Taberu食べる
Lunch = Ohirugohanお昼御飯
Together = Isshoni一緒に

Invite:

Answer:
Isshoni ohirugohan o tabemasen ka?
一緒にお昼御飯を（お）食べませんか

Te-formて一活用形

Te-form can used in a variety of different situations in japanese and is a handy part of Japanese grammar. We will cover its usages in later sections, however first we need to know how to make verbs into te form.

As with all verbs in Japanese, the conjugation will be different depending on the type of verb.

Ru-verbs:
1. Drop the final "ru"
2. Add "te"

e.g. Tabe~~ru~~ (to eat) → Tabe + te → Tabete

Ru verb usually end in "eru" or iru" however there are some exceptions.

U-verbs:
Using Te-form with u-verbs is more complicated, as these verbs are divided into five categories.

Each is conjugated differently depending on the ending of the verb.

U-verbs with final **u, tsu, ru**:
1. Drop the highlighted part.
2. Add "tte"

e.g. Ka~~u~~ (to buy) → Ka + tte
→ Katte

e.g. Ma~~tsu~~ (to wait) → Ma + tte
→ Matte

e.g. Waka~~ru~~ (to understand) → Waka + tte
→ Wakatte

U-verbs with final **mu, bu, nu**:
1. Drop the highlighted part
2. Add "nde"

e.g. No~~mu~~ (to drink) → No + nde
→ Nonde

e.g. Aso~~bu~~ (to play) → Aso + nde
→ Asonde

e.g. Shi~~nu~~ (to die) → Shi + nde
→ Shinde

U-verbs with final **ku**:
1. Drop the highlighted part
2. Add "ite"

e.g. Ka~~ku~~ (to write) → Ka + ite
→ Kaite

An exception to this rule is verb **Iku (to go)**, which is conjugated as **Itte**.

U-verbs with final **gu**:
1. Drop the highlighted part
2. Add "ide"

e.g. Oyo~~gu~~ (to swim) → Oyo + ide
→ Oyoide

U-verbs with final **su**:
1. Drop the highlighted part
2. Add "shite"

e.g. Hana~~su~~ (to talk) → Hana + shit
→ Hanashite

<u>Irregular verbs:</u>
Irregular verbs conjugate as follows:

e.g. Suru (to do) → Shite
e.g. Kuru (to come) → Kite

A common mistake students make when learning *te*-form is confusing it with the masu form conjugation. Try not to make this mistake, unforntunately te form conjugation is more complicated and we just have to try and memorise it.

<u>Exercise</u>

Practice: Write the following words in *te*-form:

Neru (to sleep)
Au (to meet)
Shinu (to die)
Matsu (to wait)
Miru (to see, to watch)
Wakaru (to understand, u-verb)
Asobu (to play)
Kiku (to ask, to listen)
Yomu (to read)
Oyogu (to swim)
Kasu (to lend)
Benkyo suru (to study)
Kuru (to come)
Iku (to go)
Taberu (to eat)
Sakebu (to scream)
Kiotukeru (to watch out)
Katu (to win)
Kau (to buy)
Kaku (to write)
Shinnjiru (to trust)
Tasukeru (to help)
Kesu (to erase)

<u>Answers</u>

Neru (to sleep) Nete
Au (to meet) Atte
Shinu (to die) Shinde
Matsu (to wait) Matte

Miru (to see, to watch) Mite
Wakaru (to understand, u-verb) Wakatte
Asobu (to play) Asonde
Kiku (to ask, to listen) Kiite
Yomu (to read) Yonde
Oyogu (to swim) Oyoide
Kasu (to lend) Kashite
Benkyo suru (to study) Benkyo shite
Kuru (to come) Kite
Iku (to go) Itte
Taberu (to eat) Tabete
Sakebu (to scream) Sakende
Kiotukeru (to watch out) Kiotukete
Katu (to win) Katte
Kau (to buy) Katte
Kaku (to write) Kaite
Shinnjiru (to trust) Shinjite
Tasukeru (to help) Tasukete
Kesu (to erase) Keshite

Present Continuous Form

現在継続の表し方

Present continuous form is used when describing actions that are ongoing. Such as "I'm eating", "she is driving", "we are going" etc.
There are two ways we use present contionous form.

To make general "-ing" sentences we have to use te form with iru/imasu

Te form + iru/imasu
(…ing)

Iru is used for informal speech and imasu is used for formal speech.

Examples

I am eating (f)
Watashi wa tabette imasu
私は食べています
(to eat = tabemasu)

She is drinking (f)
Kanojo wa nonde imasu
彼女は飲んでいます
(to drink = nomu)

I am reading a book (inf)
Ima hon o yonde iru
今本を読んでいる
(now = ima今) (to read = yomu読む)
(book = hon本)

To make more sentences we can conjugate imasu and iru just like they were any other verb:

Present negative
She is not eating
Kanojo wa tabette imasen
彼女は食べていません (f)
Kanojo wa tabette inai(inf)

Past Postive
She was eating
Kanojo wa tabette imashita (f)
彼女は食べていました
Kanojo wa tabette ita (inf)
彼女は食べていた

Past negative
She was not eating
Kanojo wa tabette imasen deshita (f)
彼女は食べていませんでした
Kanojo wa tabette inakatta (inf)
彼女は食べていなかった

<u>Using "ing" with verbs and adjectives</u>
When we have a "ing" verb and adjective in the same sentence we follow a different pattern.

In this case, the sentence doesn't mean a action that you are doing right now but is instead just talking about the topic.

Examples
Singing is fun
Studying is boring

In these examples we have a "ing" verb and an adjective. Here we cannot use "Te form + iru/imasu", instead we have to use the particle "noの".

The particle “noの” is normally used for possession but as you know, in Japanese particles can have many uses. This is just another use of “noの” particle.

Langauge pattern:

Verb plain form + no + particle + adjective + desu

“desuです” makes this sentence a polite level sentence. We can omit “desuです” to make the sentence casual.

Let’s look at some examples

Singing is fun (inf)
Utau no wa tanoshī
歌うのは楽しい
(sing = utau歌う) (fun = tanoshii楽しい)

I like studying (f)
Benkyo suru no ga suki desu
勉強するのが好きです
(to study = benkyo suru勉強する)

I like playing games (f)
Gemu o suru no wa suki desu
ゲームを（お）するのは好きです
(playing games = gemu o suruゲームを（お）する)

When we use “no” in this way, the “ing” verb actually becomes a noun.

Negative form
To create negative forms of these sentences, we simply have to use the same conjugations in previous sections:

Danicing is not fun
Odoru no wa Tanoshikunai desu
踊るのは楽しくないです

Studying Japanese is not easy (inf)
Nihongo o hanasu no wa kantan ja nai
日本語を（お）話すのは簡単じゃないです

I don't like drinking alchocol
Osake o nomu no wa suki ja nai desu
お酒を（お）飲むのは好きじゃないです

When we conjugate this pattern, we only change the adjective and the verb stays the same.

<u>Exercise:</u>
Translate the following sentences to Japanese.

1. I am watching tv
(tv = terebiテレビ) (watch = miru見る)

Answer:
Terebi o mite imasu
テレビを（お）見ています

2. The baby is sleeping
(baby = akachan赤ちゃん) (to sleep = neru寝る)

Answer:
Akachan wa nete imasu
赤ちゃんは寝ています

3. Recently I have been watching game of thrones
(recently = saikin最近) (to watch = miru見る)

Answer:
Saikin game of thrones o mite imasu
最近ゲームオブソローンを（お）見ています

4. She is teaching

(she = kanojo彼女) (to teach = oshieru教える)

Answer:
Kanojo wa oshiete imasu
彼女は教えています

5. Singing is not fun
(to sing = utau歌う) (fun = tanoshii楽しい)

Answer:
Utau no wa tanoshikunai desu

歌うのは楽しくないです

I Have私は持っています

When we want to say that we have something, we use the following phrase:

Object ga Arimasu/Imasu

I have object

Arimasuあります is used or non-living things such as a table, a chair or dead animals like fish in a market.

Imasu いますis used for living creatures such as a cat, a dog and humans.

Aru あるand iruいる are the informal versions of arimasu / imasu.

Ga is used again here, it does not contain any special meaning but is instead just used in this phrase.

Examples

I have a cat

Neko ga imasu

猫がいます

I have a car

Kuruma ga arimasu

車があります

We can also add the subject to the front of the sentence to state a person has an item.

Person wa object ga imasu/arimasu

Person has object

Example

Mr suki has a cat

Suki san wa neko ga imasu

スキさんは猫がいます

(cat = neko猫)

Ms Yudi has a younger sister (inf)

Yudi wa imoto ga iru

ユディは妹がいる

(younger sister = imoto妹)

To make this into a question we just need to add the particle "kaか" to the end of the sentence.

Mr suki has a cat

Suki san wa neko ga imasu

スキさんは猫がいます

Does Mr suki have a cat?

Suki san wa neko ga imasu ka?

スキさんは猫がいますか

Conjugation of have

The conjugation of imasu and arimasu is the same as any other masu verb.

Present Postive	=	Imasu / arimasu
Present Negative	=	Imasen / arimasen
Past Positive	=	Imashita / arimashita
Past Negative	=	Imasen deshita / arimasen deshita

Examples

Mr suki does not have a cat

Suki san wa neko ga imasen
スキさんは猫がいません

Ms Judai does not have a car
Yudi san wa kuruma ga arimasen
ユディさんは車がありません

However the conjugaton of aru and iru is slightly different

Positive Present	=	aru
Negative Present	=	nai
Positive Past	=	atta
Negative Past	=	nakkata

Positive Present	=	iru
Negative Present	=	inai
Positive Past	=	ita
Negative Past	=	inakatta

Examples
I don't have money
Okane ga nai
お金がない
(money = okaneお金)

I didn't have time
Jikan ga nakkatta
時間がなかった
(time = jikan時間)

I had a cat
Watashi wa neko ga ita
私は猫がいた
(cat = neko猫)

<u>Exercise</u>

Translate the given sentences:

1. I have a younger brother.

Answer:
Ototo ga imasu.
弟がいます

2. She had a boyfriend.

Answer:
Kanjyo wa kareshi ga imashita.
彼女は彼氏がいました

3. I have no pets.
(pet = pettoペット)

Answer:
Petto ga imasen.
ペットがいません

4. He did not have money.

Answer:
Kare wa okane ga arimasen deshita.
彼はお金がありませんでした

Existence - There is/ There are

存在 - がある

When describing the location/existence of something, we also use imasu/arimasu.
However the pattern is slightly different:

Thing + ga + location + ni + arimasu/imasu

We can also use aru/iru for informal speech
Ga particle is always used when talking about existence. We have learnt about particle "niに" in a previous section. We also use "niに" when talking about location/existence. "niに" in these situations translates to "in" or "at"

Let's look at some examples.
Gakko ni sensei ga imasu.
学校に先生がいます
(gakko学校 =school) (sensei先生 = teacher)
= There are teachers at a school
At school ..... (gakko ni)

Kyoshitsu ni tsukue to isu ga arimasu.
教室に机と椅子があります
(Kyoshitsu 教室= classroom) (Tsukue机 = desk) (Isu椅子 = chair)
= There are desks and chairs in the classroom.
In the classroom .... (kyoshitsu ni)

Watashi no heya ni terebi ga aru
私の部屋にテレビがある (inf)
(Heya部屋 = room) (terebiテレビ = TV)
= There is a TV in my room.
In my room .... (watashi no heya ni)

As you can see from these phrase we are talking about the existence of an item therefore we use imasu/arimasu. And since we are talking about where they exist, we have to use particle “ni”.

Adding pre-positions

We can also use prepositions words to further explain the location of an item.

List of pre positions

On	Ue上
In	Naka中
Under	Shita下
Front	Mae前
Behind	Ushiro後ろ
Next	Yoko横/Tonari隣
Near	Chikaku近く
Between	Aida間

When combining with a noun, such as “on the table”, “next to the school”, the preposition phrases go as follows:

Place/object + no + preposition

Examples:

On the desk = Tsukue no ue
机の上

Under the chair = Isu no shita
椅子の下

Near my house = Ie no chikaku
家の近く

Now you know how to say "there is/are" and location words.
We can now put these two phrases together to make a more descriptive sentence:

Place/object + no + pre postion + ni + object + ga + arimasu/imasu

As stated before we need to include the particle "niに" when talking about location.

Example Sentences:
Tsukue no ue ni enpitsu ga arimasu
机の上に鉛筆があります
(Pencil = Enpitsu鉛筆), (Desk = Tsukue机)
= **There is a pencil on the desk.**

Suupaa no tonari ni hanaya ga arimasu
スーパーの隣に花屋があります
(Suupaaスーパー = supermarket)
(hanaya花屋 = flower shop)
=**There is a flower shop next to the supermarket**

Yoshida san no tonari ni watashi ga iru (inf)
吉田さんの隣に私がいる
= **Yoshida is next to me**

__Asking for location of an item__
When you want to know the location of an object, you can use the question word "whereどこ" (doko). We can use this with arimasu/imasu.
The sentence structure goes as follows:

Doko + ni + object + ga + arimasu/imasu + ka?

Where is (object)?

Where is the pencil?
= Doko ni enpitsu ga arimasu ka?
どこに鉛筆がありますか

In the pencase.
= Fudebako no naka ni arimasu.
筆箱の中にあります
(Pencase = Fudebako筆箱)

<u>Exercise</u>
Translate the following sentences.
1. There is a flower shop in front of the station.
(Flower shop = Hanaya花屋), (Station = Eki駅)

Answer:
Eki no mae ni hanaya ga arimasu.
駅の前に花屋があります

2. There is a cat under the chair.
(Cat = Neko中), (Chair = Isu椅子)

Answer:
Isu no shita ni eko ga imasu.
椅子の下に猫がいます

3. There is a dog next to the man (inf)
(man = o toko男), (next to = tonari隣),
(Dog = Inu犬)

Answer:
O toko no tonari ni inu ga iru.

男の隣に犬がいる

Making Requests依頼

Since we have learnt te-form, we can now start putting it to use. Te-form can be used together with **kudasaiください**, in order to make a polite request to another person.

Verb *te*-form + kudasai
(please do ...)

Example:

Oshieru	→	**Oshiete kudasai**
Nomu	→	**Nonde kudasai**
Kaku	→	**Kaite kudasai**
Hanasu	→	**Hanashite kudasai**
Iku	→	**Itte kudasai**

Example sentences:
Please drink this medicine.
(Kusuri薬 = medicine) (drink = nomu飲む)
= Kono kusuri o nonde kudasai.
この薬を（お）飲んでください

Please speak in Japanese.
(Nihongo日本語 = Japanese)
= Nihongo de hanashite kudasai.
日本語で話してください

When talking to a close friend or a relative, you can make a less formal request by omitting **kudasaiください.**

Example sentences:
Turn on the TV.
(Tsukeru つける= turn on)
Terebi o tsukete.
テレビを（お）つけて

Do the homework.
(Shukudai宿題 = homework) (do = suruする)
Shukudai o shite.
宿題を（お）して

<u>Exercise</u>:
Translate the following requests to Japanese.
1. Please eat the vegetables.
(Vegetables = yasai野菜)

Answer:
Yasai o tabete kudasai.
野菜を（お）ください

2. Please help your parents.
(Parents = ryoshin両親) (To help = tetsudau手伝う)

Answer:
Ryoshin o tetsudatte kudasai.
両親を（お）手伝ってください

3. Open the window (inf)
(Window = mado窓) (To open = akeru開ける)

Answer:
Mado o akete.
窓を（お）開けて

4. Play with your friends outside (inf)
(To play = asobu遊ぶ) (Friends = tomodachi友達) (Outside = soto外)

Answer:
Tomodachi to soto de asonde.
友達と外で遊ぶ

Asking For Permission許可を得る

When asking for permission we also use Te-form. We put this together with "mo ii desu ka?"

Verb *te*-form + mo ii desu ka?
(may I do ...?)

Example:

Miru → **Mi**te mo ii desu ka
May I watch?
(Miru見る/観る = to see, to watch)

Hanasu → **Hana**shite mo ii desu ka
May I talk?
(Hanasu話す = to talk)

In casual speech we omit the particles and just leave the verb, "ii" and use a rising tone.

Verb te form + ii + rising tone? (inf)
(may I ... ?)

Examples
Can I sit next to you?
Tonari suwatte ii?
隣座っていい
(next to = tonari隣) (sit = suwaru座る)

Can I open the window?
Mado, akete ii?
窓、開けていい
(window = mado窓) (open = akeru開ける)

To give our response, we use the te form and "mo ii desu" to say you may. And we use "wa ikemasen" to say you may not.

Verb *te*-form + mo ii desu
(you may do ...)

Verb *te*-form + wa ikemasen
(you may/must not do ...)

Example:

Miru → **Mite mo ii desu**
You may watch
(Miru見る/観る = to see, to watch)

Hanasu → **Hanashite wa ikemasen**
You may not talk
(Hanasu話す = to talk)

Example sentences:
A: **Uchi ni kaette mo ii desu ka?**
うちに帰ってもいいですか
(Uchi うち= home)
(Kaeru帰る = to go home, return)
May I go home?

B: **Hai, kaette mo ii desu.**
はい、帰ってもいいです
Yes, you may.

A: **Shashin wo totte mo ii desu ka?**
写真を撮ってもいいですか
(Shashin写真 = picture) (Toru撮る = to take)
May I take a picture?

B: **Koko de shashin o totte wa ikemasen.**

ここで写真を撮ってはいけません
You must not take a picture here.

Exercise:
Ask for permission by forming sentences with given words.

1. Jitensha + kariru
(Jitensha自転車 = bicycle)
(Kariru借りる = to borrow)

Answer:
Jitensha o karite mo ii desu ka?
自転車を借りてもいいですか

2. Atarashii + kutsu + kau
(Atarashii 新しい= new) (Kutsu 靴= shoes)
(Kau買う = to buy)

Answer:
Atarashii kutsu o katte mo ii desu ka?
新しい靴を（お）買ってもいいですか

3. Denwa + hanasu
(Denwa 電話= telephone)
(Hanasu 話す= to speak)

Answer:
Denwa de hanashite mo ii desu ka?
電話で話してもいいですか

Expressing too much過剰表現

When we want to express “too” in a sentence we use the word “sugiruすぎる”. We place this after the verb or adjective we are talking about. In order to use this in a sentence we need to conjugate.

Language pattern

Adjective/verb + sugiru/sugimasu

Sugiru is used for informal speech
Sugimasu is used for formal speech

Let’s look at using sugiru with adjectives first:

I adjectives with sugiru
We have to remove the final I and add sigiru.
I adjective (remove final i) + sigiru

Na adjectives with sigiru
We remove the final na and add sigiru:
Na adjective (remove na) + sigiru

Let’s see some examples

Too expensive
= takasugiru高すぎる (inf)
= takasugimasu高すぎます (f)
(expensive = takai高い)

Too cold
= samusugru 寒すぎる(inf)
= samusugimasu寒すぎます (f)
(cold = samui寒い)

Too quiet
= Shizuka sugiru静かすぎる (inf)
= Shizuka sugimasu静かすぎます (f)
(quiet = shizuka na静かな)

Examples in full sentences

This watch is too expensive
Kono tokei wa takasugirimasu
この時計は高すぎます
(expensive = takai高い)

This library is too quiet
Kono toshoukan wa shizuka sugimasu
この図書館は静かすぎます
(quiet = shizuka na静かな)

This new job is too hard
Atarashi shigoto wa taihen sugiru
新しい仕事は大変すぎる
(hard = taihen na大変な)

Negations are the same as any other verb, therefore we can conjugate in the following way:

Present Positive
= Takasugimasu / sugiru
Present Negative
= Takasugimasen / sugi nai
Past Positive
= Takasugimashita / sugita
Past Negative

=	Takasugimasen deshita / suginakatta

Sugiru with verbs
When using sigiru with verbs ending in “iru” and “eru” we have to chop off the final ru and add sigiru

Misugiru見すぎる
To watch too much
(watch = miru)

Tabesugiru食べすぎる
To watch too much
(eat = taberu)

Nesugiru寝すぎる
To sleep too much
(sleep = neru)

Example sentences
I slept too much yesterday (inf)
Kinō wa nesugita
昨日は寝すぎた

My little brother always watches too much TV (f)
Otōto wa itsumo terebi o misugimasu
弟はいつもテレビを（お）見すぎます

Sugiru with u verbs
For all other verbs ending in u, take off the ‘u’ and add sigiru.

Drank too much

Nomisugiru飲みすぎる
(drink = nomu)

Wrote too much
Kakisugita書きすぎる
(kaku = write)

Don't get confused!
If you're talking about "too" as in "me too /as well", here you have to use "moも" particle and not sigiruすぎる.

I like sushi
Watashi mo sushi ga suki desu
私も寿司が好きです
(I as well like sushi)

Exercise

Translate the given sentences:

1. This pen is too cheap.

(cheap = yasui安い)

Answer:
Kono pen wa yasusugimasu.
このペンは安すぎます

2. She worked too much yesterday.

Answer:
Kanjyo wa kinou shigoto sisugimashita.
彼女は昨日仕事しすぎました

Counters数え方

Japanese does not have plural form. Instead we use counter to state the amount of an item.

In English when to count something we can simply say what it is.
1 pen, 2 photos. 3 people

However in Japanese certain objects have their own specific counters
1 pen = ippon一本
2 photos = nimai二枚
3 people = sannin三人

There are tons of counters in Japanese. But don't worry, you don't have to learn all of them to use counters.

Let's go through some common ones

Nin人 counter
For counting people we use the "nin人" counter. The first two have special names but the rest follow the pattern "nin人"

1 person = Hitori一人
2 people = Futari二人
3 people = Sanin三人
4 people = Yonin四人
5 people = Gonin五人
6 people = Rokunin六人
7 people = Shichinin七人
8 people = Hachinin八人
9 people = Kyuunin九人
10 people = Juunin十人
100 people = Hyakunin百人
1000 people = Sennin千人
How many people = Nannin? 何人

Ko個 counter

Ko個 can be used to count small objects, such as apples, eggs etc. We simply add ko個 to the number.

1 = Iko一個
2 = Niko二個
3 = Sanko三個
4 = Yonko四個
5 = Goko五個
6 = Rokko六個
7 = Nanako七個
8 = Hakko八個
9 = Kyuuko九個
10 = Juko十個
100 = hyakko百個
1000 = senko 千個
How many = nanko? 何個

Generic counter

This counter can be used for counting generic things, like icecream, keys, chairs etc. These counters only go up to 10.

1 = Hitotsu一つ
2 = Futatsu二つ
3 = Mittsu三つ
4 = Yottsu四つ
5 = Itsutsu五つ
6 = Muttsu六つ
7 = Nanatsu七つ
8 = Yattsu八つ
9 = Kokonotsu九つ
10 = Too十
How many = Ikutsuいくつ

After 10 you can use ko個 counter to count more.

Ordering注文

Now that we have learnt about counters, we can learn how to order in Japanese. We use the words "onegaishimasuお願いします" and "kudasaiください" when placing an order.

Onegaishimasu and kudasai both translate to "please", however onegaishimasu is more polite.

…. Onegaishimasu / kudasai
… please

Examples
A vegetable ramen and a beer please
Yasai ramen to bīru kudasai
野菜ラーメンとビールください
(vegetable = yasai野菜)

Can I have a menu please?
Menu onegaishimasu
メニューお願いします

When ordering more than one of something, we need to use counters. The best way to do this is by using the following language pattern:

Food/drink name + (number + ko /tsu counter) + kudasai

Example
Can I have four waters please
Mizu o yonko kudasai
水を（お）四個ください
or
Mizu o yotsu kudasai
水を（お）四つください
(water = mizu水)

Can I have 3 beer and 2 salmon please
Biru o mitsu to sāmon o futatsu kudasai
ビールを（お）三つとサーモンを（お）二つください
or
Biru o sanko to sāmon o niko kudasai
ビールを（お）三個とサーモンを（お）二個ください
(beer = biruビール)

Sometimes when ordering you might not know the name of the items you want. In this case we can use the word "koreこれ" and simply point out the items off the menu.

I want this and this please
Kore to kore o kudasai
これとこれを（お）ください

A few common phrases you may here
When entering the restaurant you will hear, "Irasshaimase". This means "welcome" and used to greet customers.

Next you'll be asked "nan nin desu ka何人ですか?" which translates to "how many people?" We can answer this with the number of people plus the people counter "nin"

3 people = sannin desu三人です
2 people = futari desu二人です

Finally when you want to call the waiter to "ask for the bill" or "to order" you can use the following phrases:

Excuse me
Sumimasen
すみません

Order please
Chumon onegaishimasu
注文お願いします

(order = chumon注文)

Check please
Okaikei onegaishimasu
お会計お願いします
(cheque = okaikeiお会計)

Exercise
Translate the given sentences:
1. Excuse me, can I have a menu please?

Answer:
Sumimasen, menu onegaishimasu.
すみません、メニューお願いします

2. Miso ramen and two beer please.

Answer:
Miso ramen to biru hutatu kudasai.
味噌ラーメンとビール二つください

3. Check please. And can I have 10 water please?
(And = soretoそれと)

Answer:
Okaikei onegaishimasu. Soreto, mizu o too kudasai.
お会計お願いします。あと、水を（お）十ください

Masho – let'sましょう

When we want to suggest to do something we use the word "masho". This translates to "let's".

Lets ……
…. Masho

To use this we simply have to take the masu part off a verb and replace it with masho.

Examples
Let's eat dinner
Bangohan o tabemasho
晩御飯を（お）食べましょう
(dinner = bangohan晩御飯)

Lets see a movie together
Issho ni eiga o mimasho
一緒に映画を（お）観ましょう
(together = issho ni一緒に)

Lets study Japanese
Nihongo o benkyo shimasho
日本語を（お）勉強しましょう
(Japanese language = nihongo日本語)

Lets study at the library
Toshokan ni benkyo shimasho
図書館に勉強しましょう
(library = toshokan図書館)

Using "let's" informally
Making "let's" sentences in informal tense can be trickier. The conjugation is slightly different depending on the verb endings.

For verbs that have “iru” and “eru” ending, we change the last “ru” to “you”.

Examples
Let’s eat (inf)
Tabeyo食べよう

Let’s eat lunch here (inf)
Koko de hirugohan o tabeyou
ここで昼ご飯を（お）食べよう

Let’s sleep (inf)
Neyou寝よう

For all other u verb endings, we change the u into ou

To go (inf)
Iku = ikou行こう

Let’s go to japan (inf)
Nihon ni ikou
日本に行こう

Let’s drink tea (inf)
Ochaa o nomou
お茶を（お）飲もう

For the two irregular verbs, they conjugate in the following way:
Suru = shiyouしよう
Kuru = koyou来よう

Exercise
Translate the given sentences:
1. Let’s go to the restaurant together.

Answer:

Issyo ni sono resutoranto ni ikimasyo.
一緒にそのレストランに行きましょう

2. Let's discuss about it.
(discuss = hanashiau 話し合う)
(about = ni tuite について)

Answer:
Sore ni tuite hanashiaimasyo.
それについて話し合いましょう

3. Let's eat lunch together. (inf)

Answer:
Issyo ni hirugohan o tabemasyo.
一緒に昼ご飯を（お）食べましょう

More than比較級ーより

In this section we are going to learn how to compare things together, for example A is better than B. To make these sentences, we use "ho ga" and "yori".
The language pattern goes as follows

A no hoga B yori C desu
A is C than B

No hoga = is more
Yori = than
C = verb or adjective you are comparing

Example
Ramen is better than pasta
Ramen no hoga pasta yori ii desu
ラーメンの方がパスタよりいいです

Snow is better than rain
Yuki no hoga ame yori ii desu
雪の方が雨よりいいです
(snow = yuki雪) (rain = ame雨)

When C is an adjective we don't have to conjugate. Literally translated this sentence means "ramen is good than pasta". However in Japanese "better" is translated as "good". Therefore we use the word "iiいい" in this situation.

We can also change C to a different adjective, to create other comparative sentences.

Example
Sam is smarter than dave
Sam no ho ga dave yori atama ga ii desu
サムの方がデイブより頭がいいです

(smart = atama ga ii頭がいい)

Hanako is cooler/handsome than Hiroko
Hanako no hoga Hiroko yori kakkoi desu
花子のほうが弘子よりかっこいいです
(cooler/handsome = kakkoiかっこいい)

I like vegetables better than meat
Yasai no hoga niku yori suki desu
野菜の方が肉より好きです
(vegetables = yasai野菜) (meat = niku肉)

What confuses most beginners, is that we can actually change the order of the sentence. However the meaning remains the same:

B yori A no hoga C desu
Than B, A is (adjective)

Example
Snow is better than rain
Ame yori yuki no hoga ii desu
雨より雪のほうがいい
Than rain, snow is better

This can be confusing to see, but just remember the meaning is still the same.

To ask someone which one they prefer, we use the following structure

Which one do you prefer A or B?
A to B to dochi no hoga suki (desu ka?)
(dochira is used for formal speech, instead of dochi)

To answer we use the same pattern as before:
I like A more than B
A no hoga b yori suki desu

If we want to say that we like both we can say this in three ways:
I like both
A mo B mo suki desu

Or
Dochi mo suki
どっちも好き
By adding mo, dochiどっち now means both
Dochiramoどちらも is more formal

Or
We can put both together
A mo b mo dochi mo suki (inf)
A mo b mo dochira mo suki desu (f)

One thing to keep in mind, is when we are asking which one you prefer, you can only use dochiどっち and dochiraどちら for 2 option. If we have more than two option we use doreどれ "which one" however this is a more advanced level pattern.

Let's see some more comparative examples
Which you prefer summer or winter?
Natsu to fuyu to dochi no hoga suki
夏と冬とどちらの方が好き
(summer = natsu夏) (winter = fuyu冬)

I prefer dogs to cats
Watashi wa inu no hoga neko yori suki desu
私は犬の方が猫より好きです
(dog = inu犬) (cat = neko猫)

Kfc is a little bit more expensive than mcdonalds
Kfc no hoga Mc'donalds yori chotto takai desu
ケー・エフ・シーの方がマクドナルドよりちょっと高いです
(little bit = chottoちょっと)

Exercise

Translate the given sentences:

1. Which do you prefer, beach or mountain? Mountain is better than beach.

(beach = biichi ビーチ) (mountain = yama 山)

Answer:

Biichi to yama dochira no hoga suki desu ka? Yama no houga biichi yori suki desu.

ビーチと山どちらの方が好きですか？山の方がビーチよりも好きです

2. Which do you prefer, coffee or tea? I like both. (inf)

Answer:

Koohii to ocha dochi ga suki? Dochi mo suki.

コーヒーとお茶どっちが好き？どっちも好き

3. British English is cooler than American English.

Answer:

Igirisu eigo no hoga amerika eigo yori kakkoii desu.

イギリス英語の方がアメリカ英語よりかっこいいです

The Most最上級

We have learnt how to compare two things, but how do we say something is the most of something. For this we use the word "ichiban一番" which translates to "number one". With this we can makes words like, fastest, cutest, longest etc.

Language pattern:

Ichiban + adjective
….. st

Ichiban一番 = number one

Let's see some examples
The cutest (literally cute no 1)
Ichiban kawaii
一番かわいい

The cutest pokemon is pickaku
Ichiban kawaii pokemon wa pickaku desu
一番かわいいポケモンはピカチュウです
(cute = kawaiiかわいい)

Yuki is the most beautiful person (no 1 beautiful person)
Ichiban kirei na hito wa yuki san desu
一番綺麗な人はゆきさんです
(beautiful = kirei na綺麗な)

Titanic is the saddest movie
Ichiban kanashi eiga wa Titanic desu
一番悲しい映画はタイタニックです
(sad = kanashi悲しい)

Exercise

Translate the given sentences:

1. Mt. Fuji is the most famous mountain in Japan.

(Mt. Fuji = fujisan 富士山)

Answer:

Nihon de ichiban yumei na yama wa fujisan desu.

日本で一番有名な山は富士山です

2. The most beautiful landscape is Japanese Alps.

(landscape = keshiki 景色)

Answer:

Ichiban kireina keshiki wa nihon alps desu.

一番綺麗な景色は日本アルプスです

3. Yoko is the kindest person.

(kind = yasashi 優しい) (person= hito 人)

Answer:

Ichiban yasashi hito wa yoko desu.

一番優しい人は洋子です

Have you ever?ーことがありますか

To state things that we have done or never dpne, we use the following language pattern:

..ta koto ga aru/arimasu
I have .. (the experience)

This often gets confused with the conjugation of verbs, let's look at the difference:

I went to japan
Nihon ni ikimashita
日本に行きました
(to go = iku行く)

I have been to japan
Nihon ni ita koto ga arimasu
日本に行ったことがありますか

So we used this phrase to state experiences we have had or we haven't had. TO make the negative form, we conjugate aru to nai and arimasu to arimasen.

Examples
I have never been to japan
Nihon ni ita koto ga nai (inf)
日本に行ったことがない
or
Nihon ni ita koto ga arimasen (f)
日本に行ったことがありません

Have you listened to this?
Kore o kita koto ga arimasu ka?
これを（お）聞いたことがありますか

(listen = kiku聞く)

I have never listened to it
Kita koto ga arimasen
聞いたことがありません

We can even simplify to say yes or no with aru/arimasu.

Have you listened to this?
Kore o kita koto ga arimasu ka?
これを（お）聞いたことがありますか

Yes
Hai arimasu / aru
はい、あります/ある

No
iee arimasen / nai
いいえ、ありません/ない

Exercise

Translate the given sentences:

1. Have you ever eaten ramen? No I have never eaten ramen.

Answer:
Ramen o tabeta koto ga arimasu ka? Iie ramen o tabeta koto ga arimasen.
ラーメンを（お）食べたことがありますか？いいえ、ラーメンを（お）食べたことがありません

2. Have you ever climbed the mountain? Yes I have.
(to climb = noboru 登る)

Answer:
Sono yama ni nobotta koto ga arimasu ka? Hai arimasu.
その山に登ったことがありますか？はい、あります

3. I have never played the game. (Inf)

Answer:
Sono geemu o shita koto ga nai.
そのゲームを（お）したことがない

Connecting Verbs動詞のつなぎ方

Previously in the book it was explained that '*to*' particle can connect two nouns, however it cannot be used with verbs.

Te-form is used to connect two or more verbs in order to describe a sequence of actions.
We only use te form to conjugate the first verb, the final verb is left in the tense you want to state (past, present, future).

Example sentences:
Shukudai o shite, yasumimasu.
宿題を（お）して、休みます
(Shukudai 宿題= homework) (Suruする = to do) (Yasumu休む = to rest)
I will do my homework and then rest.

Oishii hirugohan wo tabete, gakko ni ikimashita.
おいしい昼ご飯を（お）食べて、学校に行きました
(Oishii おいしい= delicious) (Hirugohan 昼ご飯= breakfast) (Taberu 食べる= to eat)
(Gakko 学校= school) (Iku 行く= to go)
I ate delicious breakfast and went to school.

Suupaa ni itte, kaimono o shimasho.
スーパーに行って、買い物を（お）しましょう
(Suupaaスーパー = supermarket) (Iku 行く= to go) (Kaimono suru 買い物する= to do shopping)
Let's go to the supermarket and do shopping.

Exercise:
Translate the given sentences:
1.I will work and then go back home.

Answer:
Hataraite ie ni kaerimasu.

働いて、家に帰ります

2. We will go to hot spring and then take a rest.
(hot spring = onsen 温泉)

Answer:
Watashitachi wa onsen ni itte yasumimasu.
私達は温泉に行って休みます

3. She will meet her friends and then go shopping.

Answer:
Kanojyo wa tomodachi ni atte kaimono o shimasu.
彼女は友達に会って、買い物を（お）します

Connecting Adjectives
形容詞のつなぎ方

Te – form can also be used to connect two or more adjectives, creating more descriptive sentences. In order to do that, we must learn how to transform adjectives into *te* – form.

I-adjectives:
1. Drop the final "i"
2. Add "kute"
e.g. Kawai~~i~~ (cute) → Kawai + kute → Kawaikute.

This also applies to the irregular adjective ii.
~~Ii~~ (good) → Yo + kute → Yokute.

Na-adjectives:
1. Drop the "na"
2. Add "de"
e.g. Kirei na (beautiful) → Kirei + de →
Kirei de

When connecting adjectives, the last adjective in the sequence remains normal and is not placed in te form.

Example sentences:
Piza wa yasukute, oishii desu
ピザは安くて、おいしいです
(Piza ピザ = pizza) (Yasui安い = cheap) (Oishiiおいしい = tasty)
The pizza is cheap and tasty

Tomodachi wa atama ga yokute, genki desu
友達は頭がよくて、元気です
(Tomodachi友達 = friend) (Atama ga ii 頭がいい= Smart) (Genki元気 = cheerful)
My friend is smart and cheerful

Kyou wa hima de, taikutsu desu
今日は暇で、退屈です
(Kyou 今日= today) (Hima 暇= free)
(Taikutsu 退屈= boring)
Today is free and boring

Exercise:
Connect the nouns and adjectives to form sentences
1. Tea + sweet + tasty
(Tea お茶= ocha) (Sweet 甘い= amai)
(Tasty おいしい= oishii)

Answer:
Ocha wa amakute, oishii desu.
お茶は甘くて、おいしいです

2. Puppy + small + cute
(Puppy = koinu子犬) (Small = chiisai小さい) (Cute = kawaiiかわいい)

Answer:
Koinu wa chiisakute, kawaii desu.
子犬は小さくて、かわいいです

3. Teacher + serious + strict
(Teacher = sensei先生) (Serious = majime naまじめな) (Strict = kibishii厳しい)

Answer:
Sensei wa majime de, kibishii desu.
先生はまじめで、厳しいです

4. Boyfriend + kind + handsome + wonderful + person
(Boyfriend = kareshi彼氏) (Kind = yasashii優しい) (Handsome = kakkoiiかっこいい) (Wonderful = suteki na素敵な)
(Person = hito人)

Answer:
Kareshi wa yasashikute, kakkoyokute, suteki na hito desu.

彼氏は優しくて、かっこよくて、素敵な人です

Telling Time in Japanese

日本語での時間の伝え方

In Japanese, both 12-hour and 24-hour clocks are used, however, 12-hour clock is more common in conversation.

Hour: Ji時
Minute: Hun, pun分

To tell time you just need to add "ji時" to the hour and "hun/pun分" to the minute. As you know 4, 7, 9 have two forms however we only use a certain type when talking about time:

Hours
4:00 Yo ji四時
7:00 Shichi ji七時
9:00 Ku ji九時

Minutes
1 minute Ippun一分
2 minutes Nihun二分
3 minutes Sanpun三分
4 minutes Yonhun四分
5 minutes Gohun五分
6 minutes Roppun六分
7 minutes Nanahun七分
8 minutes Happun八分
9 minutes Kyuu hun九分
10 minutes Juppun十分
...

The sentence order is the same as English. First we state the hour and then the minutes:

Example
2:15
Niji ju-go hun二時十五分

We can also use the following phrases to state am and pm:

Am = Gozen午前
Pm = Gogo午後

In Japanese AM/PM come in front of the time.

Examples
3:01pm
Gogo sanji ippun午後三時一分

8:00am
Gozen hatchiji 午前八時

Finally to ask the time we can use the question word:

Nanji? 何時 = what time?

We use this in the set phrase:

What time is it now?
Ima nanji desu ka? 今何時ですか
(now = ima今)

When talking about minutes we can also use the phrase "han半" to say half past

3:30
Sanji han三時半

1:30
Ichiji han一時半

Exercise

Translate the given sentences:

1.What time is it now? It is 8:20 am.

Answer:
Ima nanji desu ka? Gozen hachiji nijuppunn desu.
今何時ですか？午前八時二十分です

2. What time is it now? It Is 7:30 pm. (Inf)

Answer:
Ima nanji? Gogo shichi ji han.
今何時？午後七時半

3. 9:41 am.

Answer:
Gozen kuji yonju ippun.
午前九時四十一分

Time & Distance時間と距離

In this section, we will learn asking and answering how much time it takes to get from one place to another.

Question word **dono guraiどのぐらい** (how much) is used when asking how much time it takes to travel a certain distance.

A kara B made dono gurai kakarimasu ka?
How long does it take to get from A to B?
(Karaから = from) (Madeまで = to)
(Kakaru かかる= to take /time to do something)

Example:
How long does it take to get from the classroom to the library?
Kyoshitsu kara toshokan made dono gurai kakarimasu ka?
教室から図書館までどのぐらいかかりますか
(Kyoshitsu教室 = classroom)
(Toshokan図書館 = Library)

Gurai means 'approximately' or 'about'. When answering a **dono gurai** question you are expected to name an approximate time duration.

A kara B made + time + gurai kakarimasu
(It takes about + time + to get from A to B)

Example:
It takes about 5 minutes to get from the classroom to the library
Kyoshitsu kara toshokan made gofun gurai kakarimasu
教室から図書館まで五分ぐらいかかります
(Kyoshitsu教室 = classroom) (Toshokan図書館 = library) (Go-fun 五分= 5 minutes)
Or simplified
Gofun gurai kakarimasu

五分ぐらいかかります

When you want to get a more precise answer you may ask how many minutes/ hours/ days it takes to get from one place to another. In that case nan + time unit is used in a question instead of dono.

A kara B made nanjikan gurai **kakarimasu ka?**
(How many hours does it take to get from A to B?)
(hour = jikan時間)

Example:
How many minutes does it take to get from the station to your home?
Eki kara uchi made nanpun gurai kakarimasu ka?
駅からうちまで何分ぐらいかかりますか
(eki駅 = station) (uchiうち = home) (nanpun何分 = how many minutes)

When you want to answer with an exact time duration you can omit gurai:

A kara B made + time + kakarimasu
(It takes + time + to get from A to B)

Example:
It takes 30 minutes
Eki kara uchi made sanjuppun kakarimasu
駅からうちまで三十分かかります
(Eki駅 = station) (Uchi うち= home)
(Sanjuppun三十分 = 30 minutes)
Or simplified
Sanjuppun kakarimasu
三十分かかります

<u>Exercise</u>:
Fill in the blank spaces.

1. A: Basutei kara __________made _gurai kakarimasu ka?
   B:__________kara suupaa_______ juppun gurai______.

(Basuteiバス停 = bus stop) (Suupaaスーパー = supermarket)
(Juppun十分 = 10 minutes)

Answer:
A: Basutei kara suupaa made dono gurai kakarimasu ka?
バス停からスーパーまでどのぐらいかかりますか
B: Basutei kara suupaa made juppun gurai kakarimasu.
バス停からスーパーまで十分ぐらいかかります

2. A: Tokyo kara______made nanjikan___________kakarimasu__.
   B: ________________Kyoto made nijikan gurai kakarimasu.

   (Nanjikan 何時間= how many hours) (Nijikan 二時間= 2 hours)

Answer:
A:
Tokyo kara Kyoto made nanjikan gurai kakarimasu ka?
東京から京都まで何時間ぐらいかかりますか

B:
Tokyo kara Kyoto made nijikan gurai kakarimasu.
東京から京都まで二時間ぐらいかかります

3. A: Apaato kara___________made nanpun__________________ka?
   B: Apaato__________konbini______happun kakarimasu.

   (Apaato アパート= apartment) (Konbini コンビニ= convenience store) (Nanpun 何分= how many minutes) (Happun八分 = 8 minutes)

Answer:

A:

Apaato kara konbini made nanfun guraikakarimasu ka?

アパートからコンビニまで何分ぐらいかかりますか

B:

Apaato kara konbini made happun kakarimasu.

アパートからコンビニまで八分かかります

Conclusion

And there you have it, we've reached the end of our Japanese Grammar 101 book.

Congratulations, if you have studied this book thoroughly your grammar will have skyrocketed – not to mention your confidence too. Just think how far you've come. That's amazing progress.

Now you have a solid foundation which you can build on. All you need to do is combine this knowledge with new vocabulary (which we will cover in the next section) and some practice, then before you know it, your fluency will be through the roof.

The next section will contain our other book based on improving your vocabulary.

Manuscript II

Japanese Vocabulary

Put the Dictionary Down

Use These Words to Break Through Japanese Fluency in Just 90 Days

(Over 1300+ of essential words & phrases)

Introduction

Want to learn Japanese fast? You've come to the right place. Learning a new language is exciting and extremely rewarding. It helps create new relationships, break down barriers and improve your brain power.

Knowing the benefits of learning a new language, there's one main problem most students fall into. They approach learning a new language the wrong way. We know learning a language isn't easy, it challenges both your brain and your time. And if you're using the wrong approach, it makes learning seem like a nightmare. You end up getting confused too quickly, frustrated too often and overall demotivated.

I've been guilty of this aswell. When I learnt my first language I didn't know where to start. Like most new starters I thought a tutor was the best place to begin. Learning from a native speaker, what could be better?

I spent months learning, paying for lessons but things were just not sinking in. I was getting overwhelmed and frustrated. All I kept asking myself is "why is this so difficult? I'm spending all this time learning but I'm still not getting it. Maybe I need to give it more time?"

What I discovered is the reason I was struggling so much, is because I was missing the core foundation of the language. A solid vocabulary.
Did you know there was a study done in 1964, learning the 1000 most frequently used words of a language will allow you to understand 76% of all non-fiction writing, 79.6% of all fiction writing and 87.8% of all oral speech.

This is insane by just learning 1000 words out of the hundreds of thousands in a language, you can understand over 80% of all speech.

Once I realized this I starting focusing on increasing my vocabulary. But then came across another problem, finding these practical words.

Like most students in order to increase my vocabulary I would spend hours, digging through dictionaries selecting words I thought would be useful.

As you can imagine this is the last thing you want to be doing. I just wanted to learn the words rather than waste time searching for them.

What this book is about

Knowing this problem, what we've done is compiled a list of the top 1300+ most essential words in Japanese. Now you don't have to spend time going through dictionaries selecting words and instead you can just focus on learning them.
Why 1300?

We compressed a long list of vocabulary, cutting out all the uncommon words. So you don't have to waste time and energy learning words you'll hardly ever use. We're not trying to be a dictionary, instead give you a more practical approach.

What we were left with is 1300+ common and very useful words. Keep in mind that these are what you'll be coming across most often when speaking Japanese.

Getting these words down first will give you a head start and lay the ground work so you can get closer to mastering the language.

How this book is laid out

First you'll be given the word in English and the
translation next to it. After that there will be a sentence of the word used in context. Next to each translation there will be a breakdown of pronunciation and any other information about the word. Nice and simple.

One thing to keep in mind, some words will change based on context. So the listed word may appear a little different when used in context. Japanese has a lot of conjugations so certain words will change depending on tense, action etc. The important thing to note when learning these words is to remember the word stem (listed word). Once you know this then all the conjugations become easy.

How to bullet proof your memory

What's the best way to learn vocabulary? Most of the time we try to memorize a long list of words. Going through each word one by one and repeating them over and over again. But after a few minutes we totally forget them. This is one of the things I used to get frustrated over all the time. How can I make these words stick?
There's hope, below is the 3 step method you can use to bulletproof your memory and make vocabulary stick for good.

<u>Step 1: Association</u>

Memorizing a long list of words is not a practical way of learning vocabulary. A better way is to memorize with association.

Associations are things that remind you of the meaning of the word. They don't really need to make sense, they just need to help you remember the meaning. The weirder the better! Weird things make us remember better. So how do we do this? Let's take the word:

Wakai = Young

Look at the word, can see if the word either sounds like anything you know or looks like anything you know – by the way the letters come together. For me personally it kind of sounds like the word "wake".

Now that I have the term "wake" I want to association the word "wakai" with it and create a link. To do this you need to create a sentence containing both words. So we can say:
***Young** people **wake** up early.*

Now we have the association created, you next need to visualize this sentence. So visualize a young person getting up early.

As stated before, the sentence doesn't need to make perfect sense. But doing this and creating a visualization of the word, gives you a memory anchor. So you're not just trying to draw the word from nothing. You've actually have some mental imagery to anchor of and that helps you record the word.

Step 2: Use word in conversation

Once you have association of the word, we need to start using it in a sentence. This will get your brain familiar with the word and allow you to recall it in a real-time conversation.

Practice making a couple of sentences with the word. It doesn't have to be complicated, just get used to adding the word into your natural speaking.

Step 3: Review & Strengthen

Final step is to strengthen this new link in your brain. To do this you have to go over the first two steps again. Go over the word, the association you have created for it and make sentences using it. This is what really embeds that word in your mind and makes it stick.

I know this is a longer process that simply reading off a list. But the good thing about this method is when you have the word down, it's down and it's less likely for you to forget it.

It's much better to learn 2 or 3 words this way than go through a list of 20 words that you forget instantly.

Follow these steps and you'll notice the amount of words you can remember drastically increase. You'll be able to recall them much better and before you know it learning vocabulary will become a breeze, rather than a memory nightmare.

Break the fluency barrier in 90 days

Like anything in language learning it's all about breaking things down into bite size pieces.

We now know that vocabulary is the key part to fluency and by learning only the first 1000 most frequently used words, you can get 87.8% of oral speech down.

Now 1000 words may sounds like a lot but it really isn't once you break it down.

Learning 1000 words in 90 days makes up to around 12 words a day. Can learn 12 words a day? Of course you can and if you want to hit all 1300 in this book, that would just be 15 words a day.

It's entirely possible. So make a strategy and set aside time when you're going to learn. Early in the morning, at lunch, when driving or just before bed...

Stick to it and 3 months down the line you'll have completed the entire list! You'll be able to understand so much more of Japanese speech, and be able to form far more sentences. Breaking you though that fluency barrier and hitting a whole new level in your language skills. Even if you just learnt these words. You will still be able to communicate with people by just stating words.

As famous linguist David Wilkins said "while without grammar little can be conveyed. Without vocabulary, nothing can be conveyed."

Once you have these words down, all it takes is learning some grammar, a little bit of practice and you'll notice how comfortable you'll be with Japanese.

That's enough of the introduction, now let's get into learning some Japanese!

Most Essential and Common Words in Japanese

As stated in the introduction the sections have been laid out in order of frequency, starting with the most common first. So make sure to go through this book in order and try to avoid skipping sections.

The words listed maybe slightly different in context due to conjugation. The important thing is to remember the word stem (listed word). Once you know this then the conjugations will become easier to understand.
Let’s begin …

Adjectives

na = na adjective
i = i adjective

1.

Big – Oki (o-kee) *(na)* 大きい
Kanojo wa **okina** me o shite imasu
She has **big** eyes.
彼女は大きな目をしています

2.

Small – Chisai (chee-sai) *(i)* *小さい*
Anata wa totemo **chisai** inu o katte imasu
You have a very **small** dog.
あなたはとても小さな犬を飼っています

3.

Cheap – Yasui (yaa-sui) *(i)安い*
Tōkyō no tabemono wa **yasui** desu
Food in Tokyo is **cheap**.
東京の食べ物は安いです

4.

Expensive – Takai (ta-kai) *(i)高い*
Nihon wa **takai** kuni desu
Japan is an **expensive** country.
日本は高い国です

5.

Right – Tadashī (ta-da-shi) *(i)*正しい
Ane wa itumo **tadashī**
My sister is always **right**.
姉はいつも正しい

6.

Wrong – Chigaimasu (chi-gai-masu)違います
Sore wa **chigaimasu,** sore wa watashi no kurumade wa arimasen.
That's **wrong**. That is not my car.
それは違います、それは私の車ではありません

7.

Clean – Kirei (ki-rei) *(i)綺麗*
Kirei na tsukue wa shinnpin no youdesu.
The **clean** table looks new.
綺麗な机は新品のようです

8.

Dirty – Kitanai (ki-ta-nai) *(i)汚い*
Koko no toire wa totemo **kitanai**.
These toilets are very **dirty.**
ここのトイレはとても汚い

9.

Dangerous – Abunai (a-bu-nai) *(i)危ない*
Koko ni hitori de iruno wa **abunai** desu.
It's **dangerous** to be alone here.
ここに一人でいるのは危ないです

10.

Safe – Anzen (an-zen) (*na)安全*
Anata wa koko ni ireba **anzen** desu.
You're **safe** here.
あなたはここにいれば安全です

11.

Dark – Kurai (ku-rai) (*i)暗い*
Kurasugimasu, ranpu o tukete.
It's too **dark**, turn on the lamp.
暗すぎます、ランプを点けて

12.

Light – Akari (ak-ari) *(i)灯り*
Akario kesukoto ga dekimasu ka?
Can you turn off the **light**?
灯りを消すことができますか

13.

Easy – Kantan (kan-tan) *(na)簡単*
Nihongoo manabu no wa **kantan** de omoshiroi.
Learning Japanese language is **easy** and fun.
日本語を学ぶのは簡単で面白い

14.

Difficult – Muzukashī (mu-zu-ka-shi) *(i)難しい*
Eigo wa bunpou ga takusan ate **muzukashī.**
English is**difficult** because there is a lot of grammar.
英語は文法が沢山あって難しい

15.

Full – Furu (fu-ru)フル
Anatano **furu**nemu o kaite kudasai.
Please write down your **full** name here.
あなたのフルネームを書いて下さい

16.

Empty – Kara (ka-ra) 空
Kuttuki wa doko desu ka? Hako no naka wa **kara** desu.
Where are all the cookies? The box is **empty.**
クッキーはどこですか箱の中は空です

17.

Fat – Futoru (fu-to-ru) *(i)太る*
Futotte miemasu ka?
Do I look **fat**?
太って見えますか

18.

Slim – Surimu (su-ri-mu) *(na)スリム*
Kanojyo wa **surimu** na taikei desu.
She has a **slim** figure.
彼女はスリムな体系です

19.

Thick – Atsui (atsu-i) *(i)厚い*
Tosou no sou ga **atsu**sugiru.
The layer of paint is too **thick**.
塗装の層が厚すぎる

20.

Thin – Hosoi (ho-soi) *(i)細い*
Kanojyo no tekubi wa **hosoi** desu.
Her wrists are **thin**.
彼女の手首は細いです

21.

Hard – Katai (ka-tai) *(i)硬い*
Kono beddo wa totemo **katai**node sukidewa arimasen.
I don't like this bed because it is very **hard.**
このベッドはとても硬いので好きではありません

22.

Soft – Yawarakai (ya-wara-kai) *(i)柔らかい*
Anata no kaminoke wa sugoku **yawarakai**, nando kaminoke wo araimasu ka?
Your hair is so **soft.** How many times do you wash it?
貴方の髪の毛はすごく柔らかい、何度髪の毛を洗いますか

23.

Hot – Atsui (At-sui) *(i)熱い*
Sono furaipan wa mada **atsui**node kiwo tsukete.
The pan is still **hot**, be careful.

そのフライパンはまだ熱いので気を付けて

24.

Cold – Samui (Sa-mui) *(i)寒い*
Samui desu, watashi no uwagi ha doko desu ka?
I feel **cold**, where is my coat?
寒いです、私の上着はどこですか

25.

Light – Karui (ka-rui) *(i)軽い*
Watashi no kaban no jyuryou ha 2kiro, **karui** desu.
My bag weighs 2 kilos, it's **light!**
私の鞄の重量は二キロ、軽いです

26.

Heavy – Omotai (o-mo-tai) *(i)重たい*
Oki desu ga **omotaku**arimasen.
It's big but it's not **heavy.**
大きいですが重たくありません

27.

Quiet – Shizuka (shi-zuka) *(na)静か*
Kodomotachi, **shizuka**ni shinasai, otosan ga neteiru desu yo.
Children, be **quiet.** Your father is sleeping.
子供たち、静かにしなさい、お父さんが寝ていますよ

28.

Loud- Urusai (uru-sai) (*i*) *うるさい*
Koko no basyo wa hontouni **urusai.**
This place is really **loud.**
ここの場所は本当にうるさい

29.

A little – Sukoshi/Chotto (su-koshi/cho-tto)少し/ちょっと
Watashi ha **sukoshi**nihongoo hanasemasu.

I can only speak a **little** Japanese.
私は少し日本語話せます

30.

A lot – Tottemo (tot-temo)とっても
Konsātowa **tottemo** tanoshikatta desu.
The concert was a lot of fun.
コンサートはとっても楽しかったです

31.

Near – Chikai (chi-kai) *(i)近い*
Koko kara **chikai** desu ka?
Is it **near** from here?
ここから近いですか

32.

Far – Tōi (Toi) *(i)遠い*
Sono omise wa koko kara **tōi** desu.
The shop is **far** from here.
そのお店はここから遠いです

33.

Old – Otoshiyori (o-to-shi-yori)お年寄り
Watashi wa **otoshiyori** no katagata to hanasu koto ga suki desu.
I like talking to **old** people.
私は年寄りの方々と話すことが好きです

34.

Young – Wakai (wa-kai) *(i)若い*
Wakai onnanoko tachi ha kirei desu.
Young girls are pretty.
若い女の子たちは綺麗です

35.

Normal – Tsūjō (tsu-jo) *(na)通常*
Ashita wa **tsūjō** no eigyō-bi desu.

Tomorrow is just a **normal** working day.
明日は通常の営業日です

36.

Special- Tokubetsu (to-ku-bet-su) *(na)特別*
Kyō wa **tokubetsu** desu. Sono watashi no gārufurendo no tanjōbi
Today is **special**. Its my girlfriends birthday
今日は特別です　その私のガールフレンドの誕生日

37.

Poor – Mazushī (ma-zu-shi) *(i)貧しい*
Mazushī hitobito wa okaneganai
Poor people have no money.
貧しい人々はお金がない

38.

Rich – Kanemochi (ka-ne-mo-chi) *(na)金持ち*
Watashi ha ituka **kanemochi** ni narimasu.
I will be **rich** one day.
私はいつか金持ちになります

39.

Ripe – Jukusu (ju-kusu)熟す
Kago no nakano kudamono ha **jukushite** imasu.
The fruits in the basket are **ripe**.
籠の中の果物は熟しています

40.

Raw – Nama (na-ma)生
Sore wa mada **nama** desu, motto nagaku cyouri suru hituyou ga arimasu.
It's still **raw**, you need to cook it longer.
それはまだ生です、もっと長く調理する必要があります

41.

Shallow – Asai (a-sai) *(i)浅い*
Kono mizuumi ha **asai** shi tsumetai desu.

This lake is **shallow** and cold.
この湖は浅いし冷たいです

42.

Deep – Fukai (fu-kai) *(i)深い*
Kono umi ha **fukai** desu.
The ocean is **deep**.
この海は深いです

43.

Short – senohikui (se-no-hikui) *(i)背の低い*
Watashi wa **senohikui** jyosei ni aimashita.
I met a **short** woman.
私は背の低い女性に会いました

44.

Long – Nagai (na-gai) *(i)長い*
Kare no kaminoke wa kurokute **nagai.**
He has **long** black hair.
彼の髪の毛は黒くて長い

45.

Stupid – Baka (ba-ka) *(na)馬鹿*
Anata wa **baka** desu ka?
Are you **stupid**?
あなたは馬鹿ですか

46.

Clever – Kashikoi (ka-shi-koi) *(i)賢い*
Watashino chichi wa **kashikoi** dansei desu.
My father is a **clever** man.
私の父は賢い男性です

47.

Slow – Yukkuri (Yuk-ku-ri)ゆっくり
Yukkuri hanashite itadakemasu ka? Wakarimasen.

Can you speak **slowly**? I don't understand.
ゆっくり話していただけますかわかりません

48.

Fast – Hayai (ha-yai) *(i)速い*
Watashi no kanojyo wa **hayai** kuruma ga suki desu.
My girlfriend likes **fast** cars.
私の彼女は早い車が好きです

49.

Hard working – Kinben (kin-ben) *(na)勤勉*
Kanojyo no otto wa **kinben** desu.
Her husband is **hardworking**.
彼女の夫は勤勉です

50.

Lazy – Namakeru (na-ma-ke-ru)怠ける
Namakeruna, Nanika wo shiro.
Don't be lazy, do something.
怠けるな、何かをしろ

51.

Smell good – iikaori (ieekao-ri) *(i)良い香り*
Kanojyo no kousui ha **iikaori** desu.
Her perfume **smells good**.
彼女の香水は良い香りです

52.

Smell bad – Kusai (ku-sai) *(i)臭い*
Korerano hana ha **kusai.**
These flowers **smell bad**.
これらの花は臭い

53.

Weak – Yowai (yo-wai) *(i)弱い*

Watashi wa **yowai** to kanjimasu. Asa gohan o tabemasen deshita
I feel **weak**. I didn't eat breakfast.
私は弱いと感じます　朝ごはんを食べませんでした

54.

Strong – Tsuyoi (tsu-yoi) *(i)強い*
Teikiteki na undou wa anata o **tsuyoku** suru.
Regular exercise makes you **strong**.
定期的な運動はあなたを強くする

55.

Wide – Hiroi (hi-roi) *(i)広い*
Karera no Ie no aidani **hiroi**gyappuga arimasu**.**
There is a **wide**gap between their houses.
彼らの家の間には広いギャップがあります

56.

Narrow – Semai (se-mai) *(i)狭い*
Watashi no machi no tōri wa **semai**.
The streets in my town are **narrow**.
私の町の通りは狭い

57.

Wet – Nureta (nu-re-ta)濡れた
Nureta ifuku wa soto ni hoshite.
Hang your **wet** clothes outside.
濡れた衣服は外に干して

58.

Dry – Kawaita (ka-wai-ta)乾いた
Kawaita taoru o itadake masu ka?
Can I have a **dry** towel?
乾いたタオルをいただけますか

Verbs

ru = ru verb
u = u verb
suru = irr verb suru

59.

Sit – Suwaru (su-wa-ru) *(ru)座る*
Kono seki wa aite imasu ka? **Suwatte** mo ii desu ka?
Can I **sit** here or is this seat taken.
この席は空いていますか座ってもいいですか

60.

Walk – Aruku (a-ru-ku) *(u)歩く*
Watashi wa ie made 2 mairu **aruka**naitoikenai.
I have to **walk** two miles to go home.
私は家まで２マイル歩かないといけない

61.

Run – Hashiru (ha-shee-ru) *(ru)走る*
Kare wa kōen o **hashiru** koto ga suki desu.
He likes to **run** in the park.
彼は公園を走ることが好きです

62.

Read – Yomu (yo-mu) *(u)読む*
Watashi wa hon wo **yomu** koto o tanoshimi masu.
I **read** books for fun.
私は本を読むことを楽しみます

63.

Write – Kaku (kah-ku) *(u)書く*
Watashi wa daigaku o sotugyo shitara hon o **kaki**tai desu.
I want to **write** a book when finish university.
私は大学を卒業したら本を書きたいです

64.

Ride – Noru (no-ru) *(ru)乗る*
Jitensha ni **nore** masu ka?
Can you **ride** a bike?
自転車に乗れますか

65.

Drive – Unten (un-ten) *(suru)運転*
Anata wa **unten** suru koto ga suki desu ka?
Do you like to **drive**?
あなたは運転をすることが好きですか

66.

Eat – Taberu (tah-beh-ru) *(ru)*
Watashi wa okome o tabemasen**,** pasuta o **taberu** hou ga suki desu.
I don't eat rice, I prefer to **eat** pasta.
私はお米を食べません、パスタを食べる方が好きです

67.

Drink – Nomu (no-mu) *(u)飲む*
Nani ka o**nomi** mono wa ikaga desu ka?
Would you like something to **drink**?
何かお飲み物はいかがですか

68.

Kick – Keru (keh-ru) *(ru)蹴る*
Soto de bōru o **keri**nasai.
Kick the ball outside.
外でボールを蹴りなさい

69.

Ask – Kiku (kee-ku) *(u)聞く*
Kare ga saru toki ni **kiite**.
Ask him when he will leave.
彼が去る時に聞いて

70.

Answer – Kaitō (ka-iee-toh) (*suru)回答する*
Dare ka **Kaitō** ga wakarimasu ka?
Does anyone know the **answer**?
誰か回答がわかりますか

71.

Buy – Kau (kah-uh) *(u)買う*
Watashi wa atarashii kuruma o **kai**tai.
I want **buy** a new car.
私は新しい車を買いたい

72.

Sell – Uru (uh-ru) *(ru)売る*
Kare wa jibun no ie o **uritai**
He wants to **sell** his house.
彼は自分の家を売りたい

73.

Carry – Hakobu (hah-ko-boo) *(u)運ぶ*
Kore o **hako**nde kuremasu ka?
Can you **carry** this for me?
これを運んでくれませんか

74.

Come – Kuru (Ku-ru) *(u)来る*
Raisyu watashi no machi ni **ki**masu ka?
Will you **come** to my city next week?
来週私の町に来ますか

75.

Go – Iku (iee-ku) *(u)行く*
Watashi wa atode mōru ni **iki**masu.
I will **go** to the mall later.
私は後でモールに行きます

76.

Meet – Au (ah-u) *(u)会う*
Kare wa resutoran de kanojo ni **au** desu yo.
He will **meet** her at the restaurant.
彼はレストランで彼女に会います

77.

Forget – Wasureru (wah-su-reh-ru) *(ru)忘れる*
Watashi wa kagi o ie ni **wasureta.**
I **forgot** my keys at home.
私はカギを家に忘れた

78.

Remember – Oboeru (o-boh-e-ru) *(ru)覚える*
Kare no denwa bangou o **oboete** imasu ka?
Do you **remember** his phone number?
彼の電話番号を覚えていますか

79.

Give – Kudasai (ku-dah-sai)ください
Anatano denwa bangou o **kudasai.**
Give me your phone number.
あなたの電話番号をください

80.

Love – Ai (a-iee)愛
Ai wa utsukushī.
Love is beautiful.
愛は美しい

81.

Like – Suki (su-kee)好き
Watashi wa Tairyori wo tsukuru koto ga **suki** desu.
I **like** to cook Thai food.
私はタイ料理を作ることが好きです

82.

Watch – Miru (mee-ru) *(ru)見る*
Kanojo wa eiga o **miru** koto ga suki desu.
She loves to **watch** movies.
彼女は映画を見ることが好きです

83.

Glance – Hitome miru (Hee-toh-meh mee-ru) *(ru)一目見る*
Kanojo ga heya ni hairutoki kare wa **hitome mita.**
He **glanced** at her as she entered the room.
彼女が部屋に入る時彼は一目見た

84.

Search – Sagasu (sa-gah-sue) *(u)探す*
Watashi wa kaban o **sagashi** masu.
I will **search** my bag for it.
私は鞄を探します

85.

Help – Tasuke/Tetsudai (tah-sue-ke/tet-su-dai)助け/手伝い
Mary wa syukudai no **tetsudai** ga hitsuyou desu.
Mary needs **help** with her homework
メアリーは宿題の手伝いが必要です

86.

Smile – egao (e-gao)笑顔
Kanojo no **egao** wa totemo suteki desu.
Her **smile** is very beautiful.
彼女の笑顔はとても素敵です

87.

Speak – Hanasu (ha-nah-su) *(u)話す*
Sam ha mittu no gengo wo **hanasu** kotoga dekimasu.
Sam can **speak** three languages.
サムは３つの言語を話すことができます

88.

Play – Suru (su-ru) *(ru)する*
Anata wa sakka o **suru** noga suki desu ka?
Do you like to **play** football?
あなたはサッカーをするのが好きですか

89.

Wait – Matsu (mah-tsu) *(u)待つ*
Kanojo wa kare ni tsugi no densya o **matsu** youni itta.
She told him to **wait** for the next train.
彼女は彼に次の電車を待つように言った

90.

Wash – Arau (ah-ra-u) *(u)洗う*
Osara o **arau** koto o wasurenaide.
Do not forget to **wash** the dishes.
お皿を洗うことを忘れないで

91.

Borrow – Kariru (kah-ri-ru) *(ru)借りる*
Pen o **karite** mo ii desu ka?
Can I **borrow** a pen?
ペンを借りてもいいですか

92.

Complain – Monku o iu (mon-ku o iee-u) *(u)文句を言う*
Kare wa itsumo tenki ni tsuite **monku o iu**.
He always **complains** about the weather.
彼はいつも天気について文句を言う

93.

Order – chūmon (chu-mon)注文
Sumimasen**, chūmon**no jyunbi ga dekimashita.
Excuse me waiter, I am ready to **order**.
すいません、注文の準備ができました

94.

Cut – Karu (kah-ru) *(ru)刈る*
Itsu kusa o **katte** kuremasu ka?
When will you **cut** the grass?
いつ草を刈ってくれますか

95.

Listen – Kiku (ki-ku) *(u)聞く*
Otosan no iu koto o **kiki** nasai.
Listen to your teacher.
お父さんのいうことを聞きなさい

96.

Guard – Miharu (mi-hah-ru) *(ru)見張る*
Karera ga shinya 12ji made tobira o **miharu.**
They will **guard** the doors until midnight.
彼らが深夜１２時まで扉を見張る

97.

Invite – Shōtai (sho-tai) *(suru)招待*
Watashi ga kanojo o pātī ni **shōtai** shimasu.
I will **invite** my girlfriend to the party.
私が彼女をパーティに招待します

98.

Think – Omou (o-mou) *(u)思う*
Watashi wa nihongo o manabu no wa kantanda to **omou**.
I **think** learning Japaneseis easy.
私は日本語を学ぶのは簡単だと思う

99.

Pour - Sosogu (so-sogu) *(u)注ぐ*
Kare ni ippai no jūsu o **sosogu.**
Pour a glass of juice for him.
彼に一杯のジュースを注ぐ

100.

Point – Yubi sashite (yu-bi sa-shee-te)指さして
Dore ga ichiban suki ka **yubi o sashite**.
Point to which one you like the most.
どれが一番好きか指をさして

101.

Lift – Mochi ageru (mo-chee a-ge-ru) *(ru)持ち上げる*
Omotasugite, **mochi agerare** masen.
I cannot **lift** this, it's too heavy.
重たすぎて持ち上げられません

102.

To keep – Hoji (ho-ji)保持
Kono syashin o **hoji** shitai.
I want to **keep** this photo.
この写真を保持したい

103.

Hug – Hagu (ha-gu)ハグ
Kanojo wa kare ni okina **hagu** o shita.
She gave him a big hug.
彼女は彼に大きなハグをした

104.

To want - ...tai (...tai)たい
Dan ha ashitaTokyo ni iki**tai.**
Dan **wants** to go to Tokyo tomorrow.
ダンは明日東京に行きたい

105.

Understand – Wakaru (wa-ka-ru) *(ru)わかる*
Eigo wa **wakari**masu ga sukoshi shika hanasemasen.
I **understand** English language but can only speak a little bit.
英語はわかりますが少ししか話せません

106.
Shout – Sakebu (sa-ke-bu) *(u)叫ぶ*
Otera no naka dewa **sakeba**nai.
Do not **shout** in the temple.
お寺のなかでは叫ばない

107.
Argue – iiau (iee-a-u) *(u)言い合う*
Kate to Simon wa yoku **iiai** o suru.
Kate and Simon **argue** a lot.
ケイトとサイモンはよく言い合いをする

108.
Explain – Setsumei (Set-su-mei) *(i)説明*
Mou ichido **setsumei** shite moraemasu ka? Wakarimasen deshita.
Can you **explain** that again? I don't understand.
もう一度説明してもらえますかわかりませんでした

109.
To work – hataraku (hata-rah-ku) *(u)働く*
Kanojo wa machinaka de **hataraki**tai.
She wants to **work** in the city.
彼女は街中で働きたい

110.
Hear – Kiku (Kee-ku) *(u)聞く*
Kanojo ga anata ga itta koto o**kiki**mashita ka?
Did she **hear** what you said?
彼女があなたが言ったことを聞きましたか

111.
Know that – …o shitteiru (…o shee-tei-ru)…を知っている
Kanojo ga inu o kowagaru koto **o shitteiru**.
I **know that** she is scared of dogs.
彼女が犬を怖がることを知っている

112.

Laugh – Warau (wah-ra-u) *(u)笑う*
Dare ga **waratte** iruno desu ka?
Who is l**aughing**?
誰が笑っているのですか

113.

Wake up – Okiru (o-kee-ru) *(ru)起きる*
Watashi wa jimu ni ikutame ni asa hayaku **okiru**.
I **wake up** early so I can go to the gym.
私はジムに行くために朝早く起きる

114.

Cry – Naku (na-ku) *(u)泣く*
Kanojyo ga **naku**to watashi mo kanashiku kanjiru.
I feel sad when I see my girlfriend **cry**ing.
彼女が泣くと私も悲しく感じる

115.

Jump – Tobu (toh-bu) *(u)*
Dono kurai takaku **tobu** koto ga dekimasu ka?
How high can you **jump**?
どのくらい高く飛ぶことができますか

116.

Try to eat something – Nani ka tabeyouto suru
(Na-nee-ka tabe-yo-to suru) *(ru)何か食べようとする*
Anata ga byouki nano wa shitte imasu, demo **nani ka tabeyouto shite**.
I know you are sick but **try to eat something**.
あなたが病気なのは知っています、でも何か食べようとして

117.

Swim – Oyogu (o-yo-gu) *(u)泳ぐ*
Dale ha taikei o iji suru tameni teikiteki ni **oyogu**.
Dale **swims** regularly to keep fit.

デールは体系を維持するために定期的に泳ぐ

118.

Dance – Odoru (o-do-ru) *(ru)踊る*
Hitobito wa kekkonshiki de itsumo **odouru**.
People always **dance** at a wedding.
人々は結婚式でいつも踊る

119.

Sing – Utau (uh-ta-u) *(u)歌う*
Watashi wa **utau** koto ga daisuki desu.
I love to **sing**.
私は歌うことが大好きです

120.

Cook – Chōri (cho-o-ri)調理
Kare wa chikin o **chōri** suru koto wa dekimasuga, kohitsuji o chōrisuru koto wa dekimasen.
He can **cook** chicken but he cannot cook lamb.
彼はチキンを調理することはできますが、子羊を調理することはできません

121.

Blow – Fuku (fu-ku) *(u)吹く*
Anata wa nanko fūsen o **fuku** koto ga dekimasu ka?
How many balloons can you **blow**?
あなたはなんこ風船をふくことができますか

122.

Pull – Hipparu (hee-ppa-ru) *(ru)引っ張る*
Kono hōkō ni tēburu o hipparu hitsuyō ga arimasu.
You need to pull the table this way.
この方向にテーブルを引っ張る必要があります

123.

Push – Osu (o-su) *(u)押す*

Kuruma o **osu** no o tetsudatte.
Help me **push** the car.
車を押すのを手伝って

124.
Crawl – Hau (ha-uh) *(u)はう*
Akachan wa heya no mawari o **hatta.**
The baby **crawled** around the room.
赤ちゃんは部屋の周りをはった

125.
Climb – Noboru (no-boh-ru) *(ru)登る*
Shigoto de, watashi wa itumo hashigo o **noboranaito** ikenai.
At work, I have to always **climb** a ladder.
仕事で私はいつもはしごを登らないといけない

126.
Up – Agaru (a-ga-ru)上がる
Watashi wa nikai ni **agarimasu.**
I am going **up** to the second floor.
私は二階にあがります

127.
Down – Oriru (o-ri-ru)降りる
Erebētā de ikkai ni **oriru.**
Take the elevator **down** to the ground floor.
エレベーターで一階に降りる

128.
Enter – Hairu (hai-ru) *(ru)入る*
Senotakai dansei ga mise ni **haitta.**
A tall man **entered** the shop.
背の高い男性が店に入った

129.
Exit – Deguchi (deh-guchi)出口

Sumimasen, **deguchi** wa doko desu ka?
Excuse me, where is the **exit**?
すみません、出口はどこですか

130.

Close – Shimeru (shi-me-ru)閉める
Kāten o **shimete** kuremasu ka.
Can you close the curtain?
カーテンを閉めてくれますか

131.

Open – Hiraku (hira-ku)開く
Eigakan wa nanji ni **hiraki**masu ka?
What time does the cinema **open**?
映画館は何時に開きますか

132.

Receive – Uketoru (u-ke-to-ru) *(ru)受け取る*
Kinō watashi no messēji o **uketori**mashita ka?
Did you **receive** my message yesterday?
昨日私のメッセージを受け取りましたか

133.

Send – Okuru (o-ku-ru) *(ru)贈る*
Hana o **okura**naide.
Don't **send** me any flowers.
花を贈らないで

Pronouns

134.

I [male]-**Watashi/Boku/Ore** (wa-tashi/bo-ku/o-reh)私/僕/俺

Boku wa shigoto no ato ni basuke no shiai ni itta.

I went to the basketball game after work.

僕は仕事の後にバスケの試合に行った

135.

I [female]-**Watashi** (wa-tashi)私

Watashi wa sūpā ni ikimasu.

I am going to the supermarket.

私はスーパーに行きます

136.

You – Anata (a-nata)あなた

Anata wa iku jyunbi ga dekimashita ka?

Are **you** ready to go?

あなたは行く準備ができましたか

137.

We – Watashitachi (wa-tash-tachee)わたしたち

Watashitachi wa konya pattai o tabeni ikimasu.

We are going to eat Pad Thai tonight.

私たちは今夜パッドタイを食べに行きます

138.

They – Kerera/Kanojora (kare-rah/kanojo-ra)彼らは/彼女ら

Karera wa dare desu ka? **Karera** ni mioboega aru.

Who are **they**? **They** look familiar.

彼らは誰ですか彼らに見覚えがある

139.

He – Kare (ka-reh)彼

Kare wa watashi no shinyuu desu.

He is my best friend.

彼は私の親友です

140.

She – Kanojo (kano-jo)彼女

Kanojo wa shoppingmōru ni kaimono ni ikimashita.

She went shopping at the mall.

彼女はショッピングモールに買い物に行きました

141.

My – Watashi no (wata-shi no)私の

Watashi no haha wa gojugo sai desu.

My mother is fifty five years old.

私の母は５５歳です

142.

Your – Anata no (a-nata no)あなたの

Anata no kyoudai wa segatakai.

Your brother is tall.

あなたの兄弟は背が高い

143.

His – Kere no (ka-reh no)彼の

Kare no kazoku wa ōkī desu.

His family is big.

彼の家族は大きいです

144.

Her – Kanojo no (kanojo no)彼女の

Kanojo no onesan wa kodomo ga futari iru.

Her sister has two children.

彼女のお姉さんは子供が二人いる

145.

Our – Watashitachi no (wa-tash-ta-chee no)私たちの

Watashitachi no ie ni wa nanatsu no heya ga arimasu.

Our house has seven rooms.

私たちの家には７つの部屋があります

146.

Their – Karera/kanojora (kare-rah/ka-nojo-rah)彼ら/彼女ら

Karera no kazoku wa totemo ōkī desu.

Their family is very big.

彼らの家族はとても大きいです

Days of the Week

147.
Monday - Getsuyōbi (Getsu-yobi)月曜日
Getsuyōbi wa syu no hajimari desu.
Monday is the start of the week.
月曜日は週の始まりです

148.
Tuesday - Kayōbi (ka-yo-bi)火曜日
Kayōbi wa Yoga e ikimasu.
I have yoga on **Tuesday.**
火曜日はヨガへ行きます

149.
Wednesday - Suiyōbi (sui-yo-bi)水曜日
Watashitachi wa **suiyōbi** ni isya ni ikimashita.
We went to the doctor on **Wednesday.**
私たちは水曜日に医者に行きました

150.
Thursday - Mokuyōbi (mo-ku-yo-bi)木曜日
Kare no tanjōbi wa **mokuyōbi** desu.
His birthday is on **Thursday.**
彼の誕生日は木曜日です

151.
Friday - Kinyōbi (kin-yo-bi)金曜日
Kinyōbi wa shiawase na hi desu.
Friday is a happy day.
金曜日は幸せな日です

152.
Saturday - Doyōbi (do-yo-bi)土曜日
Watashitachi wa **Doyōbi** ni kyanpu ni iku.

We will go camping on **Saturday**.
私たちは土曜日にキャンプに行く

153.

Sunday - Nichiyōbi (ni-chee-yo-bi)日曜日
Nichiyōbi wa ame ga furisouda.
It will rain on **Sunday**.
日曜日は雨が降りそうだ

154.

Day before yesterday – Ototoi (o-to-toi)一昨日
Zenkai kare ni attano wa **ototoi** desu.
The last time I saw him was **the day before yesterday**.
前回彼に会ったのは一昨日です

155.

Yesterday – Kinou (ki-no)昨日
Kono kutsu o **kinou** kaimashita.
I bought these shoes **yesterday**.
この靴を昨日買いました

156.

Today – Kyō (ki-yo)今日
Watashi wa **kyō** ichiba ni iku.
Today I will go to the market.
私は今日市場に行く

157.

Tomorrow – Ashita (ash-i-ta)明日
Kanojo wa **ashita** daiji na shaken ga aru.
She has a big exam **tomorrow**.
彼女は明日大事な車検がある

158.

The day after tomorrow – Asatte (a-sa-tte)明後日
Asatte wa kyūjitsu desu.

The day after tomorrow I have a holiday.
明後日は休日です

Months of the Year

159.

January – Ichigatsu (ichi-gat-su)一月
Ichigatsu wa ichinen no hajime no tsuki desu.
January is the first month of the year.
一月は一年の始めの月です

160.

February – Nigatsu (nee-gat-su)二月
Watashitachi wa maitoshi **nigatsu** ni barentaindē o iwaimasu.
We celebrate Valentine's Day every **February**.
私たちは毎年二月にバレンタインデーを祝います

161.

March – Sangatsu (san-gat-su)三月
Kanojo wa **sangatsu** ni kunren o kaishi shimasu.
She will start her training in **March**.
彼女は三月に訓練を開始します

162.

April – Shigatsu (shee-gat-su) 4 月
Watashi wa **shigatsu** no tenki ga suki desu.
I like the weather in **April**.
私は四月の天気が好きです

163.

May – Gogatsu (goh-gat-su)五月
Watashitachi wa **gogatsu** ni gaikoku ni iku.
We will go abroad this **May**.
私たちは五月に外国に行く

164.

June – Rokugatsu (ro-ku-gat-su) 6 月
Kanojo wa **rokugatsu** ni modotte kuru.

She will come back in **June**.
彼女は六月に戻ってくる

165.

July – Shichigatsu (shee-chee-gat-su) ７月
Shichigatsu tsuki wa Tōkyō de atsui desu.
July is the hot in Tokyo.
７月　月は東京で暑いです

166.

August – Hachigatsu (ha-chee-gat-su) ８月
Watashi no atarashī keiyaku wa **hachigatsu**ni hajimarimasu.
My new contract starts in **August**.
私の新しい契約は八月に始まります

167.

September – Kugatsu (Ku-gat-su) ９月
Kanojo no kareshi no tanjōbi wa **kugatsu** desu.
Her boyfriend's birthday is in **September**.
彼女の彼氏の誕生日は９月です

168.

October – Jyugatsu (ju-gat-su)10月
Harou~īn no tsuki nanode **jugatsu** ga suki desu.
I like **October** because of the Halloween.
ハローインの月なので10月が好きです

169.

November – Jyuichigatsu (ju-ichee-gat-su)11月
Karera no gakkou ha **juichigatsu** ni hajimari masu.
Their school starts in **November**.
彼らの学校は11月に始まります

170.

December – Jyunigatsu (ju-knee-gat-su)12月
Watashi ha **jyunigatsu** ni Amerika ni ikimasu.

I will go to USA this **December**.
私は12月にアメリカに行きます

171.

Last month – Sengetsu (sen-get-su)先月
Sengetsu wa watashi no yūjin no kekkonshiki deshita.
Last month was my friend's wedding.
先月は私の友人の結婚式でした

172.

This month – Kongetsu (kon-get-su)今月
Karera wa **kongetsu** kekkon suru.
They are getting married **this month**.
彼らは今月結婚する

173.

Next month – Raigetsu (rai-get-su)来月
Watashitachi wa **raigetsu** atarashī ie ni hikkoshimasu.
We will move to the new house **next month**.
私たちは来月新しい家に引っ越します

Colours

174.

Red – Akairo (a-kai-ro)赤色
Watashi no kanojo wa **akairo** no kuruma ga suki desu.
My girlfriend likes **red** cars.
私の彼女は赤色の車が好きです

175.

Pink – Pinku (pin-ku)ピンク
Ōdorī no sukina iro wa **pinku** desu.
Audrey's favourite colour is **pink**.
オードリーの好きな色はピンクです

176.

Orange – Oreji iro (o-ren-jee iee-ro)オレンジ色
Kanojo wa **orenji iro** no sukāto o kite imasu.
She is wearing an **orange** skirt.
彼女はオレンジ色のスカートを着ています

177.

Yellow – Ki iro (keeiee-ro)黄色
Takushī wa tsūjō **kiiro** desu.
Taxis are normally **yellow**.
タクシーは通常黄色です

178.

Green – Midori iro (mi-do-ri iee-ro)緑色
Midori iro wa watashi no suki na iro desu.
Green is my favourite colour.
緑色は私の好きな色です

179.

Blue – Aoiro (ah-o iee-ro)青色
Umi to sora wa **ao iro** desu.

The sea and sky are **blue**.
海と空は青色です

180.

Dark blue- Kon iro (kon iee-ro)紺色
Watashi wa kinou heya o **kon iro** ni tosou shita.
I painted my room **dark blue** yesterday.
私は昨日部屋を紺色に塗装した

181.

Purple – Murasaki iro (mu-ra-sa-kee iee-ro)紫色
Murasaki iro no doresu wa kau na.
Don't buy a **purple** dress.
紫色のドレスは買うな

182.

Black – Kuroiro (ku-ro iee-ro)黒色
Sono **kuroiro** no doresu wa toremo kirei desu.
That **black** dress looks very beautiful.
その黒色のドレスはとても綺麗です

183.

White – Shiroi (shee-roi)白い
Kanojo no ha wa tottemo **shiroi**.
Her teeth are very **white**.
彼女の歯はとっても白い

184.

Brown – Cha iro (cha iee-ro)茶色
Cha iro no inu ga kōen o hashitte imashita.
The **brown** dog was running in the park.
茶色の犬が公園を走っていました

185.

Grey – Hai iro (hai iee-ro)灰色
Kono **hai iro** no neko wa totemo okina me o shiteiru.

This **grey** cat has very big eyes.
この灰色の猫はとても大きな目をしている

186.

Golden – Kiniro (kin iee-ro)金色
Kanojo no kaminoke wa **kin iro** de kirei desu.
She is a beautiful girl with **golden** hair.
彼女の髪の毛は金色で綺麗です

187.

Indigo – Ai iro (ai iee-ro)藍色
Kare no kuruma wa **ai-iro** desu.
His car is **indigo.**
彼の車は藍色です

188.

Colour – Iro (iee-ro)色
Anata wa kuruma o nani **iro** ni tosou shimasu ka?
What **colour** will you paint your car?
あなたは車を何色に塗装しますか

Occupation

189.

Teacher – Kyōshi (kyo-shi)教師
Kanojo wa **sensei** ni naritai desu.
She wants to be a **teacher**.
彼女は先生になりたいです

190.

Doctor – Isha (iee-sha)医者
Sono **isha** wa byōin kara tōkuhanarete sunde imasu.
The **doctor** lives far away from the hospital.
その医者は病院から遠く離れて住んでいます

191.

Dentist – Shikai (shi-kai)歯科医
Kanojo wa ii **shikai** desu.
She is a good **dentist**.
彼女は良い歯科医です

192.

Nurse – Kangoshi (kan-go-shi)看護師
Watashi wa **kangoshi** desu ga, isha ni naritai desu.
I am a **nurse** but I want to be a doctor.
私は看護師ですが、医者になりたいです

193.

Pharmacist - Yakuzaishi (ya-ku-zai-shi)薬剤師
Sono **yakuzaishi** wa kare ni kusuri o watashita.
The **pharmacist** gave him the drugs.
その薬剤師は彼に薬を渡した

194.

Policeman – Keikan (kei-kan)警官
Kuruma no naka ni sannin no **keikan** ga iru.

There are three **policemen** in the car.
車の中に3人の警官がいる

195.

Soldier – Heishi (hei-shee)兵士
Heishi ni naruto iukoto wa abunai shigoto desu.
Being a **solider** is a dangerous job.
兵士いなるということは危ない仕事です

196.

Postman - Yūbin haitatsuin (you-bin hai-tat-su-in)郵便配達員
Yūbin haitatsuin wa kyō watashi no tegami o haitatsu shinakatta.
The **postman** didn't deliver my letters today.
郵便配達員は今日私の手紙を配達しなかった

197.

Fireman – Shōbō shi (sho-boshee)消防士
Shōbō shi wa sono dansei o sukutta.
The **fireman** saved the man.
消防士はその男性を救った

198.

Engineer – Enjinia (en-ji-nia)エンジニア
Watashi wa **enjinia** ni naru tame no benkyō shite imasu.
I am studying to be an **engineer**.
私はエンジニアになるための勉強をしています

199.

Business man – Bijinesuman (bi-ji-ness-man)ビジネスマン
Kare no chichioya wa **bijinesuman** desu.
His father is a **business man**.
彼の父親はビジネスマンです

200.

Secretary - Hisho (hi-sho)秘書
Watashi no **hisho** ni shōsai o tsutaete .

Give the details to my **secretary.**
私の秘書い詳細を伝えて

201.

Lawyer – Bengoshi (ben-go-shee)弁護士
Bengoshi wa mazushī kuraianto o yōgo shita.
The **lawyer** defended the poor client.
弁護士は貧しいクライアントを擁護した

202.

Judge – Saibankan (sai-ban-kan)裁判官
Anata wa **saibankan** desu ka?
Are you a **judge**?
あなたは裁判官ですか

203.

Pilot – Pairotto (pai-rotto)パイロット
Pairotto wa doko desu ka?
Where is the **pilot**?
パイロットはどこですか

204.

Air hostess – Kyakushitsu jyomuin (kyaku-shit-su jo-mu-in)客室乗務員
Kono **kyakushitsu jyomuin** wa totemo tsukarete imasu.
This **air hostess** is very tired.
この客室乗務員はとても疲れています

205.

Receptionist – Uketsuke (u-ket-suke)受付
Uketsuke wa doko desu ka?
Where is the **receptionist**?
受付はどこですか

206.

Chef – Shefu (she-fu)シェフ
Shefu dearu koto wa sutoresu ga ōi desu.

Being a **chef** is stressful.
シェフであることはストレスが多いです

207.

Reporter – Kisha (kee-sha)記者
Watashi wa kono **kisha** ga suki desu, kare no namae wa nani desu ka?
I like this **reporter,** what is his name?
私はこの記者が好きです、彼の名前は何ですか

208.

Photographer – Shashin ka (sha-shin ka)写真家
Shashin-ka wa watashitachi no kekkonshiki no shashin o totta.
The **photographer** took pictures of our wedding.
写真家は私たちの結婚式の写真を撮った

209.

Hair dresser – Biyōshi (bi-yo-shi)美容師
Watashi wa **biyōshi**ni shitsumon o shimashita.
I asked the **hairdresser** a question.
私は美容師に質問をしました

210.

Sportsman – Supōtsuman (su-pot-su-man)スポーツマン
Supōtsuman wa katsute kyōshidatta.
The **sportsman** used to be a teacher.
スポーツマンはかつて教師だった

211.

Musician – Myūjishan (myu-ji-shan)ミュージシャン
Watashi no yūjin wa itsumo **myūjishan** ni naritai to omotte imashita.
My friend always wanted to be a **musician**.
私の友人はいつもミュージシャンになりたいと思っていました

212.

Singer – Kasyu (ka-syu)歌手
Kono **kasyu** wa dare desu ka?

Who is this **singer**?
この歌手は誰ですか

213.

Actor – Haiyū (hai-yu)俳優
Sono **haiyū** ga daisuki desu.
I love that **actor**.
その俳優が大好きです

214.

Model – Moderu (mo-de-ru)モデル
Watashi no ane/imouto wa **moderu** desu.
My sister is a **model.**
私の姉/妹はモデルです

215.

Farmer – Nōka (no-ka)農家
Kare no sofu wa **nōka** deshita.
His grandfather was a **farmer**.
彼の祖父は農家でした

216.

Fisherman – Ryoshi (ryo-shi)漁師
Sono **ryoshi** ha kinou okina sakana o tutta.
The **fisherman** caught a huge fish yesterday.
その漁師は昨日大きな魚を釣った

217.

Merchant- Shōnin (sho-nin)商人
Shōnin wa kashikoi hito desu.
The **merchant** is a clever man.
商人は賢い人です

Family

218.

Father Chichi (chi-chi)父
Watashi no **chichi** wa kibishii hito desu.
My **father** is a strict man.
私の父は厳しい人です

219.

Mother – Haha (ha-ha)母
Are wa kare no **haha** desu.
That is his **mother**.
あれは彼の母です

220.

Grandfather – Sofu (so-fu)祖父
Kanojo no **sofu** wa ninen mae ni nakunarimashita
Her **grandfather** died two years ago.
彼女の祖父は二年前に亡くなりました

221.

Grandmother – Sobo (so-bo)祖母
Deibu no **sobo** wa hachijuni sai desu.
Dave's **grandmother** is 82 years old.
デイブの祖母は８２歳です

222.

Uncle – Oji (o-ji)叔父
Watashi no **oji** wa dai teitaku o shoyū shite imasu.
My **uncle** owns a mansion.
私の叔父は大邸宅を所有しています

223.

Aunt – Oba (o-ba)叔母
Anata no **oba** wa honto ni kakkoii.

Your **Aunt** is really cool.
あなたの叔母は本当にかっこいい

224.

Older brother – Ani (a-nee)兄
Sore wa riamu desu, kare wa deibu no **ani** desu.
That's Liam, he's Dave's **older brother**.
それはリアムです、彼はデイブの兄です

225.

Older sister – Ane (a-ne)姉
Watashi no **ane** wa yoku ryoko ni iku.
My **older sister** travels a lot.
私の姉は旅行に行く

226.

Son – Musuko (mu-su-ko)息子
Watashi wa **musuko** o aishiteimasu.
I love my **son**.
私は息子を愛しています

227.

Daughter – Musume (mu-su-me)娘
Karera no ichiban okina **musume** wa ima daigakusei desu.
Their first **daughter** is now in college.
彼らの一番大きな娘は今大学生です

228.

Nephew – Oi (o-yee)甥
Karera no **oi** wa genzai nyūyōku ni sunde imasu.
Their **nephew** now lives in New York.
彼らの甥は現在ニューヨークに住んでいます

229.

Niece – Mei (me-yee)姪
Kanojo no **mei** no tanjōbi wa ashita desu.

Her **niece**'s birthday is tomorrow.
彼女の姪の誕生日は明日です

230.

Great-grandchild – Mago (ma-go)孫
Kare no **mago** wa mada akachan desu.
His **great-grandchild** is just a baby.
彼の孫はまだ赤ちゃんです

231.

Relative – Shinseki (shin-se-ki)し
Are wa Reicheru desu, kanojo wa chikai **shinseki** desu.
That's Rachel, she's a close **relative**.
あれはレイチェルです　彼女は近い親戚です

232.

Friend – Tomodachi (tomo-da-chi)友達
Kanojo wa watashi no gakko no **tomodachi** desu.
She is my **friend** from school.
彼女は私の学校の友達です

233.

Boyfriend – Kareshi (ka-reh-shee)彼氏
Anata wa **kareshi** ga imasu ka?
Do you have a **boyfriend**?
あなたは彼氏がいますか

234.

Girlfriend - Kanojo (ka-no-jo)彼女
Kare no **kanojo** wa yasashikute kirei desu.
His **girlfriend** is kind and beautiful.
彼の彼女は優しくて綺麗です

235.

Single – Dokushin (Do-ku-shin)独身
Watashi wa kanojo ga imasen, **dokushin** desu.

I do not have a girlfriend, I am **single**.
私は彼女がいません、独身です

236.

Get married – Kekkon suru (ke-kkon-su-ru)結婚する
Watashi no jōshi wa rainen **kekkon** shimasu.
My boss is **getting married** next year.
私の上司は来年結婚します

237.

Fiancé – Konyakusha (kon-yaku-sha)婚約者
Watashi no **konyakusha** wa gaikoku kara kimashita.
My **fiancé** is from a foreign country.
私の婚約者は外国から来ました

238.

Fiancée - Konyakusha (kon-yaku-sha)婚約者
Kareshi no **konyakusha** wa kirei na josei desu.
His **fiancée** is a beautiful woman.
彼氏の婚約者は綺麗な女性です

239.

Groom – Shinrou (shin-rou)新郎
Shinrou wa kekkonshiki no tame ni hayaku okita.
The **groom** got ready early for his wedding.
新郎は結婚式のために早く起きた

240.

Bride – Shinpu (shin-pu)新婦
Shinpu wa sugoku kirei deshita.
The **bride** was so beautiful.
新婦はすごく綺麗でした

241.

Husband – Otto (o-tto)夫
Kanojo no **otto** wa nintaidzuyoku shinsetsu desu.

Her **husband** is patient and kind.
彼女の夫あ忍耐強く親切です

242.

Wife – Tsuma (tsu-ma)妻
Kare no **tsuma** wa Tai kara kimashita.
His **wife** is from Thailand.
彼の妻はタイからきました

243.

Divorce – Rikon (ri-kon)離婚
Rikon tetsuzuki ga ima hajimari mashita.
The **divorce** process has now started.
離婚手続きが今始まりました

244.

Widower – Mibōjin (mi-bo-jin)未亡人
Kare wa **mibōjin** desu.
He is a **widower.**
彼は未亡人です

245.

Widow - Mibōjin (mi-bo-jin)未亡人
Kanojo wa ju-nenkan **mibōjin** desu.
She has been a **widow** for 10 years.
彼女は10年間未亡人です

246.

Stepfather – Mama chichi (mama chi-chi)ママ父
Sore wa kare no **mama chichi** desu
That is his **stepfather**.
それは彼のママ父です

247.

Stepmother – Mamahaha (mamaha-ha)ママ母
Anata no **mamahaha** wa dou desu ka?

How is your **stepmother**?
あなたのママ母はどうですか

248.

Family – Kazoku (ka-zo-ku)家族
Karera no **kazoku** wa issho ni yūshoku o toru koto ni shimashita.
Their **family** decided to have dinner together.
彼の家族は一緒に夕食をとることにしました

Fruits

249.

Fruits – Kudamono (ku-da-mo-no)果物
Iroiro na **kudamono** ga kago no nakani arimasu.
There are different types of **fruits** in the basket.
色々な果物が籠の中にあります

250.

Orange – Orenji (o-ren-ji)オレンジ
Orenji no aji wa nigai.
Oranges taste bitter.
オレンジの味は苦い

251.

Mango – Mangō (man-go)マンゴー
Mangōjūsu o ippai onegaishimasu.
I would like one **mango** juice.
マンゴージュースを一杯お願いします

252.

Water melon – Suika (sui-ka)スイカ
Suika wa amai kudamono desu.
Watermelon is a sweet fruit.
スイカは甘い果物です

253.

Lychee – Raichi (rai-chi)ライチ
Watashi wa **raichi** o tabeta koto ga nai.
I have never ate **lychee**.
私はライチを食べたことがない

254.

Papaya – Papaiya (pa-pai-ya)パパイヤ
Watashinohaha wa **papaiya** ga daisuki desu.
My mother likes **papaya** a lot.
私の母親はパパイヤが大好きです

255.

Banana – Banana (ba-na-na)バナナ
Saru wa **banana** wo tabeta.
The monkey ate the **banana.**
サルはバナナを食べた

256.

Pineapple – Painappuru (pai-nap-puru)パイナップル
Kono nomimono wa **painappuru** no aji ga suru.
This drink tastes of **pineapple.**
この飲み物はパイナップルの味がする

257.

Grape – Budō (bu-do)ブドウ
Midori no **budō** yori aka no **budō** ga suki desu.
I like red **grapes** more than green **grapes**.
緑のブドウより赤のブドウが好きです

258.

Coconut – Kokonattsu (ko-ko-natt-su)ココナッツ
Kokonattsu ga kare no atama ni ochimashita.
The **coconut** fell on his head.
ココナッツが彼の頭に落ちました

259.

Guava – Guaba (gua-ba)グアバ
Kono dezāto wa **guaba** de tsukura rete imasu.
This dessert is made with **guava**.
このデザートはグアバで作られています。

260.

Passionfruit – Passhonfurūtsu (pas-shon-fu-rutsu)パッションフルーツ
Watashi no sukina nomi-mono wa **passhonfurūtsu** desu.
My favourite drink is **passionfruit**.
私の好きな飲み物はパッションフルーツです

261.

Pear – Nashi (na-shee)梨
Ichi kiro no **nashi** wa ikura desu ka?
How much for a kilo of **pears**?
一キロの梨はいくらですか

262.

Peach – Momo (mo-mo)もも
Kanojo wa **momo** ga kirai desu.
She doesn't like **peach**.
彼女はモモが嫌いです

263.

Pomegranate – Zakuro (za-ku-ro)ざくろ
Kanojo wa kinō watashi ni **zakuro**jūsu o kureta.
She gave me a **pomegranate** juice yesterday.
彼女あ昨日私にザクロジュースをくれた

264.

Watermelon – Suika (su-ika)スイカ
Kare wa hito kire no **suika** ga daisuki desu.
He'd love a slice of **watermelon**.
彼は一切れのスイカが大好きです

265.

Plum – Puramu (pu-ra-mu)プラム
Puramu nikiro kau.
Buy two kilos of **plums**.
プラムニキロ買う

266.
Apple – Ringo (rin-go)リンゴ
Onakagasuita-ra **ringo** o tabete kudasai.
Have an **apple** if you are hungry.
お腹がすいたらリンゴを食べてください

267.
Cherry – Sakuranbo (saku-ran-bo)さくらんぼ
Kono **sakuranbo**kēki wa oishī desu.
This **cherry** cake is delicious.
このサクランボケーキはおいしいです

Numbers

268.

0 – Zero (ze-ro)ゼロ
Kion wa **zero** do desu.
The temperature is **zero** now.
気温は０度です

269.

1 – Ichi (ichi) １
Watashi wa petto o **ippiki** katteimasu.
I have **one** pet.
私はペットを一匹買ってきます

270.

2 – Ni (ni) 2
Watashi no tomodachi **futari** wa raisyu gaikoku ni ikimasu.
Two of my friends are going abroad next week.
私の友達二人は来週外国に行きます

271.

3 – San (san) ３
San-nin no hito ga sono shima ni imasu.
There are **three** people on the island.
3人の人がその島にいます

272.

4 – Yon (yon) ４
Watashi wa **yonin** no dōryō to shigoto o shite imasu.
I work with **four** colleagues.
私は4人の同僚と仕事をしています

273.

5 – Go (go) ５
Kōen ni wa **go**nin no inu ga imasu.

There are **five** dogs in the park.
公園には5匹の犬がいます

274.

6 – Roku (ro-ku) ６
Yūshoku dewa **roku**mai no osara o yōi saremashita.
Six plates were served at the dinner.
夕食では6枚のお皿を用意されました

275.

7 – Nana (na-na) ７
Nananin no hito ga kurasu ni imasu.
There are **seven** people in the class.
7人の人がクラスにいます

276.

8 – Hachi (ha-chi) ８
Sono untenshu wa **yattu** no kozutsumi wo todoke mashita.
The driver delivered **eight** packages.
その運転手は８つの小包を届けました

277.

9 – Kyu (kyu) 九
Watashi no musume wa **kyu**sai desu.
My son is **9** years old.
私の娘は九歳です

278.

10 – Ju (ju)10
Watashi wa **ju**nin no kodomo ga imasu.
I have **10** children.
私は10人の子供がいます

279.

11 – Juichi (ju-ichi)11
Ju-ichi nin no hito ga basu no naka ni imasu.
Eleven people are on the bus.

11人の人がバスの中にいます

280.

12 – Juni (ju-ni)12

Heya niwa **juni**-kyaku no isu ga arimasu.

There are **12** chairs in the room.

部屋には12脚の椅子があります

281.

13 – Jusan (ju-san)13

Watashino ani/otouto wa **jusan** sai desu.

My brother is **thirteen**.

私の兄/弟は13歳です

282.

14 – Juyon (ju-yon)14

Garēji ni wa **juyo**nin no hitobito ga imasu.

There are **fourteen** people in the garage.

ガレージには14人の人々がいます

283.

15 – Jugo (ju-go)15

Kanojo wa **jugo**ko no bōshi o motte imasu.

She owns **fifteen** hats.

彼女あ15の帽子をもっています

284.

16 - Juroku (ju-ro-ku)16

Kanojo no tanjōbi ha raisyu desu, kanojo wa **juroku**-sai ni narimasu.

It is her birthday next week, she will be **sixteen**.

彼女誕生日は来週です、彼女は16歳になります

285.

17 – Junana (ju-na-na)17

Watashi no gurūpu ni wa **junana**-nin no gakusei ga imasu.

There are **seventeen** students in my group.

私のグループには17人の学生がいます

286.

18 – Juhachi (ju-ha-chi)18
Juhachi-sai wa jūyōna nenrei desu.
Eighteen is an important age.
18歳は重要な年齢です

287.

19 – Jukyu (ju-kyu) １９
Niju hiku ichi wa **jukyu** desu.
Twenty minus one is **nineteen**.
20引く１は19です

288.

20 – Niju (ni-ju)20
Watashi no ie no bangou wa **niju** desu.
My house number is **twenty**.
私の家の番号は20です

289.

101 – Hyakuichi (hya-ku-ichi)101
Kono bin no naka ni wa **hyakuikko** no okashi ga arimasu.
There are **101** sweets in this jar.
この瓶の中には101個のお菓子があります

290.

111 – Hyakujuichi (hya-ku-ju-ichi) １１１
Densha ni wa **hyakujuichi**-nin ga notte ita.
There were **111** people on board the train.
電車には111人が乗っていた

291.

112 – Hyakujuni (hya-ku-ju-ni) １１２
Watashi wa furui ryō ni **hyakujuni**-hon no pen o nokoshimashita.
I left **112** pens in my old dorm.
私は古い寮に112本のペンを残しました

292.
200 – Nihyaku (ni-hya-ku)200
Anata wa watashi ni **nihyaku**dora karite iru.
You owe me **200**dollars.
あなたは私に200ドル借りている

293.
221 – Nihyakunijuichi (ni-hyaku ni-ju ichi) ２２１
Shūjin bangō **nihyakunijuichi** ga datsugoku shimashita.
The prisoner number **221** has escaped.
囚人番号221が脱獄しました

294.
222 – Nihyaku niju ni (Ni-hyaku ni-ju ni) ２２２
Sono eiga wa **nihyakunijuni** hun tsudukimasu.
The movie lasts **222** minutes.
その映画は222分続きます

295.
500 – Gohyaku (go hya-ku)500
Gohyaku nin ga sono kekkonshiki ni shusseki suru.
500 people are going to the wedding.
500人がその結婚式に出席する

296.
600 – Roppaku (rop-paku)600
Roppyaku nin ga kaigi ni shusseki shimashita.
600 people came to a meeting.
600人が会議に出席しました

297.
700 – Nanahyaku (na-na hya-ku)700
Watashi wa benkyō no tame ni **nanakyaku**-doru o harau hitsuyō ga arimasu.
I need **700** dollars to pay for my studies.
私は勉強のために700ドルを払う必要があります

298.

900 – Kyu hyaku (kyu hya-ku)
Watashitachi wa ima kaibatsu **kyuhyaku** mētoru desu.
We are now **900** metres above the sea level.
私たち今海抜900メートルです

299.

999 – Ku hyaku kyujukyu (kyu hya-ku kyu ju-kyu) ９９９
Kanojo wa **ku hyaku kyu jukyu**doru de atarashī denwa o kaimashita.
She bought a new phone for **999** dollars.
彼女は999ドルで新しい電話を買いました

300.

1000 – Sen (sen)千
Kare wa kazoku ni **sen-doru** o oitekita.
He left **1000** dollars to his family.
彼は家族に千ドルをおいてきた

301.

2000 – Nisen (ni-sen)二千
Nisen nen no toshi wa seiki no kawarime desu.
The year **2000** is the turn of the century.
2千年の年は世紀の変わり目です

302.

3000 – Sanzen (san-zen)3千
Sono arīna wa **sanzen**-nin made shūyō dekimasu.
The arena can seat up to **3000** people.
そのアリーナは三千人まで収容できます

303.

4000 – Yonsen (yon-sen)4千
Yonsen bon no mizu ga hinansha ni kubararemashita.
4000 bottles of water were distributed to the evacuees.
4千本の水が避難者に配られました

304.

5000 – Gosen (go-sen)5千
Kono kaisha ni wa **gosen**-ri no jūgyōin ga imasu
This company has **5000** employees
この会社には5千人の従業員がいます

305.

6000 – Rokusen (ro-ku-sen)6千
Kore wa **rokusen** desu.
This is **6000**.
これは6000です

306.

7000 – Nanasen (na-na-sen)7千
Watashi wa kakede **nanasen** peso kachitotta.
I won **7000** pesos in the bet we made.
私は賭けで7000ペソ勝ち取った

307.

8000 – Hasen (ha-sen)8千
Zaidan wa kotonaru gakkō ni **hassen** no isu o ataemashita.
The foundation gave **8000** chairs to different schools.
財団は異なる学校に8000の椅子を与えました

308.

9000 – Kyusen (kyu-sen)九千
Kore wa **kyusen** mētoru no taka-sa desu.
This is **9000** meters tall.
これは9000メートルの高さです

309.

10000 – Ichiman (ichi-man)一万
Ichi Man hito ga kare o shinrai shite iru
10000 people trust him.
一万人の人が彼を信頼している

310.

100000 – Juman (ju-man)10万
Watashi wa kuizu bee de **juman** katta.
I won **100000** in the quiz bee.
私はクイズビーで10万勝った

311.
1000000 – Hyakuman (hyaku-man)百万
Jakkupotto wa Hyakuman-doru desu
The jackpot is **1000000** dollars.
ジャックポットは100万ドルです

312.
Number – Nanbā (nan-ba)ナンバー
Watashi no rakkī**nanbā** wa go desu.
My lucky **number** is 5.
私のラッキーナンバーは５です

Weather

313.

Air – Kūki (ku-kee)空気
Tsumetai **kūki** ga fukimasu.
The cold **air** blows.
冷たい空気が吹きます

314.

Cold – Samui (sa-mu-yee)寒い
Soto wa totemo **samui** node bōshi o kaburu-yō ni shite kudasai.
Make sure to wear your hat, outside is very **cold**.
外はとても寒いので帽子をかぶるようにしてください

315.

Degrees – Do (doh)度
Kyou wa 20-**do** desu.
It is 20 **degrees** today.
今日は20度です

316.

Cloudy – Kumori (ku-mo-ri)曇り
Kinou wa **kumori** deshita.
Yesterday was a **cloudy** day.
昨日は曇りでした

317.

Fog – Kiri (kee-ri)霧
Kiri no seide nanimo mienai.
I can't see anything because of the **fog**.
霧のせいで何も見えない

318.

Freeze – Kōru (ko-ru)凍る
Tori- o **kōrasete** kudasai.
Freeze the chicken for me.

鳥お凍らせてください

319.

Hot – Hotto (hot-to)ホット
Anata wa **hotto**kōhī to kōrudokōhī dochira ga suki desu ka?
Do you like **hot** coffee or cold coffee?
あなたはホットコーヒーとコールドコーヒーどちらが好きですか

320.

Hurricane – Harikēn (hari-ken)ハリケーン
Harikēn wa kare no ie o hakai shita.
The **hurricane** destroyed his house.
ハリケーンは彼の家を破壊した

321.

Ice – Kōri (ko-ri)氷
Kōri wa ikaga desu ka?
Would you like some **ice**?
氷はいかがですか

322.

Lightning – Kaminari (ka-mee-na-ri)雷
Konya wa **kaminari** ga hassei surudarou.
Tonight will be **lightning**.
今夜は雷が発生するだろう

323.

Moon – Tsuki (tsu-ki)月
Mokuyōbi wa man**getsu** ni narimasu.
There will be a full **moon** on Thursday.
木曜日は満月になります

324.

Rain – Ame (a-me)雨
Kinyōbi wa **ame** ga furu desu yo.
It will **rain** on Friday.

金曜日は雨が降るでしょう

325.

Rainbow – Niji (ni-ji)虹
Asoko ni **niji** ga dete imasu.
There is a **rainbow** over there.
あそこに虹がでています

326.

Sky – Sora (soh-ra)空
Konya no **sora** wa sugoku kirei desu.
The **sky** looks so beautiful tonight.
今夜の空はすごく綺麗です

327.

Snow – Yuki (yu-kee)雪
Watashitachi wa **yuki** o mitakoto ga nai.
We have never seen **snow** before.
私たちは雪みたことがない

328.

Storm – Arashi (a-ra-shee)嵐
Deteikanai de, ōkina **arashi** ga kuru.
Don't go out, there is a big **storm** coming.
出ていかないで大きな嵐がくる

329.

Sun – Taiyō (tai-yo)太陽
Watashi wa **taiyō** to atsui tenki ga daisuki desu.
I love **sun** and hot weather.
私は太陽と暑い天気が大好きです

330.

Sunny – Hare (ha-reh)晴れ
Ashita wa **hare** ni naru desu yo.
Tomorrow will be a sunny day.

明日は晴れになるでしょう

331.

Typhoon – Taifū (tai-fu)台風
Watashi wa kinō **taifū** o mita.
I saw a **typhoon** yesterday.
私は昨日台風をみた

332.

Warm – Atatakai (ata-ta-kai)暖かい
Watashi wa **atatakai** ofuro ni hairu koto ga suki desu.
I like taking a bath with **warm** water.
私は暖かいお風呂に入ることが好きです

333.

Weather – Tenki (ten-ki)天気
Soto no **tenki** wa dou desu ka?
How is the **weather** outside?
外の天気はどうですか

334.

Windy – Kyōfū (kyo-fu)強風
Kinō wa**kyōfū** deshita.
Yesterday was too **windy**.
昨日は強風でした

Places

335.

Airport – Kūkō (ku-ko)
Karera wa **kūkō** de owakare o itta.
They said their goodbyes in the **airport**.
彼らは空港でお別れを言った

336.

Apartment – Apāto (a-pa-to)アパート
Anata no **apāto** wa chikaku desu ka?
Is your **apartment** close by?
あなたのアパートは近くですか

337.

Bank – Ginkou (gin-kou)銀行
Syumatsu wa **ginkou** ga shimatte imasu.
The **bank** is closed on the weekends.
週末は銀行が閉まっています

338.

Barber shop – Tokoya (to-ko-ya)床屋
Kyō wa **tokoya** ni ikimasu.
I'm going to the **barber** today.
今日は床屋に行きます

339.

Book Store – Honya (hon-ya)本屋
Kare wa **honya** ni imasu.
He is in the book store.
彼は本屋にいます

340.

Bus Stop – Basu-tei (ba-su-tei)バス停
Karera wa ichiban chikai **basutei** de au koto ni kimeta.

They decided to meet at the nearest **bus stop**.
彼らは一番近いバス停で会うことに決めた

341.

Cinema – Eiga-kan (eh-ga-kan)映画館
Karera no saisho no dēto wa **eigakan** deshita.
Their first date was at the **cinema**.
彼らの最初のデートは映画館でした

342.

Coffee shop – Kafe (ka-feh)カフェ
Anata wa **kafe** ni imasu ka?
Are you in the **coffee shop**?
あなたはカフェにいますか

343.

Convenience shop – Konbini (Kon-bee-nee)コンビニ
Sumimasen, ichiban chikai **konbini** wa doko desu ka?
Excuse me, do you know where the closest **convenience shop** is?
すみません、一番近いコンビニはどこですか

344.

Department store – Depāto (de-par-to)デパート
Depāto wa mōru no naka ni arimasu.
The **department store** is inside the mall.
デパートはモールの中にあります

345.

Fire department – Shōbōsho (sho-bo-sho)消防署
Shōbōsho wa keisatsusho no tonari ni arimasu.
The **fire department** is next to the police station.
消防署は警察署の隣にあります

346.

Home – Ie (ie)家
Kazoku ga koishī, **ie** ni kaeritai.

I miss my family, I want to go **home**.
家族が恋しい、家に帰りたい

347.

Hospital – Byōin (byo-in)病院
Byōin wa itsumo seiketsu ni tamota rete imasu.
The **hospital** is always kept clean.
病院はいつも清潔に保たれています

348.

Hotel – Hoteru (ho-te-ru)ホテル
Kono **hoteru** wa ōkikutetakai.
This **hotel** is very big and expensive.
このホテルは大きくて高い

349.

House – Jitaku (ji-ta-ku)自宅
Watashi no **jitaku** wa kono michi no owari ni arimasu.
My house is at the end of this road.
私の自宅はこの道の終わりにあります

350.

Library – Toshokan (to-sho-kan)図書館
Kanojo wa benkyō suru tame ni **toshokan** ni ikimashita.
She went to the **library** to study.
彼女は勉強をするために図書館に行きました

351.

Office – Jimusho (ji-mu-sho)
Kanojo wa chīsana **jimusho** de hataraite imasu.
She works in a small **office**.
彼女は小さな事務所で働いています

352.

Pharmacy – Yakkyoku (yak-kyo-ku)薬局
Yakkyoku wa byōin ni arimasu.

The **pharmacy** is in the hospital.
薬局は病院にあります

353.

Post Office – Yūbinkyoku (yu-bin-kyo-ku)郵便局
Kare wa **yūbinkyoku** ni nimotsu o okuri ni itta.
He went to the **post office** to send a package.
彼は郵便局に荷物を送りに行った

354.

Restaurant – Resutoran (re-su-to-ran)レストラン
Watashi wa itarian **resutoran** ni ikimashita, tabemono wa oishikatta desu.
I went to an Italian **restaurant**, the food was delicious.
私はイタリアンレストランに行きました、食べ物はおいしかったです

355.

School – Gakkō (gak-ko)学校
Kanojo wa shū ni itsuka**gakkō** ni ikimasu.
She goes to **school** 5 days a week
彼女は週に5日学校に行きます

356.

Supermarket – Sūpā (su-pah)スーパー
Anata wa nanika **sūpā** de hitsuyōna mono wa arimasu ka?
Do you need anything from the **supermarket**?
あなたは何かスーパーに必要なものはありますか

357.

Train Station – Eki (e-kee)駅
Hayaku, sanjuppun de eki ni tōchaku suru hitsuyō ga arimasu.
Quick, we need to arrive at the **train station** in 30 minutes.
速く、30分で駅に到着する必要があります

358.

Work – Shigoto (shee-go-toh)仕事
Gomennasai ikemasen. Watashi wa ashita **shigoto** ga arimasu.

I'm sorry I cannot go. I have **work** tomorrow.
ごめんなさい　行けません　私は明日仕事があります

359.

Living room – Ima (e-ma)居間
Anata no kutsu wa **ima** ni arimasu.
Your shoes are in the **living room**.
あなたの靴は居間にあります

360.

Bedroom – Shinshitsu (shin-shit-su)寝室
Watashi no **shinshitsu** wa totemo chīsai desu.
My **bedroom** is very small.
私の寝室はとても小さいです

361.

Garden – Niwa (ni-wa)庭
Niwa wa utsukushiku, hana de ippai desu.
The **garden** is beautiful and is full of flowers.
庭は美しく、花でいっぱいです

362.

Room – Heya (he-ya)部屋
Heya wa jimu ni narimashita.
The **room** is now converted into a gym.
部屋はジムになりました

363.

Kitchen – Daidokoro (dai-do-ko-ro)台所
Totemo kireina **daidokoro** ga arimasu.
You have a very clean **kitchen**.
とても綺麗な台所があります

364.

Bathroom – Toire (toy-ire)トイレ
Sumimasen, **toire** wa doko desu ka?

Excuse me, where is the **bathroom**?
すみません、トイレはどこですか

365.

Shower – Shawā (sha-waa)シャワー
Kyō wa atsuinode **shawā** o nikai abimashita.
I took a **shower** twice today because of the hot weather.
今日は暑いのでシャワーを二回浴びました

366.

Beach – Sunahama (su-na-ha-ma)
Kyō **sunahama** ni ikimasu ka?
Are you going to the **beach** today?
今日砂浜に行きますか

367.

Mountain – Yama (ya-ma)山
Ano **yama** no namae wa nan desu ka?
What is the name of that **mountain**?
あの山の名前は何ですか

368.

Island – Sima (shee-ma)島
Dare mo kono **shima** ni sunde imasen.
No one lives on this **island**.
誰もこの島に住んでいません

369.

River – Kawa (ka-wa)川
Kono **kawa** wa mizūmi ni tsunagatte imasu.
This **river** joins to the lake.
この川は湖に繋がっています

370.

Ocean – Umi (u-mie)海
Umi wa totemo kirei desu.

The **ocean** looks so beautiful.
海はとても綺麗です

371.

Desert – Sabaku (sa-ba-ku)砂漠
Watashitachiha **sabaku** o aruite oudan shimashita.
We walk across the **desert**.
私たちは砂漠を歩いて横断しました

372.

Field – Tanbo (tan-bo)田んぼ
Sore wa **tanbo** desu ka?
Is that a rice **field**?
それは田んぼですか

373.

Forest – Mori (mo-ri)森
Machi no soto ni wa **mori** ga arimasu
There is a **forest** outside the city.
町の外には森があります

Directions & Pre-positions

374.

Turn left – Sasetsu (sa-set-su)左折
Tsugi no deguchi o**sasetsu** shimasu.
Turn left at the next exit.
次の出口を左折します

375.

Turn right – Usetsu (u-set-su)右折
Sono michi no saki o **usetsu** shimasu.
Turn right at the end of the road.
その道の先を右折します

376.

Go straight – Massugu saki (mas-su-gu sa-ki)まっすぐ先
Eigakan wa **massugu saki** no kado ni arimasu.
Go straight the cinema is on the corner.
映画館はまっすぐ先の角にあります

377.

Junction – Jyankusyon (jyan-ku-syon)ジャンクション
Dono **jyankusyon** o riyō shimasu ka?
Which **junction** do I take?
どのジャンクションを利用しますか

378.

Bridge – Hashi (ha-shee)橋
Kore wa nagai **hashi** desu.
This is a long **bridge.**
これは長い橋です

379.

Traffic light – Shingō (shin-go)信号
Takushī wa **shingō** de tomatta.

The taxi stopped at the **traffic light**.
タクシーは信号で止まった

380.

Corner – Kado (ka-do)角
Watashinoie wa kono **kado** noatari desu.
My house is around this **corner**.
私の家はこの角のあたりです

381.

Left hand – Hidarigawa (Hi-da-ri-ga-wa)左側
Hoteru wa **hidarigawa** ni arimasu.
The hotel is on the **left hand** side.
ホテルは左側にあります

382.

Right hand – Migigawa (Mi-gi-ga-wa)右側
Ginkō wa **migigawa** ni arimasu.
The bank is on the **right hand** side.
銀行は右側にあります

383.

Cross the street - **Tōri o wataru** (to-ri o wa-ta-ru)通りを渡る
Tōri o watareba bā ni tsuku koto ga dekimasu.
If you **cross the street** you can reach the bar.
通りを渡ればバーに着くことができます

384.

Left – Hidari (hi-da-ri)左
Eki ni iku niwa **hidari** ni magatte massugu susumimasu.
To get to the station take a **left** and then go straight.
駅に行くには左に曲がってまっすぐ進みます

385.

Right – Migi (mi-gi)右
Watashi wa **migi**kiki desu.

I am **right** handed.
私は右利きです

386.

On – Ue (u-eh)上
Neko wa tēburu no **ue** ni imasu.
The cat is **on** the table.
猫はテーブルの上にいます

387.

Upstairs – Kaijō (kai-jo)階上
Depāto wa **kaijō** desu.
The department store is **upstairs.**
デパートは階上です

388.

Downstairs – Kaika (kai-ka)階下
Bā wa **kaika** ni arimasu.
The bar is **downstairs**.
バーは階下にあります

389.

Under – Shita (shi-ta)下
Inu wa beddo no **shita** ni imasu.
The dog is **under** the bed.
犬はベッドの下にいます

390.

In front of - Mae ni (ma-e ni)前に
Toire wa erebētā no **mae ni** arimasu.
The toilet is **in front of** the lift.
トイレはエレベーターの前にあります

391.

Behind – Ushiro (u-shi-ro)後ろ
Sono shōjo wa otōsan no **ushiro** ni tatte ita.

The girl stood **behind** her dad.
その少女はお父さんの後ろに立っていた

392.

In – Naka (na-ka)中
Hako no **naka** ni omocha ga arimasu
There is a toy **in** the box.
箱お中におもちゃがあります

393.

Out – Dekaketa (de-ka-ke-ta)出かけた
Kare wa sanpo ni **dekaketa**.
He went **out** for a walk.
彼は散歩に出かけた

394.

Besides – Tonari (to-na-ri)隣
Shiriaru wa orenji no **tonari**ni arimasu.
The cereal is **beside** the oranges.
シリアルオレンジの隣にあります

395.

Between – Aida (ai-da)間
Jitensha wa kuruma no **aida** ni arimasu.
The bike is **between** the cars.

396.

Opposite – Mukai (mu-kai)
Toire wa erebētā no **mukai** ni arimasu.
The toilet is **opposite** the lift.
トイレはエレベーターの向かいにあります

397.

Above – Zujō (zu-jo)頭上
Kanojo wa ryōte o **zujō** ni oita.
She put her hands **above** her head.

彼女は両手を頭上においた

398.

Below – Shita (shi-ta)下
Shio wa tēburu no **shita** ni arimasu.
The salt is **below** the table.
塩はテーブルの下にあります

Body Parts

399.

Head – Atama (a-ta-ma)頭
Atama ga itai desu.
My **head** is hurting.
頭が痛いです

400.

Face – Kao (kao)顔
Kanojo wa totemo utsukushī **kao** o shite iru.
She has a very beautiful **face**.
彼女はとても美しい顔をしている

401.

Hair – Kaminoke (ka-mi-no-ke)髪の毛
Kanojo wa senshū **kaminoke** o kaeta.
She changed her **hair** last week.
彼女は先週髪の毛を変えた

402.

Ears – Mimi (mi-mi)耳
Kare no **mimi** wa ōki sugiru.
His **ears** are too big.
彼の耳は大きすぎる

403.

Eyes – Me (me)目
Josei wa aoi **me** o shite imasu.
The woman has blue **eyes**.
女性は青い目をしています

404.

Eyebrows – Mayuge (ma-yu-ge)眉毛
Anata wa**mayuge** o tsumubeki desu

You should pluck your **eyebrows**.
あなたは眉毛をつむべきです

405.

Nose – Hana (ha-na)鼻
Watashi wa **hana** o ni-do otta.
I have broken my **nose** twice.
私は鼻を二度折った

406.

Mouth – Kuchi (ku-chi)口
Kuchi o akenaide kudasai.
Don't open your **mouth**.
口を開けないでください

407.

Lips - Kuchibiru (ku-chi-bi-ru)唇
Anata no **kuchibiru** wa yawarakai.
You have soft **lips**.
あなたの唇は柔らかい

408.

Tongue – Shita (shi-ta)舌
Hebi wa nagai **shita** o motte imasu.
Snakes have long **tongues.**
蛇は長い舌をもっています

409.

Chin – Ago (a-go)顎
Kare no **ago** wa ōki sugimasu.
His **chin** is too big.
彼の顎は大きすぎます

410.

Jaw – Ago (a-go)顎
Ago ga itai desu.

My **jaw** is hurting.
顎が痛いです

411.
Cheek – Hoho (ho-ho)頬
Akachan wa futotta **hoho** o motte imasu.
The baby has fat **cheeks**.
赤ちゃんは太った頬をもっています

412.
Beard – Agohige (a-go-hi-ge)顎髭
Kāru wa nagai **agohige** o hayashite imasu.
Carl has a long **beard**.
カールは長いあごひげを生やしています

413.
Moustache – Kuchihige (ku-chi-hi-ge)口ひげ
Watashi wa **kuchihige** o hayashitai desu.
I want to grow a **moustache**.
私は口ひげを生やしたいです

414.
Neck – Kubi (ku-bi)首
Watashi wa itsumo **kubi** ni sukāfu o tsukete imasu.
I always wear a scarf around my **neck**.
私はいつも首にスカーフをつけています

415.
Chest – Mune (mu-ne)胸
Sekio suruto **mune** ga itaku Narimasu.
When I cough, my **chest** hurts.
咳をすると胸が痛くなります

416.
Breast – Mune (mu-ne)胸
Kare wa watashi no **mune** ni fureta.

He touched my **breast**.
彼は私の胸に触れた

417.

Shoulders – Kata (ka-ta)肩
Suieisenshu wa ōkina **kata** o shite imasu.
Swimmers have big **shoulders**.
水泳選手は大きな肩をしています

418.

Arms – Ude (u-de)腕
Watashi no **ude** wa jimu ni ittekara itai desu.
My **arms** are hurting from the gym.
私の腕はジムに行ってから痛いです

419.

Hands – Te (te)手
Te o sashinobete kudasai.
Give me your **hand** and follow me.
手を差し伸べてください

420.

Fingers – Yubi (yu-bi)指
Kono pianisuto wa hosonagai **yubi** o shite imasu.
This pianist has long thin **fingers**.
このピアニストは細長い指をしています

421.

Thumbs – Oyayubi (o-ya-yu-bi)親指
Anata ga shiawasenara, **oyayubi** o tatete kudasai.
Put your **thumbs** up if you are happy.
あなたが幸せなら親指を立ててください

422.

Knuckles – Yubi no kansetsu (yu-bi no kan-set-su)指の関節
Watashi wa tatakai de **yubi no kansetsu** o kizutsuketa.

I hurt my **knuckle** in the fight.
私は戦いで指の関節を傷つけました

423.

Nails – Tsume (tsu-me)爪
Naze anata wa mada **tsume** o kitte inai no desu ka?
Why haven't you cut your **nails** yet?
何故あなたはまだ爪を切っていないのですか

424.

Back – Senaka (se-na-ka)背中
Jiko no ato, watashi no **senaka** ga itai.
My **back** hurts after the accident.
事故のあと、私の背中が痛い

425.

Lower back – Koshi (ko-shi)腰
Lower back pain – Yōtsū (yo-tsu)
Watashi wa ichinenkan **yōtsū** ni kurushinde iru.
I have had **lower back pain** for 1 year.
私は一年間腰に苦しんでいる

426.

Stomach – I (ee)胃
I ga itai desu, nanika o taberu hitsuyō ga arimasu.
My **stomach** is hurting, I need to eat something.
胃が痛いです、何かを食べる必要があります

427.

Abs – Fukkin (fuk-kin)腹筋
Kare wa tsuyoi **fukkin** ga hoshii desu.
He wants to have strong **abs.**
彼は強い腹筋がほしいです

428.

Hips – Hippu (hi-ppu)ヒップ

Odorutoki **hippu** o tsukai nasai.
Use your **hips** when you are dancing.
踊るときヒップを使いなさい

429.

Bum – Oshiri (o-shi-ri)おしり
Watashi wa subette**oshiri** kara kokemashita, totemo hazukashikatta desu.
I slipped and fell on my **bum**, it was so embarrassing.
私は滑っておしりからこけました、とても恥ずかしかったです

430.

Penis – Inkei (in-kei)陰茎
Dansei ni wa **inkei**ga arimasu.
Men have a **penis**.
男性には陰茎があります

431.

Vagina – Chitsu (chit-su)膣
Josei ni wa **chitsu** ga arimasu.
Women have a **vagina**.
女性には膣があります

432.

Legs – Ashi (a-shi)足
Nagai sanpo de **ashigai**tai.
My **legs** hurt after the long walk.
長い散歩で足が痛い

433.

Thighs – Futomomo (fu-to-mo-mo)太もも
Kanojo wa **futomomo** ni yobun'na shibō ga tsuite imasu.
She has extra fat on her **thighs**.
彼女は太ももに余分な脂肪がついています

434.

Knee – Hiza (hee-za)膝

Hashitte iru uchi ni **hiza**mazuita
I fell on my **knee** while running.
走ってるうちにひざまづいた

435.

Calf - Fukura hagi (fu-ku-ra-ha-gi)ふくらはぎ
Kare no **fukura hagi** wa totemo ōkī desu.
His **calf** is very big.
彼のふくらはぎはとても大きいです

436.

Foot – Ashi (a-shee)足
Watashi wa **ashi** no shujutsu o shimashita.
I had an operation for my **foot.**
私は足の手術をしました

437.

Ankle – Ashikubi (a-shi-ku-bi)足首
Haikingu shinagara **ashikubi** o hinetta.
He twisted his **ankle** while hiking.
ハイキングをしながら足首をひねった

438.

Toes – Tsumasaki (tsu-ma-sa-kee)つま先
Akachan ni wa chīsana **tsumasaki** ga arimasu.
Babies have tiny **toes**.
赤ちゃんには小さなつま先があります

439.

Toe nails – Tsumasaki no tsume (tsu-ma-sa-ki no tsu-me)つま先の爪
Tsumasaki no tsume o kitte imasu.
I am cutting my **toe nails.**
つま先の爪を切っています

440.

Heart – Kokoro (ko-ko-ro)心

Kare no hahaoya wa ōkina **kokoro** o motte imasu.
His mother has a big **heart**.
彼の母親は大きな心をもっています

441.
Lungs – Hai (hai)肺
Kenkōna **hai** ga hoshī nonara, kitsuen o yameru hitsuyō ga arimasu.
If you want healthy **lungs**, you need to quit smoking.
健康な肺が欲しいのなら、喫煙をやめる必要があります

442.
Liver – Kanzō (kan-zo)肝臓
Arukōru wa **kanzō** ni warui desu.
Alcohol is bad for your **liver**.
アルコールは肝臓に悪いです

443.
Brain – Nō (noh)脳
Watashi wa totemo tsukarete imasu, **nō** wa kinō shinaku narimashita.
I'm so tired, my **brain** has stop working.
私はおても疲れています、脳は機能しなくなりました

444.
Intestines – Chō (cho)腸
Anata no **chō** wa yoi jyoutai desu.
Your **intestines** are in a good condition.
あなたの腸は良い状態です

445.
Skin – Hada (ha-da)肌
Hada o hoshitsu shite kudasai.
Keep your **skin** moisturized daily.
肌を保湿してください

446.
Teeth – Ha (hah)歯

Mainichi**ha** o migaite kudasai.
Brush your **teeth** every day.
毎日歯を磨いて下さい

447.

Elbow – Hiji (hee-ji)肘
Watashi wa taiikukan de **hiji** o itameta.
I hurt my **elbow** at the gym.
私は体育館で肘を痛めた

Clothes

448.

Belt – Beruto (be-ru-to)ベルト
Betsu no **beruto** wa arimasu ka?
Do you have another **belt**?
別のベルトはありますか

449.

Vest – Besuto (be-su-to) ベスト
Anata wa watashi no **besuto** o mimashita ka?
Have you seen my **vest**?
あなたは私のベストを見ましたか

450.

Shopping – Kaimono (kai-mo-no)買い物
Watashi wa kaimono ni iku no ga suki desu
I like to go **shopping.**
私は買い物に行くのが好きです

451.

Pants – Zubon (zu-bon)ズボン
Anata wa kono mise de yasui **zubon** o kau koto ga dekimasu.
You can buy cheap **pants** in this store.
あなたはこの店で安いズボンを買うことができます

452.

Bra - Burajā (bu-ra-ja)ブラジャー
Kanojo wa pinku no **burajā** o kite imashita.
She was wearing a pink **bra**.
彼女はピンクのブラジャーを着ていました

453.

Boots – Būtsu (bu-tsu)ブーツ
Kanojo wa kuroi doresu to kuroi **būtsu** o minitsukete ita.

She wore a black dress and black **boots**.
彼女は黒いドレスと黒いブーツを身に着けていた

454.

Cap – Bōshi (bo-shee)帽子
Kare wa kuroi **bōshi** o kabutte ita.
He was wearing a black **cap**.
彼は黒い帽子をかぶっていた

455.

Coat – Uwagi (u-wa-gi)上着
Kare wa **uwagi** o kurabu ni oitekimashita.
He left his **coat** in the club.
彼は上着をクラブに置いてきました

456.

Dress – Doresu (do-re-su) ドレス
Sono **doresu** wa kirei desu.
That **dress** looks beautiful.
そのドレスは綺麗です

457.

Gloves – Tebukuro (te-bu-ku-ro)手袋
Watashi wa atarashī **tebukuro** o kaimashita.
I bought a new pair of **gloves**.
私は新しい手袋を買いました

458.

Hat – Bōshi (bo-shi)帽子
Sore wa don'na **bōshi** desu ka?
What type of **hat** is that?
それはどんな帽子ですか

459.

Jacket – Jaketto (ja-ketto)ジャケット
Kono **jaketto** wa motto chīsai saizu no mono ga arimasu ka?

Do you have this **jacket** in a smaller size?
このジャケットはもっと小さいサイズのものがありますか

460.

Jeans – Jīnzu (jin-zu)ジーンズ
Watashinoie no daremoga **jīnzu** o kite imasu.
Everyone in my house wears **jeans**.
私の家のだれもがジーンズを着ています

461.

Knickers – Pantī (pan-ti)パンティ
Watashi no**pantī**no hotondo wa pinku desu.
Most of my **knickers** are pink.
私のパンティのほとんどはピンクです

462.

Pyjamas – pajama (pa-ja-ma)パジャマ
Kanojo wa yoru ni **pajama** o kite imasu.
She wears **pyjamas** at night.
彼女は夜にパジャマを着ています

463.

Trousers – Zubon (zu-bon)ズボン
Korera no **zubon** wa kitsu sugiru.
These **trousers** are too tight.
これらのズボンはきつすぎる

464.

Scarf – Sukāfu (su-ka-fu)スカーフ
Watashi wa kanojo no ie ni **sukāfu** o oitekita.
I left my **scarf** at her house.
私は彼女の家にスカーフを置いてきた置いてきた

465.

Shirt – Shatsu (shat-su)シャツ
Ashita wa kanarazu shiroi **shatsu** o kite kudasai.

Make sure to wear a white **shirt** tomorrow.
明日は必ず白いシャツを着てください

466.

Shorts – Shōtopantsu (sho-to-pant-su)ショートパンツ
Kanojo wa **shōtopantsu** o kimasen.
She doesn't want to wear **shorts**.
彼女はショートパンツを着ません

467.

Shoes – Kutsu (kut-su)靴
Watashi wa atarashī **kutsu** o kau hitsuyō ga arimasu.
I need to buy new **shoes**.
私は新しい靴を買う必要があります

468.

Skirt - Sukāto (su-ka-to)スカート
Sono **sukāto** wa doko de kōnyū shimashita ka?
Where did you buy that **skirt** from?
そのスカートはどこで購入しましたか

469.

Slippers – Surippa (su-rip-pa)スリッパ
Watashi wa **surippa** o haku no ni narete imasen.
I am not used to wearing **slippers**.
私はスリッパを履くのに慣れていません

470.

Socks – Kutsushita (ku-tsu-shi-ta)靴下
Kutsushita o taiikukan ni oitekita.
I left my **socks** in the gym.
靴下を体育館に置いてきた

471.

Suit – Sūtsu (sut-su)スーツ
Otto wa shigoto de**sūtsu** o kinakereba narimasen.

My husband has to wear a **suit** to work.
夫は仕事でスーツを着なければなりません

472.

Sweater – Sētā (se-ta)セーター
Soto wa samuinode, **sētā** o kite kudasai.
It's cold outside, put on a **sweater**.
外は寒いのでセーターを着てください

473.

T-shirt – Tīshatsu (ti-shat-su) Ｔシャツ
Kare no **tīshatsu** wa mō kare ni wa aimasen.
His **t-shirt** does not fit him anymore.
彼のＴシャツはもう彼には合いません

474.

Tie – Nekutai (ne-ku-tai)ネクタイ
Watashitachi wa pātī de onaji **nekutai** o tsukemashita.
We wore the same **tie** to the party.
私たちはパーティで同じネクタイをつけました

475.

Trousers – Zubon (zu-bon)ズボン
Watashi wa kiiroi **zubon** o sagashiteimasu.
I am looking for yellow **trousers**.
私は黄色いズボンを探しています

476.

Underwear – Shitagi (shi-ta-gi)下着
Shitagi wa kaitekidenakereba narimasen.
Underwear should be comfortable.
下着は快適でなければなりません

477.

Socks – Kutsushita (kut-su-shi-ta)靴下
Kare wa shūshin-ji ni **kutsushita** o haite iru.

He wears **socks** when he goes to sleep.
彼は就寝時に靴下をはいている

478.

Sunglasses – Sangurasu (san-gu-ra-su)サングラス
Kanojo wa yasui **sangurasu** o kaimasu.
Itsumo sorera o ushinau node.
She buys cheap **sunglasses** because she always loses them.
彼女は安いサングラスを買います
いつもそれらを失うので

479.

Shoe – Kutsu (kut-su)靴
Watashi no **kutsu** o mimashita ka?
Have you seen my **shoes**?
私の靴を見ましたか

Seasons

480.

Spring – Haru (ha-ru)春
Haru wa otozureru no ni yoi jiki desu.
Spring is a good time to visit.
春は訪れるのによい時期です

481.

Summer – Natsu (nat-su)夏
Konkai wa hontōni atsui **natsu** deshita.
This has been a really hot **summer**.
今回あ本当に暑い夏でした

482.

Autumn – Aki (a-kee)秋
This Autumn – **Konshū** (kon-syu)
Konshū Jamaika e ikimasu
We will travel to Jamaica this **Autumn**.
今秋ジャマイカに行きます

483.

Winter – Fuyu (fu-yu)冬
Igirisu no **fuyu** wa hijō ni samui desu.
Winter is very cold in England.
イギリスの冬は非常に寒いです

Vegetables

484.

Asparagus – Asuparagasu (asu-para-ga-su)アスパラガス
Kenkō-tekinanode **asuparagasu** ga suki desu.
I like **asparagus** because it is healthy.
健康的なのでアスパラガスが好きです

485.

Aubergine – Nasu (na-su)ナス
Nasu mo tabemashita ka?
Have you even eaten **aubergine**?
ナスも食べましたか

486.

Broccoli – Burokkorī (bu-rok-kori)ブロッコリー
Watashi no musuko wa **burokkorī** ga daikirai desu.
My son hates **broccoli**.
私の息子はブロッコリーが大嫌いです

487.

Cabbage – Kyabetsu (kya-bet-su)キャベツ
Kyabetsu wa mumida to omoimasu
I think **cabbage** is tasteless.
キャベツは無味だと思います

488.

Carrot – Ninjin (nin-jin)人参
Ninjin wa totemo herushī desu.
Carrots are very healthy.
人参はとてもヘルシーです

489.

Cauliflower – Karifurawā (kari-fura-wa)カリフラワー
Karifurawā o ichiba de kaimashita.

We bought **cauliflower** from the market.
カリフラワーを市場で買いました

490.

Sweetcorn – Suītokōn (sui-to-kon)スイートコーン
Kyūri no kawari ni **suītokōn** o taberu no ga suki desu.
I prefer to eat **sweetcorn** instead of cucumber.
きゅうりの代わりにスイートコーンを食べるのが好きです

491.

Cucumber – Kyūri (kyu-ri)きゅうり
Anata wa **kyūri** o dorekurai tabemasu ka?
How many **cucumbers** would you like?
あなたはきゅうりをどれくらい食べますか

492.

Garlic - Nin'niku (nin-ni-ku)ニンニク
Nin'niku no kaori ga daisuki desu.
I love the smell of **garlic**.
ニンニクの香りが大好きです

493.

Ginger – Shōga (sho-ga)ショウガ
Watashi no kanojo wa **shōga** ga sukide wa arimasen.
My girlfriend doesn't like **ginger**.
私の彼女はショウガが好きではありません

494.

Lettuce – Retasu (re-ta-su)レタス
Motto **retasu** o taberu hitsuyō ga arimasu.
I need to eat more **lettuce**.
もっとレタスを食べる必要があります

495.

Mushroom – Kinoko (ki-no-ko)キノコ
Kono shokuji ni ha**kinoko**to tamanegi ga arimasu.

This meal has **mushrooms** and onions.
この食事にはキノコと玉ねぎがあります

496.

Okra – Okura (o-ku-ra)オクラ
Kon'ya wa **okura** o tabemasu.
We will eat **okra** tonight.
今夜はオクラを食べます

497.

Olive – Orību (o-ri-bu)オリーブ
Watashi wa **orību** ga doko ni aru no ka wakarimasen.
I don't know where the **olives** are.
私はオリーブがどこにあるのかわかりません

498.

Onion – Tamanegi (ta-ma-ne-gi)玉ねぎ
Tamanegi wa doko ni arimasu ka?
Where are the **onions**?
玉ねぎはどこにありますか

499.

Peas - Endō mame (en-do ma-me) えんどう豆
Watashi wa **endō mame** o tabeta koto ga nai.
I have never eaten **peas** before.
私はエンドウ豆を食べたことがない

500.

Peppers – Pīman (pi-man)ピーマン
Pīman soretomo aka **pīman**?
Green **peppers** or red **peppers**?
ピーマンそれとも赤ピーマン

501.

Potatoes – Jagaimo (ja-gai-mo)ジャガイモ
Shinsen na **Jagaimo**ga saikō desu.

Fresh **potatoes** are the best.
新鮮なジャガイモが最高です

502.

Radish – Daikon (dai-kon)大根
Kono **daikon** wa juku shite imasen.
This **radish** is not ripe.
この大根は熟していません

503.

Red onion – Aka tamanegi (a-ka ta-ma-ne-gi)赤玉ねぎ
Kono piza wa **aka tamanegi** ga haitte imasu ka?
Does this pizza have **red onions**?
このピザは赤玉ねぎが入っていますか

504.

Spinach – Hōrensō (ho-ren-so)ほうれん草
Kare wa **hōrensō** igai no subete o tabeta.
He ate everything except the **spinach**.
彼はほうれん草以外の食べ物をすべて食べた

505.

Sweet potatoes – Satsumaimo (sat-su-mai-mo)さつまいも
Kanojo wa **satsumaimo** o ichiba de kaimashita.
She bought **sweet potatoes** from the market.
彼女はさつまいもを市場で買いました

506.

Tomatoes – Tomato (to-ma-to) トマト
Korera no **tomato** wa totemo ōkī desu.
These **tomatoes** are very big.
これらのトマトはとてもも大きいです

507.

Turnip – Kabu (ka-buh)カブ
Sumimasen, **kabu** wa doko ni arimasu ka?

Excuse me, where are the **turnips**?
すみません　カブはどこにありますか

508.

Vegetables – Yasai (ya-sai)　野菜

Watashi no musuko wa kesshite **yasai** o tabemasen.
My son never eats his **vegetables**.
私の息子は決して野菜を食べません

Animals

509.

Alligator – Wani (wa-ni)わに
Kyō watashi wa **wani** ni aimashita.
I saw an **alligator** today.
今日私はワニに会いました

510.

Cockroach – Gokiburi (go-ki-bu-ri)ゴキブリ
Karera wa resutoran no tēburu no shita ni gokiburi o mimashita.
They saw a **cockroach** under the restaurant's table.
彼はレストランのテーブルの下にゴキブリをみました

511.

Crow – Karasu (ka-rah-su)からす
Karasu wa hitobanju urusakatta desu.
The **crow** was very loud all night.
カラスは一晩中うるさかったです

512.

Ant – Ari (a-ri)あり
Daidokoro ni **ari** ga imasu.
There are **ants** in the kitchen.
台所にありがいます

513.

Bear - Kuma (ku-ma)熊
Dōbutsuen no **kuma** wa ōkikute kowakatta desu.
The **bear** in the zoo was big and scary.
動物園の熊は大きくて怖かったです

514.

Bee – Hachi (ha-chee)はち
Hachi ga kare no ude o sashita.

A **bee** stung him on his arm.
はちが彼の腕をさした

515.

Bird – Tori (to-ri)鳥
Kanojo wa ie de petto no **tori** o katte imasu.
She has a pet **bird** at home.
彼女は家でペットの鳥を飼っています

516.

Camel – Rakuda (ra-ku-da)ラクダ
Watashi wa **rakuda** o mita koto ga nai.
I have never seen a **camel**.
私はラクダを見たことがない

517.

Cat – Neko (ne-ko)猫
Watashi no yūjin wa nora**neko** o mitsukemashita.
My friend found a stray **cat**.
私の友人あ野良猫を見つけました

518.

Cheetah – Chītā (chee-tah)チーター
Chītā wa hayai dōbutsu desu.
The **cheetah** is a fast animal.
チーターは早い動物です

519.

Chicken – Toriniku (tori-ni-ku)鶏肉
Watashitachiha yūshoku ni **toriniku** o yoku tabemasu.
We often eat **chicken** for dinner.
私たちは夕食に鶏肉をよく食べます

520.

Chimpanzee – Chinpanjī (chin-pan-ji)チンパンジー
Chinpanjī no kazoku ga imasu.

There is a family of **chimpanzees**.
チンパンジーの家族がいます

521.

Cow – Ushi (u-shee)牛
Nohara ni wa santō no **ushi** ga imasu.
There are three **cows** in the field.
野原には三頭の牛がいます

522.

Crocodile – Wani (wa-ni)ワニ
Ano **wani** ni wa ōkina ha ga arimasu
That **crocodile** has big teeth.
あのワニは大きな歯があります

523.

Deer – Shika (shee-ka)鹿
Kinō watashi ga unten shiteita toki ni ayauku**shika** ni butsukatta.
Yesterday I almost hit a **deer** when I was driving.
昨日私が運転していた時に危うく鹿にぶつかった

524.

Dog – Inu (ee-nu)犬
Sore wa anata no **inu** desu ka? **Inu** no namae wa?
Is that your **dog**? What's his name?
それはあなたの犬ですか犬の名前は

525.

Dolphin – Iruka (iru-ka)イルカ
Watashitachiha bōto no chikaku de **iruka** o mimashita.
We saw **dolphins** near our boat.
私たちはボートの近くでイルカを見ました

526.

Duck – Ahiru (a-he-ru)アヒル
Imamadeni **ahiru** o tabeta koto ga arimasu ka?

Have you even eaten **duck** before?
今までにアヒルを食べたことがありますか

527.

Donkey – Roba (ro-bah)ロバ
Roba wa ashi o kegashita.
The **donkey** injured its leg.
ロバは足を怪我した

528.

Eagle – Washi (wa-shi)わし
Washi wa surudoi me o shite imasu.
An **eagle** has a sharp eye.
わしは鋭い目をしています

529.

Elephant – Zō (zoh)像
Zō wa Afurika ni sunde imasu.
Elephants live in Africa.
象はアフリカに住んでいます

530.

Fish – Sakana (sa-ka-na)魚
Ichiba wa shinsen na **sakana** o utte imasu.
The market sells fresh **fish.**
市場は新鮮な魚を売っています

531.

Fly – Hae (ha-e)ハエ
Kono **hae** wa watashi o nayama sete imasu.
This **fly** is annoying me.
このハエは私を悩ませています

532.

Fox – Kitsune (kit-su-ne)狐
Kitsune wa watashitachi no gomi o tabete imashita.

The **fox** was eating our rubbish.
狐は私たちのごみを食べていました

533.

Frog – Kaeru (kae-ru)カエル
Kaeru wa kimochiwarui desu.
I think **frogs** are disgusting.
カエルは気持ち悪いです

534.

Giraffe – Kirin (ki-rin)キリン
Raion wa **kirin** o kōgeki shimashita.
The lion attacked the **giraffe**.
ライオンはキリンを攻撃しました

535.

Goat – Yagi (ya-gi)やぎ
Yagi no miruku wa oishikute bitamin ga hōfu desu.
Goat milk tastes good and is full of vitamins.
やぎのミルクはおいしくてビタミンが豊富です

536.

Goldfish – Kingyo (kin-gyo)金魚
Ie de petto no **kingyo** o katte imasu
I have a pet **goldfish** at home.
家でペットの金魚を飼っています

537.

Hamster – Hamusutā (ha-mu-su-ta)ハムスター
Hamusutā ga watashi no ressha no kippu o tabeta.
The **hamster** ate my train ticket.
ハムスターが私の列車の切符を食べた

538.

Hippo – Kaba (ka-ba)カバ
Watashinohaha wa omocha no **kaba** o atsumete imasu.

My mom collects toy **hippos**.
私の母はおもちゃのカバを集めています

539.

Horse – Uma (u-mah)馬
Kanojo wa tanjōbi ni **uma** ni notta.
She rode a **horse** for her birthday.
彼女は誕生日に馬に乗った

540.

Kangaroo – Kangarū (kan-ga-ru)カンガルー
Kangarū wa ōsutoraria ni sunde imasu.
Kangaroos live in Australia.
カンガルーはオーストラリアに住んでいます

541.

Kitten – Koneko (ko-ne-ko)子猫
Koneko wa samukute kūfukudatta.
The **kitten** was cold and hungry.
子猫あ寒くて空腹だった

542.

Lion – Raion (rai-on)ライオン
Kono **raion** wa rippana tategami o motte imasu.
This **lion** has a gorgeous mane.
このライオンは立派なたてがみをもっています

543.

Lobster – Robusutā (ro-bu-su-ta)ロブスター
Sono resutoran dewa totemo oishī **robusutā** o dasu.
The restaurant served very tasty **lobsters**.
そのレストランではとても美味しいロブスターをだす

544.

Monkey – Saru (sa-ru)サル
Kanojo wa petto no **saru** o kaitai to omotte imasu.

She wants to have a pet **monkey**.
彼女はペットのサルを飼いたいと思っています

545.

Octopus – Tako (ta-ko)たこ
Karera wa chūka resutoran de **tako** o chūmon shimashita.
They ordered **octopus** at the Chinese restaurant.
彼らは中華レストランでタコを注文しました

546.

Owl – Fukurou (fu-ku-rou)フクロウ
Kyō wa **fukurou**kafe ni ikimashita.
We went to an **owl** café today.
今日はフクロウカフェに行きました

547.

Panda – Panda (pan-da)パンダ
Watashi watada **panda** o miru tame ni Chūgoku ni ikimashita.
I went to China just to see a **panda**.
私はただパンダを見るために中国に行きました

548.

Pig – Buta (bu-tah)豚
Buta wa akachan o unda bakari desu.
The **pig** has just had babies.
豚は赤ちゃんを産んだばかりです

549.

Puppy – Koinu (koi-nu)子犬
Kare wa **koinu** o oka no ue made hakonda.
He carried the **puppy** up the hill.
彼は子犬を丘の上まで運んだ

550.

Rabbit – Usagi (u-sa-gi)ウサギ
Watashi no **usagi** wa ichinen mae ni shinimashita.

My **rabbit** died one year ago.
私のウサギは一年前に死にました

551.

Rat- Ratto (ra-tto)ラット
Watashi wa **ratto** ga kowai desu.
I am scared of **rats**.
私はラットが怖いです

552.

Scorpion – Sasori (sa-so-ri)サソリ
Sasori wa kiken'na konchū desu.
Scorpion are dangerous insects.
サソリは危険な昆虫です

553.

Seal – Azarashi (a-za-ra-shi)アザラシ
Kono suisō ni wa totemo takusan no **azarashi** ga imasu.
There are so many **seals** in this aquarium.
この水槽にはとてもたくさんのアザラシがいます

554.

Shark – Same (sa-meh)サメ
Watashi wa **same** ni tsuite no dokyumentarī o mimashita.
I watched a documentary about **sharks**.
私はサメについてのドキュメンタリーを見ました

555.

Sheep – Hitsuji (hit-su-ji)羊
Sore wa **hitsuji**dewa naku, yagi desu.
It isn’t a **sheep**, it’s a goat.
それは羊ではなくヤギです

556.

Snail – Katatsumuri (ka-tat-su-mu-ri)かたつむり
Anata wa **katatsumuri** no yō ni arukimasu, totemo osoi desu.

You walk like a **snail**, very slow.
あなたはかたつむりのように歩きますとても遅いです

557.
Snake – Hebi (he-bi)へび
Kanojo wa ie ni pettono **hebi** o katte imasu.
She has a pet snake at home.
彼女は家にペットのへびを飼っています

558.
Spider – Kumo (ku-mo)蜘蛛
Tasukete, watashinoheya ni **kumo** ga iru
Help, there is a **spider** in my room
助けて、私の部屋に蜘蛛がいる

559.
Squirrel – Risu (ri-su)リス
Watashi wa **risu** no tame ni kōen ni konomi o suuko oitekita.
I left a few nuts for the **squirrel** in the park.
私はリスのために公園に木の実を数個置いてきた

560.
Tiger – Tora (toh-ra)とら
Tora wa ori kara nigeta.
The **tiger** escaped from the cage.
トラはおりから逃げた

561.
Turtle – Umigame (u-mi-ga-me)ウミガメ
Sore wa umi**game** desu ka? Soretomo rikugame ka?
Is that a **turtle** or a tortoise?
それはウミガメですかそれともリクガメですか

562.
Wolf – ōkami (o-ka-mi)狼
Anata no inu wa **ōkami** mitai desu.

Your dog looks like a **wolf**.
あなたの犬は狼みたいです

563.

Zebra – Shimauma (shi-ma-u-ma)シマウマ
Shimauma wa shiroi to kurono shima desu.
Zebra is black with white stripes.
シマウマは白いと黒のしまです

564.

Animal – Dōbutsu (do-but-su)動物
Dōbutsu no ōkoku wa kyōryokuna ikimono de ippai desu.
The **animal** kingdom is full of mighty creatures.
動物の王国は強力な生き物でいっぱいです

565.

Pigeon – Hato (ha-toh)鳩
Kono kōen ni wa takusan no **hato** ga imasu.
There are a lot of **pigeons** in this park.
この公園にはたくさんの鳩がいます

566.

Mosquito – Ka (kah)蚊
Koko ni wa **ka** ga takusan imasu.
There is too many **mosquitos** here.
ここには蚊が沢山います

Food and Drink

567.

Delicious – Oishī (oi-shi)美味しい
Tai ryōri wa **oishī** desu.
Thai food is **delicious.**
タイ料理は美味しいです

568.

Flavour – Fūmi (fu-mi)風味
Kare wa tabemono no **fūmi** ga sukidatta.
He liked the **flavour** of the food.
彼は食べ物の風味が好きだった

569.

Lemon – Remon (re-mon)ラーメン
Remon-jiru wa karada o kirei ni suru kouka ga arimasu.
Drinking **lemon** juice can help clean your body.
ラーメン汁は体を綺麗にする効果があります

570.

Sour – Suppai (sup-pai)酸っぱい
Watashi wa chīsana kyōdai ni **suppai** ame o tabe sasemasu.
I let my small siblings eat **sour** candy.
私は小さな兄弟に酸っぱい飴を食べさせます

571.

Menu – Menyū (men-yu)メニュー
Menyū o onegaishimasu.
Can I have a menu please.
メニューお願いします

572.

Meat – Niku (ni-ku)肉
Karera wa pātī no tame ni shinsen'na **niku** o yaita.

They grilled fresh **meat** for the party.
彼らはパーティのために新鮮な肉を焼いた

573.

Seafood – Kaisen (kai-sen)海鮮
Sono chihou ni wa yasui **kaisen**ga arimasu.
There are cheap **seafood** in the province.
その地方には安い海鮮があります

574.

Food – Tabemono (ta-be-mo-no)食べ物
Watashi no yūjin wa ekizochikkuna **tabemono** o taberu no ga suki desu.
My friend likes eating exotic **food**.
私の友人はエキゾチックな食べ物を食べるのが好きです

575.

Wheat – Komugi (ko-mu-gi)小麦
Pan wa **komugi** de dekite imasu.
Bread is made of **wheat**.
パンは小麦でできています

576.

Vinegar – Su (su)酢
Karera wa **su** de subete no mono o taberu.
They eat everything with **vinegar**.
彼らは酢ですべてのものを食べる

577.

Tea – Ocha (o-cha)お茶
Ocha o ippainomimashō.
Have a cup of **tea** with us.
お茶を一杯飲みましょう

578.

Beer – Bīru (bi-ru)ビール
Kono **bīru** to wa nani desu ka?
What is this **beer** called?

このビールとは何ですか

579.

Pork – Butaniku (bu-ta-ni-ku)豚肉
Sumimasen, watashi wa **butaniku** o tabemasen.
I am sorry, I don't eat **pork.**
すみません私は豚肉を食べません

580.

Rice – Okome (oko-me)お米
Yūshoku ni yasai to issho ni **okomeo** takimashou.
Let's cook some **rice** with vegetables for dinner.
夕食に野菜と一緒にお米を炊きましょう

581.

Cook – Ryōri (ryo-ri)料理
Kare wa gesuto no tame ni Ajia **ryōri** o tsukuritai to omotte imasu.
He wants to **cook** Asian food for his guests.
彼はゲストのためにアジア料理を作りたいと思っています

582.

Spicy – Karai (ka-rai)辛い
Indo ryōri wa **karai** desu.
Indian food is **spicy**.
インディアン料理は辛いです

583.

Water – Mizu (mi-zu)水
Koppuippai no **mizu** o morae masu ka?
Can I have a glass of **water**, please?
コップ一杯の水をもらえますか

584.

Spice – Supaisu (su-pai-su)スパイス
Watashi wa ryōri ni **supaisu** o amari tsukawanai.
I don't use a lot of **spice** when I cook.

私は料理にスパイスをあまり使わない

585.

Cheese – Chīzu (chi-zu)チーズ
Watashi wa **chīzu** nashi de pasuta o tabemasen.
I don’t eat pasta without **cheese.**
私はチーズなしでパスタを食べません

586.

Salt – Shio (shi-o)塩
Kanojo wa tabemono ni takusan no **shio** o kakeru.
She puts lots of **salt** on her food.
彼女は食べ物に沢山の塩をかける

587.

Butter – Batā (ba-ta)バター
Kono reshipi ni wa **batā** ga hitsuyō desu.
I need **butter** for this recipe.
このレシピにはバターが必要です

588.

Squid – Ika (i-ka)イカ
Watashi wa **ika** o tabemasen.
I will never eat **squid**.
私はイカを食べません

589.

Lamb – Hitsuji (hit-su-ji)羊
Ko**hitsuji** wa totemo kawaii desu.
The baby **lamb** is very cute.
子羊はとてもかわいいです

590.

Pizza – Piza (pi-za)ピザ
Watashi wa ima ryōri suru koto wa dekimasen, **piza** o chūmon shimashou.
I can’t cook now, let’s order a **pizza**.

私は今料理をすることができません、ピザを注文しましょう

591.

Noodles – Men (men)麺
Watashi wa chōshoku ni **men** o tabemashita.
I ate **noodles** for breakfast.
私は朝食に麺を食べました

592.

Vegetarian – Bejitarian (be-ji-ta-ri-an)ベジタリアン
Bejitarian no syoku wa kenkō desu.
Vegetarian food is healthy.
ベジタリアンの食は健康です

593.

Fruit Juice – Furūtsujūsu (fu-rut-su-ju-su)フルーツジュース
Asa wa **furūtsujūsu** o nomimasu.
I drink **fruit juice** in the morning.
朝はフルーツジュースを飲みます

594.

Seasoning – Chōmiryō (cho-mi-ryo)調味料
Kono tabemononiwa **chōmiryō** ga hitsuyō desu.
This food needs some **seasoning**.
この食べ物には調味料が必要です

595.

Pasta – Pasuta (pa-su-ta)パスタ
Pasuta wa watashi no suki natabemono desu.
Pasta is my favourite food.
パスタは私の好きな食べ物です

596.

Bread – Pan (pan)
Watashi wa **pan** o tabemasen.
I don't eat **bread**.

私はパンを食べません

597.

Yogurt – Yōguruto (yo-gu-ru-to)ヨーグルト
Kono **yōguruto** ni wa takusan no satō ga fukumarete imasu.
This **yoghurt** has a lot of sugar in it.
このヨーグルトにはたくさんの砂糖が含まれています

598.

Sugar – Satō (sa-toh)砂糖
Satō wa arimasu ka?
Do you have any **sugar**?
砂糖はありますか

599.

Milk – Gyūnyū (gyu-nue)牛乳
Kare wa kōhī ni **gyūnyū** o ireta.
He put **milk** in his coffee.
彼はコーヒーに牛乳を入れた

600.

Coffee – Kōhī (ko-hi)コーヒー
Rara wa itsumo asa **kōhī** o nomimasu.
Lara always drinks **coffee** in the morning.
レラはいつも朝コーヒーを飲みます

601.

Juice – Jūsu (ju-su)ジュース
Maiasa shinsen na orenji**jūsu** o tsukurimasu.
I make fresh orange **juice** every morning.
毎朝新鮮なオレンジジュースを作ります

602.

Sandwich – Sandoitchi (san-do-itchi)サンドイッチ
Kanojo wa chikin**sandoitch**i o katta
She bought a chicken **sandwich**

彼女はチキンサンドイッチを買った

603.

Cooked Rice – Gohan (go-han)ご飯
Oishisouna **gohan** no kaori.
Gohansmells good.
美味しそうなご飯の香り

604.

Beef – Gyuniku (gyu-ni-ku)牛肉
Gyūniku o tabenai no ga zan'nen desu.
I'm sorry I don't eat **beef**.
牛肉を食べないのが残念です

605.

Eggs – Tamago (ta-ma-go)卵
Karera wa chōshoku ni **tamago** o tabeta.
They ate **eggs** for breakfast.
彼らは朝食に卵を食べた

606.

Wine – Wain (wa-in)ワイン
Aka**wain** to shiro**wain** no dochira ga suki desu ka?
Would you like red **wine** or white **wine**?
赤ワインと白ワインのどっちが好きですか

607.

Non Vegetarian – Bejitarian igai (beji-ta-ri-an i-gai)ベジタリアン以外
Kono resutoran ni wa **bejitarian igai** no tabemono ga takusan arimasu
This restaurant has a lot of **non-vegetarian**food.
このレストランにはベジタリアン以外の食べ物が沢山あります

608.

Dessert – Dezāto (de-za-to)デザート
Kono **dezāto** ni wa banana to aisukurīmu ga arimasu.
This **dessert** has bananas and ice-cream.

このデザートにはバナナとアイスクリームがあります

609.

Black Tea – Kōcha (ko-cha)紅茶
Kōcha ga suki desu ga, totemo tsuyoi desu.
I like **black tea** but it is very strong.
紅茶が好きですがとても強いです

610.

Tasteless – Aji ga nai (aji ga nai)味がない
Kono tabemono wa **aji ga nainode**, sukidewa arimasen.
This food is **tasteless**, I don't like it.
この食べ物は味がないので、好きではありません

611.

Tuna – Maguro (ma-gu-ro)マグロ
Kanojo wa **chūshoku** ni ōkina maguro kan o tabeta.
She ate a big can of **tuna** for lunch.
彼女は昼食に大きなマグロ缶を食べた

612.

Biscuit – Bisuketto (bi-su-ket)ビスケット
Bisuketto wa hitotsu de jūbun desu.
One **biscuit** is enough.
ビスケットは一つで十分です

Positions

613.

First – Saisho (sai-sho)最初
Dare ga **saisho** ni ikitai desu ka?
Who wants to go **first**?
誰が最初に行きたいですか

614.

Second – Ni banme (ni ban-me)二番目
Kore wa kanojo no **nibanme** no kodomo desu.
This is her **second** child.
これは彼女の二番目の子供です

615.

Third – San banme (sanban-me)三番目
Sanbanme no hito wa dōmedaru o kakutoku shimasu.
The person who comes **third** gets a bronze medal.
三番目の人は銅メダルを獲得します

616.

Fourth – Yon banme (yon ban-me) ４番目
Kare wa rēsu de **yonbanme** ni narimashita.
He came **fourth** in the race.
彼はレースで四番目になりました

617.

Fifth – Go kai (gokai)五回
Watashi no jimusho wa **gokai** ni arimasu.
My office is on the **fifth** floor.
私の事務所は五階にあります

618.

Sixth – Roku daime (ro-ku dai-me) ６台目
Kore wa watashi ga katta **roku daime** no kuruma desu.

This is the **sixth** car I have bought
これは私が買った６台目の車です

619.

Seventh – Nana kai (na-nakai) ７回
Watashino heya wa **nanakai** ni arimasu.
My room is on the **seventh** floor.
私の部屋は７階にあります

620.

Eighth – Hachi kaime (ha-chikai-me) ８回目
Watashi ga anata ni itta no wa kore ga **hachi kaime** desu.
This is the **eighth** time I have told you.
私があなたに言ったのはこれが八回目です

621.

Ninth – Kyu kai (kyu kai)九回
Kono erebētā wa **kyukai** ni ikimasu ka?
Does this elevator go to the **ninth** floor?
このエレベーターは9階に行きますか

622.

Tenth – Jui (ju-i)十位
Kanojo wa rēsu de **jui**ni natta.
She came **tenth** in the race.
彼女はレースで十位になった

Directions – Part 2

623.
North – Kita (ki-ta)
Kita wa tsuneni samui desu.
It is always colder in the **north**.
北は常に寒いです

624.
West – Nishi (ni-shi)西
Amerika wa Igirisu no **nishi** desu.
America is **west** to England.
アメリカはイギリスの西です

625.
East – Higashi (hi-ga-shi)東
Itaria wa Supein no **higashi** desu.
Italy is **east** of Spain.
イタリアはスペインの東です

626.
South – Minami (mi-na-mi)南
Mekishiko wa Amerika no **minami** desu.
Mexico is **south** of America.
メキシコはアメリカの南です

627.
North East – Hokutō (ho-ku-to) 北東
Kawa wa koko kara **hokutō** desu.
The river is **north east** from here.
川はここから北東です

628.
South East – Nantō (nan-to)南東
Nantō o aruku hitsuyō ga arimasu.

We need to walk **south east**.
南東を歩く必要があります

629.

North West – Hokusei (ho-ku-sei)北西
Yama wa **hokusei** desu.
The mountain is **north west**.
山は北西です

630.

South West – Nansei (nan-sei)南西
Mori no **nansei** ni mura ga arimasu.
There is a village **south west** from the forest.
森の南西に村があります

Furniture

631.

Chair – Isu (i-su)
Korera no **isu** wa ugokasu hitsuyō ga arimasu.
These **chairs** need to be moved.
これらの椅子は動かす必要があります

632.

Bed – Beddo (be-ddo)ベッド
Kono heya ni wa ikutsu no **beddo** ga arimasu ka?
How many **beds** does this room have?
この部屋にはいくつのベッドがありますか

633.

Curtain – Kāten (ka-ten)カーテン
Kanojo wa **kāten** o shimeta.
She closed the **curtains**.
彼女はカーテンを閉めた

634.

Lamp – Ranpu (ran-pu)ランプ
Ranpu ga heya zentai o terashita.
The **lamp** lit up the whole room.
ランプが部屋全体を照らした

635.

Mirror – Kagami (ka-ga-mi)鏡
Subete no josei wa kaban no naka ni **kagami** o motte imasu.
Every woman has a **mirror** in their handbag.
すべての女性は鞄の中に鏡を持っています

636.

Table – Tēburu (te-bu-ru)テーブル
Anata ga tabetaato ni **tēburu** o sōji shite kudasai.

Clean the **table** after you eat.
貴方あ食べた後にテーブルを掃除してください

637.

Pillow – Makura (ma-ku-ra)枕
Mō hitotsu-**makura** o moraemasu ka?
Can I have one more **pillow** please?
もう一つ枕をもらえますか

638.

Sofa – Sofa (sofah)ソファ
Kon'ya, kare wa **sofa** de nenakereba narimasen.
Tonight, he has to sleep on the **sofa**.
今夜彼はソファで寝なければなりません

Time

639.

Morning – Gozen chu/Asa gohan (go-zen chu/asa go-han)午前中/朝ごはん
Gozen-chū ni kaigi ga arimasu.
I have a meeting in the **morning**.
午前中に会議があります

640.

Lunch – Chūshoku (chu-sho-ku)昼食
Watashitoisshoni **chūshoku** o tabete hoshī.
I want you to have **lunch** with me.
私と一緒に昼食を食べて欲しい

641.

Noon – Shōgo (sho-go)正午
Watashitachiha tsūjō **shōgo** ni chūshoku o tabemasu.
We usually eat lunch at **noon**.
私たちは通常正午に昼食を食べます

642.

Afternoon – Gogo (go-go)午後
Kanojo wa **gogo** kara gakkō ni itta.
She went to school in the **afternoon**.
彼女は午後から学校に行った

643.

Evening – Ban (ban)晩
This evening – Konban (kon-ban)
Anata wa **konban** nani o shimasu ka?
What are you do this **evening**?
あなたは今晩何をしますか

644.

Night – Yoru (yo-ru)夜
Nan yoru ni ikimasu ka?
What night are we going?
何夜に行きますか

645.

Midnight – Shinya reiji (shin-ya reiji) 深夜零時
Watashi wa **shinyareiji** mae ni ie ni kaeranakereba naranai.
I have to go back home before **midnight**.
私は深夜零時前に家に帰らなければならない

646.

Quarter past – Jugo fun (ju-go fun)15分
Ibento wa Ju-ji **jugo-fun**ni kaishi saremasu.
The event will start at **quarter past** 10.
イベントは10時15分に開始されます

647.

Half past – San-jyuppun/han (san-ju-ppun/han)30分/半
Ima hachi-jihan.
Its half past 8pm.
今8時半

648.

Quarter to – Yonjugofun (yon ju-go fun)45分
Ima nana-ji yonjugo fun.
It's quarter to 8.
今7時45分

649.

Seconds – Byō (byo)秒
Ichi bu ni nan byo?
How many seconds in 1 minute?
1分に何秒

650.

Minute- Fun (fun)分
Gofun kudasai.
Give me five**minute** please.
5分ください

651.
Hour – Jikan (ji-kan)時間
Watashi wa sono jimusho ni tsuku no ni ichi-**jikan** kakaru.
It takes me an **hour** to get to the office.
私はその事務所に着くのに一時間かかる

Introductions

652.

What's Your Name? – Anata no namae nan desu ka?
(a-na-tano na-ma-e wa nan de-su ka)あなたの名前は何ですか
Hajimemashite, anata no namae nan desu ka?
Nice to meet you, **what's your name**?
初めまして、あなたの名前は何ですか

653.

Welcome – Yokoso (yo-ko-so)ようこそ
Nihon e yōkoso.
Welcome to Japan.
日本へようこそ

654.

I'm Good – Daijobu (da-jo-bu)大丈夫
Watashi wa **daijōbu** desu. Ogenki desu ka?
I'm good. How are you?
私は大丈夫です　お元気ですか

655.

So-so - Mā Mā (ma-ma)まぁまぁ
Eiga wa **ma-ma** desu.
The movie was **so-so.**
映画はまぁまぁです

656.

My Name Is … - Watashi no namae (wa-ta-shi no na-ma-e)私の名前
Watashinonamae ha George Smith desu. Hajimemashite.
My name is George Smith, nice to meet you.
私の名前はジョージスミスです　はじめまして

657.

Hello – Konnichiwa (kon-ni-chi-wa)こんにちは

Konnichiwa. Ogenki desu ka?
Hello, how are you?
こんにちは　お元気ですか

658.

How are you? – Ogenki desu ka? (o-gen-ki de-su ka)お元気ですか
Ohayōgozaimasu. Ogenki desu ka?
Good morning, how are you?
おはようございます　お元気ですか

659.

Good Bye – Wakare (wa-ka-re)別れ
Kare wa tomodachi ni **wakare** o tsugeta.
He said **goodbye** to his friends.
彼は友達に別れを告げた

660.

Yes – Hai (ha-i)はい
Kanojo wa kare no puropōzu ni "**hai**"to itta.
She said **yes** to his engagement proposal.
彼女は彼のプロポーズに"はい"と言った

661.

No – iie (ii-e)いいえ
Īe watashi wa sakana o tabemasen.
No i don't eat fish.
いいえ私は魚を食べません

662.

And you? – Anata wa (a-na-tawa)あなたは
Watashi wa genki desu. **Anata wa**?
I'm am fine. **And you**?
私は元気です　あなたは

Useful Words

663.

Fire – Hi (hie)火
Hi o mite.
Look at the **fire**.
火を見て

664.

Woman – Josei (jo-sei)女性
Warui shirase o kiita **josei** wa naita.
The **woman** cried when she heard the bad news.
悪い知らせを聞いた女性は泣いた

665.

Sneeze – Kushami (ku-sha-mi)くしゃみ
Kanojo wa daijōbu desu ka? Kanojo wa **kushami** o shite imasu.
Is she ok? She is **sneezing** a lot.
彼女は大丈夫ですか彼女はくしゃみをしています

666.

Put on – Haku (ha-ku)はく
Fuyu-yō no būtsu o **haite**, yuki ga futte imasu.
Put on your winter boots, it's snowing.
冬用のブーツを履いて、雪が降っています

667.

Believe – Shinjiru (shin-ji-ru)信じる
Dōshite anata wa watashi o **shinji**nai no desu ka?
Why don't you **believe** me?
どうしてあなたは私を信じないのですか

668.

Last time – Saigo (sai-go)最後
Watashi ga **saigo** ni itta toki, michinimayotta.

The **last time** I went there, I got lost.
私が最後に行った時、道に迷った

669.

Infection – Enshō (en-sho)炎症
Kono **enshō** wa kōseibusshitsu de chiryō suru koto ga dekimasu.
This **infection** can be cured with antibiotics.
この炎症は抗生物質で治療することができます

670.

Rock – Iwa (i-wa)岩
Sono shōnen wa mizūmi ni **iwa** o nageta.
The boy threw a **rock** into the lake.
その少年は湖に岩を投げた

671.

Permanent – Eikyū (ei-kyu)永久
Kono irezumi wa **eikyū**-tekina monode wa arimasen.
This tattoo is not **permanent**.
この入れ墨は永久的なものではありません

672.

Shade – Hikage (hi-ka-ge)日陰
Atsuinode **hikage** ni ite kudasai
Stay in **shade** because it is hot.
暑いので日陰にいてください

673.

Coach – Kōchi (ko-chi)コーチ
Kōchi wa watashi o ōini tasukete kuremashita.
My **coach** has helped me a lot.
コーチは私をおおいに助けてくれました

674.

Mud – Doro (do-ro)泥
Hōmuresu no inu wa **doro** de ōwa rete imashita.

The homeless dog was covered in **mud**.
ホームレスの犬は泥でおおわれていました

675.

Wild – Yasei (ya-se-i)野生
Yasei dōbutsu kara hanarete kudasai.
Stay away from **wild** animals.
野生動物からはなれてください

676.

Bruise – Aoaza (a-o-a-za)青あざ
Kare wa hiza ni ōkina **aoaza** ga aru.
He has a big **bruise** on his knee.
彼は膝に大きな青あざがある

677.

Net – Ami (a-mi)あみ
Koko de wa **ami-**gyou wa yurusarete imasen.
You are not allowed to use a **net** for fishing here.
ここでは網業は許されていません

678.

Recommend – Susumeru (su-su-meru)勧める
Kono resutoran wa **osusume** shimasen.
I don't **recommend** this restaurant.
このレストランはお勧めしません

679.

Once – Ichido (i-chi-do)一度
Watashi wa **ichido** dake itta koto ga arimasu.
I've only been there **once**.
私は一度だけ行ったことがあります

680.

Twice – ni kai (ni-kai)二回
Tesuto o teishutsu suru mae ni **ni-kai** kakunin shimasu.

Ceck **twice** before submitting your test.
テストを提出する前に二回確認します

681.

Piece – Kire (ki-re)切れ
Hito **kire** no kēki o moraemasu ka?
Can I have a **piece** of cake?
一切れのケーキをもらえますか

682.

Thief – Dorobō (do-ro-bo)泥棒
Dorobō wa Jugo-saidatta.
The **thief** was only 15 years old.
泥棒あ15歳だった

683.

Conversation – Kaiwa (kai-wa)会話
Watashi wa yūjin to nagai **kaiwa** o shimashita.
I had a long **conversation** with my friend.
私は友人と長い会話をしました

684.

Dancing – Odoru (o-do-ru)踊る
Watashi wa kekkonshiki de kanojo to **odotte** imashita.
I was **dancing** with her at the wedding.
私は結婚式で彼女と踊っていました

685.

Proud – Hokori (ho-ko-ri)誇り
Ryōshin ga**hokori**omou yō ni shitai desu.
I want to make my parents **proud**.
両親が誇り思うようにしたいです

686.

Fear – Kyōfu (kyo-fu)恐怖
Watashi no saidai no **kyōfu** wa kumo desu.

My biggest **fear** is spiders.
私の最大の恐怖は蜘蛛です

687.

Shy – Hazukashi (ha-zu-ka-shee)恥ずかしい
Kare ga hajimete kanojo ni atta toki**hazukashi**gariyadatta.
He was **shy** the first time he met her.
彼が初めて彼女に会った時恥ずかしがりやだった

688.

Prepare – Junbi (jun-bi)準備
Kakunin dekiru yō ni bunsho o **junbi** shimasu.
Prepare the documents so I can check them.
確認できるように文書を準備します

689.

Get a Job - Shūshoku suru (shu-sho-ku su-ru)就職する
Kanojo no hahaoya wa **shūshoku suru** yō ni kanojo ni itta.
Her mother told her to **get a job**.
彼女の母親は就職するように彼女に言った

690.

Pond – Ike (i-ke)池
Kono **ike** ni wa takusan no sakana ga imasu.
This **pond** has a lot of different fish.
この池には沢山の魚がいます

691.

See You Later – Mata aimasho (ma-ta ai-ma-sho)また会いましょう
Watashi wa ikanakereba ikemasen, **mata aimasho**.
I have to go, **see you later**.
私は行かなければいけません、また会いましょう

692.

Vet – Jūi (ju-i)獣医
Watashi wa **jūi** ni naru koto o benkyō shite imasu.

I am studying to become a **vet**.
私は獣医になることを勉強しています

693.

Sweet – Amai (a-ma-i)甘い
Kanojo wa **ama**tou desu.
She has a **sweet** tooth.
彼女は甘党です

694.

Get – Toru (to-ru)とる
Kuruma kara kaban o **totte** kitte moraemasu ka?
Can you **get** the bag from the car?
車から鞄をとってきてもらえますか

695.

By - …ni yotte (ni yot-te)…によって
Kanojo no kēki wa kareshi**ni yotte** tsukura reta.
Her cake was made **by** her boyfriend.
彼女のケーキは彼氏によってつくられた

696.

Break Out – Boppatsu (bop-pa-tsu)勃発
Ima sugu sensō ga **boppatsu** suru kamo shiremasen.
A war may **break out** any moment now.
今すぐ戦争が勃発するかもしれません

697.

Beige – Bēju (bei-ju)ベージュ
Kare wa heya o **bēju** ni nutta.
He painted his room **beige**.
彼は部屋をベージュに塗った

698.

Later – Atode (a-to-de)後で
Atode kimasu.

I would come **later**.
後で来ます

699.

Which day? – Dono hi (do-no hi)どの日
Anata wa **dono hi** ni haisha ni iku no desu ka?
Which day are you going to the dentist?
あなたはどの日に歯医者に行くのですか

700.

Jewellery Store – Hōseki ten (ho-se-ki ten)宝石店
Hōseki-ten wa depāto no mukai ni arimasu.
The **jewellery store** is opposite the department store.
宝石店はデパートの向かいにあります

701.

Throw – Nageru (na-ge-ru)投げる
Watashi ni rimokon o **nagete**.
Throw the remote to me.
私にリモコンを投げて

702.

Winner – Shōsha (sho-sha)勝者
Watashi no imōto wa shiai no **shōsha** deshita.
My sister was the **winner** in the competition.
私の妹は試合の勝者でした

703.

Ceremony – Shikiten (shi-ki-ten)式典
Kon'ya wa **shikiten**ni ikimasu ka?
Are you going to the **ceremony** tonight?
今夜は式典に行きますか

704.

Age - Nenrei (nen-rei)年齢
Kanojo no **nenrei** wa nan-sai desu ka?

What is her **age**?
彼女の年齢は何歳ですか

705.

Thirsty – Nodo ga kawaku (no-do ga ka-wa-ku)喉が渇く
Watashi wa maiasa **nodo ga kawaite** imasu.
I am **thirsty** every morning.
私は毎朝喉が渇いています

706.

Company – Kaisha (kai-sha)会社
Dono **kaisha** ni tsutomete imasu ka?
Which **company** do you work for?
どの会社に勤めていますか

707.

Interesting – Omoshiroi (o-mo-shi-roi)面白い
Kono hon wa **omoshiroku**nai desu.
This book is not **interesting**.
この本は面白くないです

708.

Thanks – Arigatōgozaimasu (ari-ga-to go-zai-ma-su)ありがとうございます
Gokyōryoku itadaki **arigatōgozaimasu**.
Thanks for your help.
ご協力いただきありがとうございます

709.

Bar – Bā (ba)バー
Kono **bā** wa shin'ya 0-ji made eigyō shite imasu.
This bar is open until **midnight**.
このバーは深夜0時まで営業しています

710.

Sale – Sēru (se-ru)セール
Kinō depāto de **sēru** ga arimashita.

There was a **sale** in the department store yesterday.
昨日デパートでセールがありました

711.

Confident – Jishin ga aru (ji-shin ga aru)自信がある
Kanojo wa **jishin** ga ari tsuyoi josei desu.
She is a **confident** and strong woman.
彼女は自信があり強い女性です

712.

Healthy – Kenkō (ken-ko)健康
Watashi no musuko wa **kenkō**de tsuyoi desu.
My son is **healthy** and strong.
私の息子は健康で強いです

713.

Secret – Himitsu (hi-mi-tsu)秘密
Watashi wa tomodachi ni ōkina **himitsu** o hanashimashita.
I told my friend a big **secret**.
私は友達に大きな秘密を話しました

714.

Cancel – Kyanseru (kyan-se-ru)キャンセル
Yoyaku o **kyanseru** shitai no desu ga.
I would like to **cancel** my appointment.
予約をキャンセルしたいのですが

715.

Stinky – Kusai (ku-sai)臭い
Kare no kutsushita wa **kusai** desu.
His socks are **stinky**.
彼の靴下は臭いです

716.

Looking For - Sagasu (sa-ga-su)探す
Watashi wa atarashī uwagi o **sagashite**imasu.

I am **looking for** a new coat.
私は新しい上着を探しています

717.

Plan – Keikaku (kei-ka-ku)計画
Keikaku dewa pātī no chokugo ni ie ni kaerimasu.
The **plan** is to go home right after the party.
計画ではパーティの直後に家に帰ります

718.

Bottle – Ippon (i-ppon)一本
Ippon no wain o itadakemasu ka?
Can you give me the **bottle** of wine?
一本のワインをいただけますか

719.

Street – Tōri (to-ri)通り
Kono **tōri** no namae wa nani desu ka?
What is the name of this **street**?
この通りの名前は何ですか

720.

Price – Kakaku (ka-ka-ku)価格
Kono **kakaku** wa ikura desu ka?
What is the **price** for this?
この価格はいくらですか

721.

Eyelash – Matsuge (ma-tsu-ge)まつ毛
Watashi wa tokidoki **matsuge** ni masukara o nuru koto ga arimasu.
I sometimes put mascara on my **eyelashes**.
私は時々まつ毛にマスカラを塗ることがあります

722.

Text Message – Mēru (me-ru)メール
Anata wa kanojo no **mēru** o jushin shimashita ka?

Did you receive her **text message**?
あなたは彼女のメールを受信しましたか

723.

Bite – Kamu (ka-mu)かむ
Watashi no inu wa **kama**nai.
My dog doesn't **bite**.
私の犬は噛まない

724.

Wifi – Musen ran (mu-sen ran)無線ラン
Sumimasen, **musen ran no** pasuwādo o shitte imasu ka?
Excuse me, do you know the **wifi** password?
すみません無線ランのパスワードを知っていますか

725.

Go With – Isshoni iku (issho-ni iku)一緒に行く
Kareshi to **isshoni iku** tsumori desu ka?
Are you going to **go with** your boyfriend?
彼氏と一緒に行くつもりですか

726.

Boil – Wakasu (wa-ka-su)沸かす
Mizu o **wakashi**te kudasai.
Can you **boil** some water, please?
水を沸かしてください

727.

Clear – Katazukeru (ka-ta-zu-ke-ru)片づける
Tēburu o**katazukeru** hitsuyō ga arimasu.
We need to **clear** the table.
テーブルを片づける必要があります

728.

Build – Kenchiku (ken-chi-ku)建築
Anata no ie wa **kenchiku** ni dono kurai kakarimashita ka?

How long did your how take to **build**?
あなたの家は建築にどのくらいかかりましたか

729.

Therefore - ...node (...no-de)...ので
Watashi wa unten dekinai**node**, kuruma o motte imasen.
I cannot drive, **therefore** I don't have a car.
私は運転できないので車をもっていません

730.

What kind of? – **Donna** (don-na)どんな
Jeimī tte **donna** hito?
What kind of person is Jamie?
ジェイミーってどんな人

731.

Plate – Osara (o-sa-ra)お皿
Betsu no **osara**o motte kite moraemasu ka?
Can you bring me different **plate**?
別のお皿を持ってきてもらえますか

732.

Sore Throat – Nodonoitami (no-do-no-i-ta-mi)喉の痛み
Nodonoitami no tame ni shiroppu o nomimasu.
Drink some syrup for your **sore throat**.
喉の痛みのためにシロップを飲みます

733.

Boring – Taikutsu (tai-ku-tsu)退屈
Sono eiga wa **taikutsu**datta, nemuri ni ochite shimatta.
The movie was **boring**, I feel asleep.
その映画は退屈だった、眠りにおちてしまった

734.

Liar – Usotsuki (u-so-tsu-ki)嘘つき
Kare o shin'yō shinaide kudasai, kare wa **usotsuki** desu.

Don’t trust him, he is a **liar**.
彼を信用しないでください、彼は嘘つきです

735.

Money – Okane (o-ka-ne)お金
Okane wa ikura gurai motte imasu ka?
How much **money** do you have?
お金はいくらぐらいもっていますか

736.

Map – Chizu (chi-zu)地図
Moshi michinimayotta-ra **chizu** o tsukatte kudasai.
If you are lost use the **map**.
もし道に迷ったら地図を使ってください

737.

Answer – Kotae (ko-ta-e)答え
Kono shitsumon ni taisuru **kotae** wa nan desu ka?
What is the **answer** to this question?
この質問に対する答えは何ですか

738.

Turn On – Tsukeru (tsu-ke-ru)つける
Okyakusan no tame ni ongaku o**tsukete**.
Turn on the music for the guests.
お客さんのために音楽をつけて

739.

Tell – Oshieru (o-shi-e-ru)教える
Mondai ga nanika **oshiete** kuremasu ka?
Tell me what the problem is?
問題が何か教えてくれますか

740.

Convenience Store – Konbini (kon-bi-ni)コンビニ
Chikaku ni **konbini** ga arimasu.

There is a **convenience store** near me.
近くにコンビニがあります

741.

Nervous – Kinchō (kin-cho)緊張
Kare wa kanojo ni atta toki**kinchō** shite ita.
He was **nervous** when he met her.
彼は彼女に会った時緊張していた

742.

Honest – Shōjiki (sho-ji-ki)正直
Anata wa itsumo **shōjiki**dearubeki desu.
You should always be **honest**.
あなたはいつも正直であるべきです

743.

Weight – Taijū (tai-ju)体重
Watashi wa natsu made ni **taijū** o herasanakereba narimasen.
I have to lose some **weight** by summer.
私は夏までに体重減らさなければなりません

744.

Fry – Ageru (a-ge-ru)あげる
Anata wa toriniku o **age**masuka soretomo yakimasu ka?
Do you **fry** or grill your chicken?
あなたは鶏肉を揚げますかそれとも焼きますか

745.

Yet – Mada (ma-da)まだ
Mada junbi ga dekite imasen.
We are not ready **yet**.
まだ準備ができていません

746.

Birth – Seinen (sei-nen)生年
Koko ni anata no **seinen**gappi o kinyushite kudasai.

Write down your date of **birth** here.
ここにあなたの生年月日を記入してください

747.

Country – Kuni (ku-ni)国
Watashi wa jibun no **kuni** ga koishī desu.
I miss my **country**.
私は自分の国が恋しいです

748.

Cough – Seki (se-ki)
Seki o shitara kuchi o ōimashou.
Cover your mouth when you **cough**.
咳をしたら口を覆いましょう

749.

This Way – Kono michi (ko-no mi-chi)この道
Anata wa **kono michi** o iku hitsuyō ga arimasu.
You need to go **this way**.
あなたはこの道を行く必要があります

750.

No Problem - Mon dai arimasen (mon dai ari-ma-sen)問題ありません
Mondaiarimasen, watashi wa betsu no mono o nyūshu shimasu.
No problem, I will get another one.
問題ありません　私は別のものを入手します

751.

Departure – Shuppatsu (shup-pa-tsu)出発
Watashitachi no **shuppatsu**jikan wa itsu desu ka?
What time is our **departure**?
私たちの出発時間はいつですか

752.

Start – Hajimaru (ha-ji-ma-ru)始まる
Eiga wa itsu **hajimari**masu ka?

When will the movie **start**?
映画はいつ始まりますか

753.

Computer - Konpyūta (kon-pyu-ta)コンピューター
Watashi no **konpyūta** wa kowarete imasu.
My **computer** is broken.
私のコンピューターは壊れています

754.

Temple – Otera (o-te-ra)お寺
Karera wa inori no tame ni **otera**ni ikimashita.
They went to the **temple** to pray.
彼らは祈りのためにお寺に行きました

755.

Size – Saizu (sai-zu)サイズ
Anata wa motto ōkī **saizu** ga arimasu ka?
Do you have a bigger **size**?
あなたはもっと大きいサイズがありますか

756.

Is – wa…desu (wa..de-su)…です
Kanojo **wa** kyōshi **desu.**
She **is** a teacher.
彼女は教師です

757.

Lip – Kuchibiru (ku-chi-bi-ru)唇
Kanojo wa yawarakai **kuchibiru** o shite iru.
She has soft **lips**.
彼女は柔らかい唇をしている

758.

Cooking – Ryōri (ryo-ri)料理
Kanojo wa yasai **ryōri** ga daisuki desu.

She loves **cooking** vegetables.
彼女は野菜料理が大好きです

759.

Simple – Kantan/Tanjun (kan-tan/tan-jun)簡単/単純
Muzukashī kotode wa arimasen deshita, **kantan** deshita.
It wasn't difficult, it was **simple**.
難しいことではありませんでした、簡単でした

760.

Surprise – Sapuraizu (sa-pu-rai-zu)サプライズ
Uwa , nante subarashī **sapuraizu**. Arigatō.
Wow, what a nice **surprise**. Thank you.
うわ、なんて素晴らしいサプライズ、ありがとう

761.

Torch – Tōchi (to-chi)トーチ
Tōchi o watashite moraemasu ka?
Can you pass me the **torch**?
トーチを渡してもらえますか

762.

Sink – Nagashi (na-ga-shi)ながし
Purēto o **nagashi** ni iremasu.
Put the plates in the **sink**.
プレートを流しにいれます

763.

Kind – Yasashī (ya-sa-shee)優しい
Kanojo no sobo wa **yasashī** josei desu.
Her grandmother is a **kind** woman.
彼女の祖母は優しい女性です

764.

Highway – Kōsokudōro (ko-so-ku-do-ro)高速道路
Kōsokudōro wa heisa sarete imasu.

The **highway** is closed.
高速道路は閉鎖されています

765.

Tall – Se no takai (se no ta-ka-i)背の高い
Senotakai dansei ga mise ni haitta.
A **tall** man entered the shop.
背の高い男性が店に入った

766.

Measure – Sokutei (so-ku-te-i)測定
Kono tēburu o **sokute**i suru hitsuyō ga arimasu.
We need to **measure** this table.
このテーブルを測定する必要があります

767.

Anniversary – Kinenbi (ki-nen-bi)記念日
Kyō wa watashi no ryōshin no kekkon **kinenbi** desu.
Today is my parents' wedding **anniversary**.
今日は私の両親の結婚記念日です

768.

Deal – Taisho (tai-sho)対処
Kono mondai ni dō **taisho** shimasu ka?
How will you **deal** with this problem?
この問題にどお対処しますか

769.

Fatigue – Hirō (hi-ro)疲労
Kare wa **hirō** de kurushinde imasu.
He is suffering with **fatigue**.
彼は疲労で苦しんでいます

770.

Tasty – Oishī (oishi-yee)美味しい
Tabemono wa totemo **oishi**katta desu.

The food was very **tasty**.
食べ物はとても美味しかったです

771.

Lonely – Sabishī (sa-bi-shyee)寂しい
Tomodachi ga inakute **sabishī** desu.
I feel **lonely** without my friends.
友達がいなくて寂しいです

772.

Road – Michi (mi-chi)道
Kare no kuruma wa tsugi no **michi** ni chūsha shimashita.
His car is park on the next **road**.
彼の車は次の道に駐車しました

773.

True – Hontō (hon-to)本当
Sore wa **hontō** desu ka?
Is it **true**?
それは本当ですか

774.

Are You Ok – Daijōbu desu ka? (dai-jo-bu de-su ka)大丈夫ですか
Kanojo wa kare ni **daijōbu**ka tazuneta?
She asked him, **are you ok**?
彼女は彼に大丈夫か尋ねた

775.

Back Door – Uraguchi no to tobira (u-ra-gu-chi no to-bi-ra)裏口の扉
Kanarazu **uraguchi no tobira**o shimete kudasai.
Make sure to close the **back door**.
必ず裏口の扉を閉めてください

776.

And - …to (toh)…と
Kochira wa watashi no ani **to** ane desu.

This is my older brother **and** older sister.
こちらは私の兄と姉です

777.

List – Risuto (ri-su-to)リスト
Konya suru koto no **risuto** ga arimasu.
I have a **list** of things to do tonight.
今夜することのリストがあります

778.

All day – Ichinichijū (i-chi-ni-chi-ju)一日中
Watashi no musuko wa i**chinichijū** nemurimashita.
My son slept **all day**.
私の息子は一日中眠りました

779.

Soap – Sekken (sek-ken)石鹸
Kono **sekken** wa hana no yōna kaori ga shimasu.
This **soap** smells like flowers.
この石鹸は花のような香りがします

780.

Floor – kai (kai)階
Kissaten wa nan-**kai** desu ka?
Which **floor** is the coffee shop on?
喫茶店は何階ですか

781.

Shampoo – Shanpū (shan-pu)シャンプー
Dono **shanpū** o shiyō shimasu ka?
Which **shampoo** do you use?
どのシャンプーを使用しますか

782.

More – Motto (mot-to)もっと
Motto okane ga hitsuyō desu.

I need **more** money.
もっとお金が必要です

783.

Shoe Store – Kutsuya (kut-su-ya)靴屋
Karera wa **kutsuya** ni ikimashita.
They went to the **shoe store.**
彼は靴屋に行きました

784.

I'd like To … -…tai (…tai)…たい
Rainen Chūgoku ni iki**tai** desu.
I'd like to visit China next year.
来年中国に行きたいです

785.

Crazy – Atamagaokashī (a-ta-ma-gao-ka-shee)頭がおかしい
Watashi no imōto wa sushi ga sukide wa arimasen.
Kanojo wa **atamagaokashī** desu.
My sister doesn't like sushi. she is **crazy**.
私の妹は寿司が好きではありません
彼女は頭がおかしいです

786.

Mouse – Nezumi (ne-zu-mi)ねずみ
Watashinohaha wa **nezumi**o mite sakebi hajimeta.
My mom saw a **mouse** and started screaming.
私の母はねずみを見て叫び始めた

787.

Confused – Konran (kon-ran)混乱
Watashi wa **konran** shite imasu, kare wa kōsai-chū desu ka, soretomo dokushin desu ka?
I'm **confused,** is he in a relationship or single?
私は混乱しています　彼は交際中ですかそれとも独身ですか

788.

Principle – Gensoku (gen-so-ku)原則
Yoi **gensoku** o motsu koto ga jūyō desu.
Its important to have good **principles**.
良い原則をもつことが重要です

789.

Paper – Yōshi (yo-shi)用紙
Ichi-mai no **yōshio** watashi ni watashite moraemasu ka?
Can you hand me a sheet of **paper**?
一枚の用紙を私に渡してもらえますか

790.

Cash – Genkin (gen-kin)現金
Genkin wa ikura arimasu ka?
How much **cash** do you have?
現金はいくらありますか

791.

Smoking – Kitsuen (kit-su-en)喫煙
Quit smoking- Kinen (kin-en)禁煙
Watashi wa **kinen** suru hitsuyō ga arimasu.
I need to **quitsmoking**.
私は禁煙する必要があります印遠

792.

Ignore – Mushi (mu-shi)無視
Mushi shite kudasai.
Just try to **ignore** him.
無視してください

793.

Call – Denwa o suru (den-wa o su-ru)電話をする
Jeimī ni **denwa o shite** kare ga itsu kuruka kiite kuremasu ka?
Can you **call** Jamie and ask when he is coming?
ジェイミーに電話をして彼がいつくるか聞いてくれますか

794.

There – Arimasu / Soko (a-ri-ma-su/so-ko)あります／そこ
Eki ga **arimasu**.
There is a train station.
駅があります

795.

Injection – chūsha (chu-sha)注射
Kanojo wa **chūsha** o suru no o osorete iru.
She is afraid of getting **injections**.
彼女は注射をするのを恐れている

796.

Never – koto ga nai (koto ga nai)ことがない
Kanojo wa Amerika ni itta **koto ga nai**.
She has **neve**r been to America.
彼女はアメリカに行ったことがない

797.

Alcohol – Arukōru (a-ru-ko-ru)アルコール
Kare wa sakuya **arukōru** o takusan nonda.
He drank a lot of **alcohol** last night.
彼は昨夜アルコールを沢山飲んだ

798.

Gift – Okurimono (o-ku-ri-mo-no)ギフト
Kare no **okurimono** wa itsumo kōka desu.
His gifts are always expensive.
彼の贈り物はいつも高価です

799.

On – Ue (u-e)上
Neko wa tēburu no **ue** ni imasu.
The cat is **on** the table.
猫はテーブルの上にいます

800.

Naughty – Itazurazuki (i-ta-zu-ra-zu-ki)いたずら好き
Watashi no mei wa totemo **itazurazuki** desu.
My niece is so **naughty**.
私の姪はとてもいたずら好きです

801.

Nice – Suteki (su-te-ki)素敵
Watashitachi wa resutoran de **suteki**na yūshoku o tabemashita.
We had a **nice** dinner at the restaurant.
私たちはレストランで素敵な夕食を食べました

802.

Already – Sudeni (su-de-ni)すでに
Watashi wa kesa **sudeni** jimu ni ikimashita.
I **already** went to the gym this morning.
私は今朝すでにジムに行きました

803.

Mean – Imi (i-mi)意味
Kare wa kaigi-chū ni itta koto o **imi** shinakatta.
He did not **mean** what he said during the meeting.
彼は会議中に言ったことを意味しなかった

804.

Open – Aku (a-ku)開く
Mise wa nanji ni **aki**masu ka?
What time does the store **open**?
店は何時に開きますか

805.

Escape – Nigeru (ni-ge-ru)逃げる
Kono basho kara **nigeru** koto wa dekimasen.
You can't **escape** from this place.
この場所から逃げることはできません

806.

Lose – Ushinau (u-shi-na-u)失う
Watashi wa **ushinau** no ga kirai desu.
I hate to **lose**.
私は失うのが嫌いです

807.

Forward – Zenshin (zen-shin)前進
Anata wa **zenshin** dekimasu ka, miemasen.
Can you move **forward**, I cannot see.
あなたは前進できますか　見えません

808.

Take – Toru (to-ru)とる
Kanojo wa kare kara nani o **totta** no desu ka?
What did she **take** from him?
彼女は彼から何をとったのですか

809.

Follow – Shitagau (shi-ta-ga-u)従う
Kare ni **shitagatte** kudasai, Kare wa anata o ie ni tsurete ikimasu.
Follow him, he will take you home.
彼に従ってください、彼はあなたを家に連れていきます

810.

Student – Gakusei (ga-ku-sei)学生
Kore wa watashi no yūjin no Risa desu, kanojo wa **gakusei** desu.
This is my friend Lisa, she is a **student**.
これは私の友人のリサです、彼女は学生です

811.

Miss – Koishī (koi-shee)恋しい
Watashi wa kanojo ga **koishī**.
I **miss** my girlfriend so much.
私は彼女が恋しい

812.

Become – Naru (na-ru)なる
Watashi wa ochitsuita hito ni **nari**mashita.
I have **become** a calm person.
私は落ち着いた人になりました

813.

Part – Bubun (bu-bun)部分
Saiaku no **bubun** wa owakare no shin desu.
The worst **part** was saying goodbye.
最悪の部分はお別れのしんです

814.

Example – Rei (re-i)例
Rei o agete moraemasu ka?
Can you give me an **example**?
例をあげてもらえますか

815.

Whiskey – Uisukī (ui-su-ki)ウイスキー
Uokka no kawari ni **uisukī** o nomu no ga suki desu.
I prefer to drink **whiskey** instead of vodka.
ウォッカのかわりにウイスキーお飲むのが好きです

816.

O'clock – ..Ji (...ji)...時
Kanojo wa kyō go-**ji** ni okita.
She woke up at five **o'clock** today.
彼女は今日五時に起きた

817.

Song- Uta (u-ta)歌
Kono **uta** no namae wa nani desu ka?
What is the name of this **song**?
この歌の名前は何ですか

818.

Alright – iine (ee ne)いいね
Iine, sore wa tanoshisou dane.
Alright, that sounds fun.
いいね　それは楽しそうだね

819.

Accident – Jiko (ji-ko)事故
Watashi wa **jiko** o okoshi, denwa o kowashite shimatta.
I had an **accident** and broke my phone.
私は事故を起こし、電話を壊してしまった

820.

Adult – Otona (o-to-na)大人
Kare wa **otona** desu ga, kodomo no yō na kōdō o shite imasu.
He is an **adult** but he is acting like a child.
彼は大人ですが、子供のような行動をしています

821.

Bug – Mushi (mu-shi)虫
Watashino heya ni **mushi** ga imasu.
There is a **bug** in my room.
私の部屋い虫がいます

822.

Stay – Tomaru (to-ma-ru)泊まる
Watashi wa inu ni **tomaru** yō ni iimashitaga, inu wa hashirisarimashita.
I told my dog to **stay** but he ran off.
私は犬いとまるように言いましたが犬は走り去りました

823.

Marry – Kekkon suru (kekkon su-ru)結婚する
Nīna wa kanojo no kareshi to **kekkon**shitai to omotte imasu.
Nina wants to **marry** her boyfriend.
ニーナは彼女の彼氏と結婚したいと思っています

824.

Knock – Nokku (no-kku)
Mishiranu hito ga tobira o **nokku** shita.
A stranger **knocked** on the door.
見知らぬ人が扉をノックした

825.

Medicine – Kusuri (ku-su-ri)薬
Kare wa **kusuri** o kai ni yakkyoku ni ikimashita.
He went to the pharmacy to buy some **medicine**.
彼は薬を買いに薬局に行きました

826.

I'm a …. – Watashi wa…desu (watashi wa …desu)私は・・・です
Watashi wa keisatsukan **desu**.
I'm a police officer.
私は警察官です

827.

Flour – Komugiko (ko-mu-gi-ko)小麦粉
Mearī **Komugiko** wa doko no?
Mary where is the **flour**?
メアリー小麦粉はどこの

828.

Visa – Biza (bi-za)ビザ
Tai ni nyūkoku suru ni wa **biza** ga hitsuyō desu.
I have to get **visa** to enter Thailand.
タイい入国するにはビザが必要です

829.

Village – Mura (mu-ra)村
Kare no **mura** wa koko kara tōkuarimasen.
His **village** is not too far from here.
彼の村はここから遠くありません

830.

Where Are You From? – Shusshin wa dochira desu ka?
(shu-sshin wa doko de-su ka)出身はどちらですか
Anata no kuchō wa kakkoī desu, **shusshin wa dochira desu ka**?
Your accent is cool, **where are you from**?
あなたの口調はカッコいいです、出身はどちらですか

831.

That – Ano/Sore (ano/so-re)あの/それ
Ano kuruma wa anata desu ka?
Is **that** car yours?
あの車はあなたですか

832.

Tourism – Kankō (kan-ko)観光
Tai no **kankō** wa totemo ninki ga arimasu.
Tourism in Thailand is very popular.
タイの観光あとても人気があります

833.

Fighting – Tatakau (ta-ta-kau)たたく
Kyō ni-hiki no inu ga **tatakatte** iru no o mita.
I saw two dogs **fighting** today.
今日にひきの犬がたたかっているのを見た

834.

Buy – Kau (ka-u)買う
Atarashī kutsu o **kai**tai no desu ga, okane ga arimasen.
I want to **buy** new shoes but I don't have any money.
新しい靴を買いたいのですがお金がありません

835.

Test – Shiken (shi-ken)試験
Shiken wa muzukashiku arimasen deshita.
The **test** wasn't difficult.
試験は難しくありませんでした

836.

Clothing – Fuku (fu-ku)服

Karera wa sono mise no **fuku** o kaemasu.

They different **clothing** in that store.

彼らはその店の服をかえます

837.

First Time – Hajimete (ha-ji-me-te)はじめて

Watashi ga pūketto o otozureru no wa konkai ga **hajimete** desu.

This is the **first time** I am visiting Phuket.

私がプーケットを訪れるのは今回が初めてです

838.

Meeting – Kaigi (kai-gi)会議

Watashi wa shokuba de **kaigi** ga arunode, ikanakereba ikemasen.

I have to go I have a **meeting** at work.

私は職場で会議があるので、行かなければいけません

839.

Usually – Tsūjō (tsu-jo)通常

Watashi wa **tsūjō** maishū kayōbi ni oyogi ni ikimasu.

I **usually** go swimming every Tuesday.

私は通常毎週火曜日に泳ぎに行きます

840.

Pain – Itai (i-tai)痛い

Doko ga **itai** desu ka?

Where do you feel **pain**?

どこが痛いですか

841.

Cup – Kappu (kap-pu)カップ

Anata wa **kappu** ga hitsuyō desu ka?

Do you need a **cup**?

あなたはカップが必要ですか

842.

Body – Karada (ka-ra-da)体
Chārī wa **karada** ni irezumi o ireta.
Charlie got a tattoo on his **body**.
チャーリーは体に入れ墨をいれた

843.

Photo – Shashin (sha-shin)写真
Watashitachi no **shashin** o totte itadakemasu ka?
Can you take a **photo** of us?
私たちの写真を撮っていただけますか

844.

Scary – Kowai (ko-wai)怖い
Ano ie wa obakeyashiki desu ka? **Kowa**sou desu.
Is that house haunted? It looks **scary**.
あの家はお化け屋敷ですか怖そうです

845.

Thing – Mono (mo-no)もの
Kanojo wa funshitsu shita**mono** o mitsuketa.
She found the **thing** she lost.
彼女は紛失したものを見つけた

846.

Every Week – Maishū (mai-shu)毎週
Kanojo wa **maishū** ryōshin no ie ni ikimasu.
She goes to her parent's house **every week**.
彼女は毎週両親の家に行きます

847.

Running – Hashiru (ha-shi-ru)走る
Kanojo wa kōen o **hashitte** ita.
She was **running** in the park.
彼女は公園を走っていた

848.

Key – Kagi (ka-gi)鍵

Watashi wa kanojo ni watashinoie no **kagi** o watashita.

I gave her the **key** to my house.

私は彼女い私の家の鍵を渡した

849.

Allergy – Arerugī (a-re-rugi)アレルギー

Watashi wa nattsu ni **arerugī** ga arimasu.

I have an **allergy** to nuts.

私はナッツにアレルギーがあります

850.

Strict – Kibishī (ki-bi-shee)厳しい

Watashi no ryōshin wa totemo **kibishī** desu.

My parents are very **strict**.

私の両親とても厳しいです

851.

Moustache – Kuchi hige (ku-chihi-ge)くちひげ

Kare wa **kuchihige** o hayasu koto ga dekimasuga, sukide wa arimasen.

He can grow a **moustache** but he doesn't like it.

彼は口ひげを生やすことができますが　好きではありません

852.

Eat – Taberu (ta-be-ru)食べる

Kyō wa nani o **taberu** tsumori desu ka?

What are you going to **eat** today?

今日は何を食べるつもりですか

853.

Discount – Waribiki (wa-ri-bi-ki)割引

Waribiki wa arimasu ka?

Can you give any **discount**?

割引はありますか

854.

Neighbour – Rinjin (rin-jin)隣人
Kare no **rinjin** wa itsumo kare ni tabemono o ataemasu.
His **neighbour** always gives him food.
彼の隣人はいつも彼に食べ物を与えます

855.

Message – Dengon (den-gon)伝言
Kanojo wa sono **dengon** o osoku uketotta.
She received the **message** late.
彼女はその伝言を遅く受け取った

856.

Clock – Tokei (to-kei)時計
Tokei wa doko desu ka?
Where is the **clock**?
時計はどこですか

857.

Year – Nen (nen)年
Rai**nen** wa Girisha e ikimasu.
We will go to Greece next **year**.
来年はギリシャへ行きます

858.

Park – Kōen (ko-en)
Kono **kōen** de inu o sanpo suru koto wa dekimasen.
You cannot walk your dog in this **park**.
この公園で犬の散歩することはできません

859.

Last Time – Saigo (sai-go)最後
Watashi ga **saigo** ni itta no wa ni-nen mae desu.
The **last time** I went, it was 2 years ago.
私が最後に行ったのは二年前です

860.

Fan – Senpūki (sen-pu-ki)扇風機
Kanojo wa atarashī heya ni **senpūki**o motte kita.
She brought a **fan** for her new room.
彼女は新しい部屋に扇風機をもってきた

861.

Study – Benkyō (ben-kyo)勉強
Watashi wa takusan **benkyō** shinakereba narimasen.
I have to **study** a lot.
私は沢山勉強をしなければなりません

862.

Chilli – Tōgarashi (to-ga-ra-shi)とうがらし
Kanojo wa **tōgarashi** no aji ga sukidewa arimasen.
She does not like the taste of **chilli**.
彼女はとうがらしの味が好きではありません

863.

Worry – Shinpai (shin-pai)心配
Shinpaishinaide, rirakkusu shite mite kudasai.
Don't **worry**, try to relax.
心配しないで、リラックスしてください

864.

Every Year – Maitoshi (mai-toshi)
Maitoshi, atashitachiha atarashī kuni o otozuremasu.
Every year, we visit a new country.
毎年私たちは新しい国を訪れます

865.

Drivers License - Unten menkyoshō (un-ten men-kyo-sho)運転免許証
Unten menkyoshō o funshitsu shimashita.
I've lost me **drivers license**.
運転免許証を紛失しました

866.

Criticize – Hinan (hi-nan)非難
Anataga hitobito kara **hihan** sarete mo daijōbu desu.
It is okay to let people **criticize** you.
あなたが人々から批判されても大丈夫です

867.

Final – Kimatsu (ki-mat-su)期末
Kimatsu shiken wa raishū okonawa remasu.
The **final** exam will happen next week.
期末試験は来週行われます

868.

Week – Shū (shu)週
Kon**shū** wa, jūyōna tesuto ga arimasu
This **week**, we have an important test.
今週は重要なテストがあります

869.

Or - ...ya... (yah)・・や
Kare wa toriniku **ya** sakana ga sukidewa arimasen.
He doesn't like chicken **or** fish.
彼は鶏肉や魚が好きではありません

870.

Lot – Takusan (ta-ku-san)沢山
Kashikoi hito wa **takusan** yomimasu.
Smart people read a **lot**.
賢い人は沢山読みます

871.

Marriage – Kekkon (keh-kon)結婚
Kekkon wa jinsei no ōkina bubun desu.
Marriage is a big part of life.
結婚は人生の大きな部分です

872.

If – Moshi (mo-shi)もし
Moshi ittara modottekonai.
If I go, I won't come back.
もし行ったら戻ってこない

873.

How Many – Donokurai (do-no-ku-rai)どのくらい
Dono kurai no hito ga pātī ni ikimasu ka?
How many people are going to the party?
どのくらいの人がパーティに行きますか

874.

Travel – Ryokō (ryo-koh)旅行
Watashinochichi wa **ryokō** ga sukidewa arimasen.
My father doesn't like to **travel**.
私の父は旅行が好きではありません

875.

Mold – Kabi (ka-bi)カビ
Sore o tabete wa ikenai,**kabi** ga haeteimasu.
Don't eat that, it has **mold** on it.
それを食べてはいけません　カビがはえています

876.

Prison – Keimusho (kei-mu-sho)刑務所
Kare wa **keimusho** ni imasu.
He is in **prison**.
彼は刑務所にいます

877.

Sweat – Ase (a-se)汗
Kare wa sutoresu o kanjiruto **ase**okaku.
He **sweats** a lot when he is stressed.
彼はストレスを感じると汗をかく

878.
Less – Sukunai (su-ku-nai)少ない
Kanojo wa kare yori mo okane ga **sukunai**.
She has **less** money than him.
彼女は彼よりもお金が少ない

879.
Without – Tōgarashi (to-ga-ra-shi)とうがらし
Watashi wa **tōgarashi** nashi chikin ga hoshī desu.
I want my chicken without **chilli**.
私はとうがらしなしチキンが欲しいです

880.
Towel – Taoru (ta-o-ru)タオル
Kaminoke ni wa kawaita **taoru** ga hitsuyō desu.
I need a dry **towel** for my hair.
髪の毛には乾いたタオルが必要です

881.
Cool – Heisei (hei-sei)平静
Heisei o tamotte, shinpaishinaide kudasai.
Stay **cool** and don't worry.
平静を保って、心配しないでください

882.
How Old Are You? – Anata wa nan sai desu ka? (ana-ta wa nan sai de-su ka)あなたは何歳ですか
Anata wa totemo wakaku mimasu, **anata wa nan-sai desu ka**?
You look very young, **how old are you**?
あなたはとても若く見えます、あなたは何歳ですか

883.
Lake – Mizuumi (mizu-umi)湖
By the lake - Kohan (ko-han)湖畔
Konshūmatsu wa **kohan** de pikunikku o shimashou.

Let's have a picnic **by the lake** this weekend.
今週末は湖畔でピクニックをしましょう

884.

Fever – Netsu (ne-tsu)熱
Kanojo wa itsukakan **netsu** ga atta.
She has had a **fever** for five days.
彼女は５日間熱があった

885.

Fix – Shūsei (shu-sei)修正
Kore o **shūsei** suru hōhō o shitte imasu ka?
Do you know how to **fix** this?
これを修正する方法を知っていますか

886.

Mine – Watashi no mono (wa-ta-shi no mo-no)私のもの
Sumimasen, sono sukāfu wa **watashi no mono** desu.
Excuse me, that scarf is **mine**.
すみません、そのスカーフは私のものです

887.

Alive – Ikiru (i-ki-ru)生きる
Saiwaina koto ni, kare wa mada **ikite** imasu.
Luckily, he is still **alive**.
幸いなことに彼はまだ生きています

888.

Come In – Haitte (hai-tte)入って
Haitte cyakuseki shite.
Come in and take a seat.
入って着席して

889.

Movie – Eiga (ei-ga)映画
Sore wa subarashī **eiga** deshita.

That was an amazing **movie**.
それは素晴らしい映画でした

890.

Pool – pūru (pu-ru)プール
Kono hoteru ni wa **pūru** ga arimasu ka?
Does this Hotel have a **pool**?
このホテルにはプールがありますか

891.

Afterwards – Atode (a-to-de)あとで
Pātī ni itte, **atode** mukae ni ikimasu.
Go to the party, I'll pick you up **afterwards**.
パーティに行って、あとで迎えにいきます

892.

Put Away – Katazukeru (ka-ta-zu-ke-ru)かたずける
Keitaidenwa o **katadzuke** nasai, shitsurei desu.
Put away your phone, it is rude.
携帯電話を片づけなさい、失礼です

893.

Trust – Shinyō (shin-yo)信用
Kanojo wa mō kare o **shinyō** dekinai.
She cannot **trust** him anymore.
彼女はもう彼を信用できない

894.

Boss – Jōshi (jo-shi)上司
Watashitachi no atarashī **jōshi** wa watashi yori wakai desu.
Our new **boss** is younger than me.
私たちの新しい上司は私より若いです

895.

Found – Mitsukeru (mit-su-ke-ru)見つける
Kagi o mitsukemashita

I **found** my keys.
鍵を見つけました

896.

Really? - Hontōni? (hon-to-ni?)本当に
Hontōni? Anata wa aisukurīmu ga kirai desu ka?
Really? You don't like ice cream?
本当にあなたはアイスクリームが嫌いですか

897.

Shit – Tawagoto (ta-wa-go-to)たわごと
Watashi wa kono **tawagoto** ni unzari shite imasu.
I am tired of this **shit.**
私はこのたわごとにうんざりしています

898.

Grass – Shiba (shi-ba)芝
Kyō wa **shiba** o karu hitsuyō ga arimasu.
You need to cut the **grass** today.
今日は芝を刈る必要があります

899.

Make – Tsukuru (tsu-ku-ru)作る
Dono yōna kēki o **tsukuru** koto ga dekimasu ka?
What kind of cakes can you **make**?
どのようなケーキを作ることができますか

900.

Leave – Saru (sa-ru)去る
Naze kare wa **satta** no desu ka?
Why did he **leave**?
なぜ彼は去ったのですか

901.

Sly – Zurui (zu-ru-i)ずるい
Watashi wa Samu ga kirai desu, kare wa totemo **zurui** desu.

I don't like Sam, he is very **sly**.
私はサムが嫌いです、彼はとてもずるいです

902.

Sentence – Bun (bun)文
Kono **bun** o mitekudasai.
Look at this **sentence**.
この文を見てください

903.

Little Bit – Sukoshi (su-ko-shi)少し
Watashi wa **sukoshi** Tai-go o hanashimasu.
I speak a **little bit** of Thai language.
私は少しタイ語を話します

904.

Forehead – Hitai (hi-tai)
Kanojo no **hitai** wa totemo hiroi desu.
Her **forehead** is very big.
彼女のひたいはとても広いです

905.

Different – Kotonaru (koto-na-ru)異なる
Tai-go wa eigo to wa hijō ni **kotonari**masu.
Thai language is very **different** to English.
タイ語は英語とは非常に異なります

906.

Do – Suru (su-ru)する
Gēmu o yamete, benkyō o **shite** kudasai.
Stop playing games and **do** some studying.
ゲームをやめて、勉強をしてください

907.

Waiter – u eitā (u ei-ta)ウェイター
Kare wa sono okanjō no tame ni **u eitā** o yonda.

He called the **waiter** for the bill.
彼はそのお勘定のためにウェイターを呼んだ

908.

Real – Honmono (hon-mo-no)本物
Kono shokubutsu wa **honmono** ka dō ka?
Is this plant **real** or not?
この植物は本物かどうか

909.

Police Station – Keisatsu sho (kei-sat-su sho)警察署
Moyori no **keisatsusho** wa doko desu ka?
Where is the closest **police station**?
最寄りの警察署はどこですか

910.

Wallet – Saifu (sai-fu)財布
Watashi wa **saifu** o kuruma no naka ni oitekita.
I left my **wallet** inside the car.
私は財布を車のなかに置いてきた

911.

Every weekend – Maishū matsu (mai-shu ma-tsu)毎週末
Kare wa **maishū matsu**ryōshin o tazunemasu.
He visits his parents **every weekend**.
彼は毎週末両親を訪ねます

912.

Pocket – Poketto (po-ke-tto)ポケット
Watashi no denwa wa **poketto** kara ochita.
My phone dropped out of my **pocket**.
私の電話はポケットから落ちた

913.

Funeral – Sōgi (so-gi)葬儀
Sōgi wa raishū ni narimasu.

The **funeral** will be next week.
葬儀は来週になります

914.

Puke – Haku (ha-ku)吐く
Watashi wa**haki** sou desu.
I feel like I'm going to **puke**.
私は吐きそうです

915.

No – Īe (iee-e)いいえ
Īe, hoshiku arimasen.
No, I do not want any.
いいえ、欲しくありません

916.

Employee – Shain (sha-in)社員
Kono shinnyū **shain** wa yarukiganai.
This new **employee** is lazy.
この新入社員はやる気がない

917.

Amazing – Subarashī (su-ba-ra-shee)素晴らしい
Kono kuni wa **subarashī** desu.
This country is **amazing**.
この国は素晴らしいです

918.

View – Nagame (na-ga-me)眺め
Kono hoteru kara no **nagame** wa subarashī desu.
The **view** from this hotel is amazing.
このホテルからの眺めは素晴らしいです

919.

Clear Up – Seiri (sei-ri)整理
Korera no shorui o **seiri** shitekara benkyō shimashou.

Let's **clear up** these paper, then we can study.
これらの書類を整理してから勉強しましょう

920.

Hold – Motsu (mot-su)持つ
Chotto watashi no kagi o **motte** moraemasu ka?
Can you **hold** my key for a minute?
ちょっと私の鍵を持ってもらえますか

921.

What Happened? – Nani ga okottano? (na-ni ga oko-tta-no)何が起こったの
Nani ga okottano? Naze anata wa okotte imasu ka?
What happened? Why are you upset?
何が起こったのなぜあなたは怒っていますか

922.

I'm from …. – Kara kimashita (ka-raki-ma-shi-ta)…から来ました
Watashi wa Kanada **kara kimashita**.
I'm from Canada.
私はカナダから来ました

923.

Nowhere – Dokonimo (do-ko-ni-mo)どこにも
Kanojo no inu wa **dokonimo** imasen.
Her dog was **nowhere** to be found.
彼女の犬はどこにもいません

924.

Baby – Akachan (a-ka-chan)赤ちゃん
Akachan wa nan-sai desu ka?
How old is the **baby**?
赤ちゃんは何歳ですか

925.

Eat Out – Gaishoku (gai-sho-ku)外食

Watashi wa **gaishoku** suru koto wa amari arimasen, Takai desu.
I don't often **eat out**, it's expensive.
私は外食することはありません、高いです

926.
Don't Worry – Shinpaishinaide (shin-pai-shi-nai-de)心配しないで
Shinpaishinaide, subete mondai naidesho.
Don't worry, everything will be alright.
心配しないで、すべて問題ないでしょう

927.
Tear / Rip – Yaburu (ya-bu-ru)やぶる
Kinō watashi wa ōkiniiri no T-shatsu o **yaburi**mashita.
Yesterday I **tore** my favourite shirt.
昨日私はお気に入りのTシャツをやぶりました

928.
Sea – Umi (u-mi)海
Umi wa kirei ni mimasu.
The **sea** looks beautiful.
海は綺麗に見ます

929.
Radio – Rajio (ra-ji-o)ラジオ
Watashi wa **rajio** o kiku koto wa amari arimasen.
I don't often listen to the **radio**.
私はラジオを聴くことはあまりありません

930.
Bush – Shigemi (shi-ge-mi)しげみ
Shigemi wa ki yori mo chīsai.
A **bush** is smaller than a tree.
しげみは木よりも小さい

931.
Respect – Sonkei (son-kei)尊敬

Watashi wa chichi o **sonkei** shimasu.
I **respect** my father.
私は父を尊敬します

932.

Bullet – Jūdan (ju~-dan)銃弾
Real bullet – Jitsudan (ji-tsu-dan)実弾
Kare no jū ni wa **jitsudan** ga arimashita.
There was a real **bullet** in his gun.
彼の銃には実弾がありました

933.

Africa – Afurika (a-fu-ri-ka)アフリカ
Watashi wa **Afurika** ni itta koto ga nai.
I have never been to **Africa.**
私はアフリカに行ったことがない

934.

Day – Nichi (ni-chi)日
Shiken wa nan **nichi** desu ka?
Which **day** is the exam?
試験は何日ですか

935.

Music – Ongaku (on-gaku)音楽
Kare wa **ongaku** o kiku no ga suki desu.
He likes listening to **music**.
彼は音楽を聴くのが好きです

936.

Quick – Hayaku (ha-ya-ku)早く
Hayaku shite, matteimasu.
Be **quick**, I am waiting.
早くして、待っています

937.

Has – Kau (ka-u)飼う
Kanojo wa san-biki no kuroi neko o **katte** imasu
She **has** 3 black cats
彼女は三匹の黒い猫を飼っています

938.

Rash – Hosshin (ho-shin)発疹
Watashi wa ude ni **hosshin** ga arimasu.
I have a **rash** on my arm.
私は腕に発疹があります

939.

Fridge – Reizōko (rei-zo~-ko)冷蔵庫
Gyūnyū wa **reizōko** ni haitte imasu.
The milk is in the **fridge**.
牛肉は冷蔵庫に入っています

940.

Captain – Senchō (sen-cho~)船長
Senchō wa rōjindatta.
The **captain** was an old man.
船長は老人だった

941.

Departure Gate - Shuppatsu gēto (shu-ppatsu-ge-to)出発ゲート
Shuppatsu gēto wa D10 desu.
Our **departure gate** is D10.
出発ゲートはD１０です

942.

Partner – Pātonā (pa-to-na~)パートナー
Kare wa kono dansu o odoruni wa**pātonā** ga hitsuyō desu.
He needs a **partner** for this dance.
彼はこのダンスを踊るにはパートナーが必要です

943.

Rib – Rokkotsu (roh-kot-su)肋骨
Kare no **rokkotsu** wa jiko no tame ni oreta.
His **rib** was broken because of the accident.
彼の肋骨は事故のために折れた

944.

To - …Ni (ni)…に
Sore wo watashi **ni** kudasai, Onegaishimasu.
Give it **to** me, please.
それを私にください、お願いします

945.

Birthday – Tanjōbi (tan-jo-bi)誕生日
Raishū wa Hayley no **tanjōbi** pātī desu.
Its Hayley's **birthday** party next week.
来週はハレーの誕生日パーティです

946.

Headache – Zutsū (zut-su)頭痛
Anata no **zutsū** wa dō desu ka, kibun wa yokunari mashita ka?
How is your **headache**, are you feeling better?
あなたの頭痛はどうですか、気分は良くなりましたか

947.

Bicycle – Jitensha (ji-ten-sha)自転車
Jitensha ni noremasen.
I can't ride a **bicycle**.
自転車に乗れません

948.

Memory – Kioku (ki-o-ku)記憶
Dokusho wa anata no **kioku** o kōjō sasemasu.
Reading improves your **memory.**
読書はあなたの記憶を向上させます

949.

Mix – Kongō (kon-go)混合
Kono eiga wa komedi to dorama no **kongō** desu.
This movie is a **mix** of comedy and drama.
この映画はコメディとドラマの混合です

950.

Move – Idou (i-dou)移動
Idou shite itadakemasuka, miemasen.
Can you please **move**, I cannot see.
移動していただけますか、見えません

951.

Nothing – Nanimo nai (na-ni-mo nai)何もない
Watashi wakonshūmatsu **nanimo** shinakatta.
I did **nothing** this weekend.
私は今週末何もしなかった

952.

Kilometre – Kiro (ki-ro)キロ
Gakkō wa watashitachi no ie kara san-**kiro** no tokoro ni arimasu.
The school is 3 **kilo**metres away from our house.
学校は私たちの家から三キロのところにあります

953.

Do – Desu ka/Suru (de-su-ka/su-ru)ですか/する
Kōcha ka kōhī dchira ga osuki **desu ka**?
Do you prefer tea or coffee?
紅茶かコーヒーどっちがお好きですか

954.

Meeting Friends – Tomodachi to au (to-mo-da-chi to a-u)友達と会う
Watashi wa konya **tomodachi to au** yotei desu.
I will be **meeting friends** tonight.
私は今夜友達と会う予定です

955.

Need – Hitsuyou (hit-su-you)必要
Otetudai ga **hitsuyou** desu ka?
Do you **need** help?
お手伝いが必要ですか

956.

Which Person? – Dare to (da-re to)誰と
Anata wa **dare to** tsukiaitai desu ka?
Which person would you like to date?
あなたは誰と付き合いたいですか

957.

Problem – Mondai (mon-dai)問題
Watashi wa **mondai** o kakaete imasu, tasukete moraemasu ka?
I have a **problem**, can you help me?
私は問題を抱えています、助けてもらえますか

958.

Last Night – Sakuya (sa-ku-ya)昨夜
Sakuya watashi wa osoku kitaku shimashita.
Last night I came home late.
昨夜私は遅く帰宅しました

959.

Question – Shitsumon (shit-su-mon)質問
Kare wa amarini mo ōku no **shitsumon** o shite imasu.
He is asking too many **questions**.
彼はあまりにも多くの質問をしています

960.

Put – Nuru (nu-ru)塗る
Anata wa takusan no keshō o **nutte** imasu.
You **put** on a lot of makeup.
あなたは沢山の化粧を塗っています

961.

Find – Mitsukeru (mit-su-ke-ru)見つかる
Pasupōto wa **mitsukari**mashita ka?
Did you **find** your passport?
パスポートは見つかりましたか

962.
District – Chiku (chi-ku)地区
Raishū watashitachi wa betsu no **chiku** ni hikkoshimasu.
We are moving to another **district** next week.
来週私たちは別の地区に引っ越します

963.
Always – Itsumademo (it-su-ma-de-mo)いつまでも
Watashi wa anata no koto o **itsumade** mo aishimasu.
I will **always** love you.
私はあなたのことをいつまでも愛します

964.
Basement – Chika (chi-ka)地下
Watashi no furui jitensha wa **chika** ni arimasu.
My old bicycle is in the **basement**.
私の古い自転車は地下にあります

965.
Bone – Hone (ho-ne)骨
Kare no hone ga orete iru
His bone is broken.
彼の骨が折れている

966.
Possible – Kanō (ka-no)可能
Sore wa **kanō** desu ka?
It is **possible** to make that?
それは可能ですか

967.

Cute – Kawaī (ka-wa-i)かわいい
Kanojo no akachan wa hontōni **kawaī** desu.
Her baby is really **cute**.
彼女の赤ちゃんは本当にかわいいです

968.

Girl – On nanoko (on na-no-ko)女の子
Kono **on nanoko** wa utsukushikute atamagaī desu.
This **girl** is beautiful and smart.
この女の子は美しくて頭がいいです

969.

Relax – Rirakkusu (ri-rak-ku-su)リラックス
Rirakkusu shite hirune o shite kudasai.
Relax and take a nap.
リラックスして昼寝をしてください

970.

Cry – Naku (na-ku)泣く
Akachan wa onaka ga suite iru toki ni **naki**masu.
Babies **cry** when they are hungry.
赤ちゃんはお腹がすいているときに泣きます

971.

Burn – Yakedo (ya-ke-do)焼けど
Yakedo shinaide kudasai.
Be careful, don't **burn** yourself.
焼けどしないでください

972.

Word – Kotoba (ko-to-ba)言葉
Kanojo wa kare ga itta subete no **kotoba**o oboete iru.
She remembers every **word** he said.
彼女は彼が言ったすべての言葉を覚えている

973.

War – Sensō (sen-so)戦争
Sensō wa kowakute kiken desu.
War is scary and dangerous.
戦争は怖くて危険です

974.

Favour – Kiku/Ageru (ki-ku/age-ru)きく/あげる
Onegai o **kiite** moraemasu ka?
Can you do me a **favour**?
お願いを聞いてもらえますか

975.

Handsome – Kakkoī (ka-kko-i)かっこいい
Tai ni wa takusan no **kakkoī** dansei ga imasu.
There are many **handsome** men in Thailand.
タイには沢山カッコいい男性がいます

976.

Allow – Yurusu (yu-ru-su)許す
Okāsan wa neko ga sotoni desuno o **yurushi**masen.
Mom doesn't **allow** the cat to go out.
お母さんは猫が外にでるのを許しません

977.

Arrive – Tōchaku (to-cha-ku)到着
Jikandōrini **tōchaku** suru yō ni shite kudasai.
Make sure to **arrive** on time.
時間通りに到着するようにしてください

978.

Don't - ...naide (nai-de)・・・ないで
Atsuinode fure**naide** kudasai.
Don't touch that, its hot.
熱いので触れないでください

979.

Letter – Tegami (te-ga-mi)手紙
Watashi wa kinō no asa kono **tegami** o uketorimashita.
I received this **letter** yesterday morning.
私は昨日の朝この手紙を受け取りました

980.

Injured – Fushō (fu-sho)負傷
Kare wa jidōsha jiko de jū**shō** o otta
He was badly **injured** in a car accident.
彼は自動車事故で重傷を負った

981.

Dinner – Yūshoku (yu-sho-ku)夕食
Yūshoku wa oishikatta desu.
The **dinner** was delicious.
夕食はおいしかったです

982.

Bottom – Saikabu (sai-ka-bu)最下部
Anata no shomei o pēji no **saikabu**ni oite kudasai.
Put your signature at the **bottom** of the page.
あなたの署名をページの最下部においてください

983.

Look – Miru (mi-ru)見る
Anata ga **mireba**hinode o miru koto ga dekimasu.
If you **look** you can see the sunrise.
あなたが見れば日ノ出を見ることができます

984.

So that's why - ...dakara (da-ka-ra)・・・だから
Anata wa tabete inai**kara**, okotte iru no desu.
You haven't eaten, **so that's why** you're angry.
あなたは食べていないから怒っているのです

985.

People – Hitobito (hi-to-bi-to)人々
Watashi wa ryokō de ōku no samazamana**hitobito** ni aimashita.
I met so many different **people** on my trip.
私は旅行で多くの様々な人々に会いました

986.

Cloth – Nuno (nu-no)布
Karera wa sono iro de saigo no **nuno** o katta.
They bought the last piece of **cloth** in that colour.
彼らはその色で最後の布を買った

987.

Date – Dēto (de-to)デート
Kare wa saisho no **dēto** no ato koi ni ochita.
He fell in love after the first **date**.
彼は最初のデートのあと恋に落ちた

988.

Fork – Fōku (fo-ku)フォーク
Tēburu ni wa **fōku** to naifu o tsukaubeki desu.
You should use a **fork** and a knife at the table.
テーブルにはフォークとナイフを使うべきです

989.

Upset – Okoru (oko-ru)おこる
Kanojo wa sōgi de **okotte**ita.
She was **upset** at the funeral.
彼女は葬儀でおこっていた

990.

Diarrhoea – Geri (ge-ri)げり
Sono resutoran de tabetaato, min'na **geri** o shita.
Everyone had **diarrhoea** after eating from that restaurant.
そのレストランで食べたあとみんな下痢をした

991.

All – Subete (su-be-te)すべて
Subete no kuruma wa kōka desu
All the cars are expensive.
すべての車は高価です

992.

Blow – Fuku (fu-ku)ふく
Watashi wa pātī no tame ni goju-ko no fūsen o **fuka**nakereba narimasen.
I have to **blow** 50 balloons for the party.
私はパーティのために50個の風船を吹かなければなりません

993.

Visit – Tazuneru (ta-zu-ne-ru)たずねる
Kanojo wa itsu oba o **tazune** mashita ka?
When did she **visit** her aunt?
彼女はいつ叔母を訪ねましたか

994.

Present – Purezento (pu-re-zen-to)プレゼント
Watashitachi ga kanojo ni okutta **purezento** wa kanojo o nakasemashita.
The **present** we gave her made her cry.
私たちが彼女に送ったプレゼントは彼女を泣かせました

995.

Is It Enough? – Sorede jūbun desu ka? (so-re-de ju-bun de-su ka)それで充分ですか
Tamago ga futatsu arimasu, **sorede jūbun desu ka**?
I have two eggs, **is it enough**?
卵が二つあります、それで十分ですか

996.

Glass – Garasu (ga-ra-su)ガラス
Watashi wa ima-yō no **garasu**tēburu ga hitsuyō desu.
I need a **glass** table for my living room.
私は今用のガラステーブルが必要です

997.

Muscle – Kin'niku (kin-ni-ku)　筋肉
Watashi no **kin'niku** wa torēningu no ato ni itai.
My **muscles** hurt after the workout.
私の筋肉はトレーニングのあとに痛い

998.

Email - Denshi mēru (den-shi me-ru)電子メール
Shashin o **denshi mēru** de okutte kudasai.
Email me the photos.
写真を電子メールで送ってください

999.

Knife – Naifu (nai-fu)ナイフ
Hanbāgā o **naifu** de kitte kudasai, sousuruto tabe yasuku narimasu.
Use a **knife** to cut the burger, it will be easier to eat.
ハンバーガーをナイフで切ってください、そうすると食べやすくなります

1000.

Come On – Sā (Sa)さぁ
Sā, issho ni odorimashou.
Come on, dance with us.
さぁ一緒に踊りましょう

1001.

Health – Kenkō (ken-ko)健康
Kenkō dato iukoto wa mottomo jūyōna koto desu.
Health is the most important thing you have.
健康だということは最も重要なことです

1002.

Embarrassed – Hazukashī (ha-zu-ka-shi)恥ずかしい
Watashi wa imamade konnani **hazukashi** kata koto wa nai.
I have never been so **embarrassed** before.
私は今までにこんなに恥ずかしかったことはない

1003.
To Manage – Kanri suru (kan-ri su-ru)管理する
Kanri suru koto ga takusan arimasu.
I have a lot of things **to manage**.
管理することが沢山あります

1004.
To Smoke – Kitsuen suru (kit-su-en su-ru)喫煙する
Kanojo wa gakusei no koro **kitsuen shite** imashita.
She used **to smoke** when she was a student.
彼女は学生の頃喫煙していました

1005.
Person – Hito (hi-to)
Watashitachiha kono shigoto ni fusawashī **hito** o sagashiteimasu.
We are looking for the right **person** for this job.
私たちはこの仕事にふさわしい人を探しています

1006.
Lost – Maigo (mai-go)迷子
Kono machi de **maigo** ni naritakunai.
I don't want to get **lost** in this city.
この町で迷子になりたくない

1007.
Boat – Fune (fu-ne)船
Anata wa soko de fune o kariru koto ga dekimasu
You can rent a **boat** there.
あなたはそこで船を借りることができます

1008.
Index Finger – Hitosashi yubi (hi-to-sa-shi yu-bi)人差し指
Doawoshimeru to **hitosashi-yubi** ga itai.
I hurt my **index finger** when I closed the door.
ドアを閉めると人差し指が痛い

1009.

Soon – Suguni (su-gu-ni)すぐに
Watashi wa **sugu ni** shuppatsu shimasu.
I will be leaving **soon**.
私はすぐに出発します

1010.

Man – Otoko (o-to-ko)男
Watashi wa kono **otoko** o shin'yō shimasen.
I do not trust this **man**.
私はこの男を信用しません

1011.

Flag – Hata (ha-ta)旗
Country's flag – Kokki (ko-kki)
Anata no kuni no **kokki** wa nani iro desu ka?
What colour is your **country's flag**?
あなたの国の国旗は何色ですか

1012.

Center – Mannaka (man-na-ka)真ん中
Heya no **mannaka** ni funsui ga arimashita.
There was a fountain in the **center** of the room.
部屋の真ん中に噴水がありました

1013.

Ring – Yubiwa (yu-bi-wa)指輪
Watashi wa kekkon **yubiwa** o hameru dake desu.
I only wear my wedding **ring**.
私は結婚指輪をはめるだけです

1014.

Enemy – Teki (te-ki)敵
Kare wa watashi no **teki** dewa arimasen.
He is not my **enemy**.
彼は私の敵ではありません

1015.

Electricity – Denki (den-ki)電気
Denki o mudani shinaide, akari o keshite kudasai.
Don’t waste **electricity**, turn off the light.
電気を無駄にしないで、灯りを消してください

1016.

Taste – Ajimi (a-ji-mi)味見
Kono kēki no **ajimi** o shite mimashou.
Let me **taste** this cake.
このケーキの味見をしてみましょう

1017.

Nut – Nattu (nat-tu)ナッツ
Burajiru no **nattsu** wa totemo herushī desu.
Brazilian **nuts** are very healthy.
ブラジルのナッツはとてもヘルシーです

1018.

Been – Itta koto (itta ko-to)いったこと
Watashi wa takusan no kuni ni **itta koto** ga arimasu
I have **been** to many countries.
私は沢山の国に行ったことがあります

1019.

Urinate – Hainyō (hai-nyo)排尿
Kokode de**hainyō** shinaide kudasai.
You shouldn’t **urinate** here.
ここで排尿しないでください

1020.

Buttocks – Oshiri (o-shi-ri)おしり
Watashi no **oshiri** wa amarini mo nagaiaida suwatte irukara itai desu.
My **buttocks** are hurting from sitting down for too long.
私のおしりはあまりにも長い間座っているから痛いです

1021.

Hungry – Onaka ga suku (o-na-ka gasu-ku)お腹がすく
Jimugo wa itsumo **onaka ga suki**masu.
I am always get **hungry** after the gym.
ジムの後はいつもお腹がすきます

1022.

Until – Made (ma-de)まで
Karera wa asunoasa **made** koko ni iru koto ga dekimasu.
They can stay here **until** tomorrow morning.
彼らは明日の朝までここにいることができます

1023.

Loose – Yurui (yu-ru-i)ゆるい
Watashi wa taijū ga hetta, watashi no jīnzu wa ima **yurunde** iru.
I've lost weight, my jeans are **loose** now.
私は体重が減った、私のジーンズは今緩いです

1024.

Tissue – Tisshu (ti-shu)ティッシュ
Tisshu no hako wa shokkitana no naka ni arimasu.
The box of **tissues** is in the cupboard.
ティッシュの箱は食器棚の中にあります

1025.

Incorrect – Machigai (ma-chi-gai)間違い
Anata no kotae wa **machiga**tte imasu.
Your answer is **incorrect**.
あなたの答えは間違っています

1026.

Round – En (en)えん
Kono **en**taku wa kōka ni mimasu.
This **round** table looks expensive.
この円卓は高価に見えます

1027.

Arrived – Tōchaku (to-cha-ku)到着
Watashitachi no hikōki wa jikandōrini **tōchaku** shita.
Our plane **arrived** on time.
私たちの飛行機は時間通りに到着した

1028.

Airplane – Hikōki (hi-ko-ki)飛行機
Chīsana **hikōki** ga jōkyaku o matte imashita.
A small **airplane** was waiting for the passengers.
小さな飛行機が乗客を待っていました

1029.

Exercise – Undō (un-do)運動
Suiei wa kodomo ni totte yoi **undo** desu.
Swimming is good **exercise** for kids.
水泳は子供にとって良い運動です

1030.

Begin – Hajimaru (ha-ji-ma-ru)始まる
Kōgi ga **hajimarou** to shite imasu.
The lecture is about to **begin**.
講義がはじまろうとしています

1031.

Dig – Horu (ho-ru)
Heishitachi wa ōkina ana o **hora**nakereba narimasen deshita.
The soldiers had to **dig** a big hole.
兵士たちは大きな穴をほらなければなりませんでした

1032.

Ticket – Chiketto (chi-ketto)チケット
Karera wa watashitachi ni shō no muryō **chiketto** o kureta.
They gave us free **tickets** to the show.
彼らは私たちにショーの無料チケットをくれた

1033.

Spit – Haku (ha-ku)はく
Anata wa dōro ni tuba o **haite** wa ikemasen.
You cannot **spit** on the roads.
あなたは道路につばをはいてはいけません

1034.

Panties - Pantī (pan-tie)パンティ
Atarashī **pantī** o kau no o wasurenaide kudasai.
Don’t forget to buy new **panties**.
新しいパンティを買うのを忘れないでください

1035.

Change – Kōkan (ko-kan)交換
Taiya o **kōkan** suru hitsuyō ga arimasu.
I need to change the tire.
タイヤを交換する必要があります

1036.

Alone – Hitori (hi-to-ri)一人
Watashi o koko ni**hitori** ni shinaide kudasai.
Don’t leave me **alone** here.
私をここに一人にしないでください

1037.

Not Everyone – Daremoga (da-re-mo-ga)だれもが
Daremoga kono shigoto o dekiru wakede wa arimasen.
Not everyone can do this job.
誰もがこの仕事をできるわけではありません

1038.

Quickly – Hayaku (ha-ya-ku)はやく
Karera ga anata o miru mae ni, **hayaku** tachisarou.
Leave **quickly**, before they see you.
彼らがあなたを見る前に早く立ち去ろう

1039.

Ask – Kiku (ki-ku)きく

Watashi ni shitsumon ga areba **kiite**mo ī desu.

You can**ask** me any questions.

私に質問があればきいてもいいです

1040.

Pen – Pen (pen)ペン

Pen karite mo ī?

Can I borrow a **pen**?

ペン借りてもいい

1041.

Noisy – Sōzōshī (so-zo-shee)騒々しい

Kono basho wa **sōzōshī** desu, dokoka shizuka ni ikimashou.

This place is **noisy**, let's go somewhere quiet.

この場所は騒々しいです、どこか静かにいきましょう

1042.

Absent Minded – Uwanosora (u-wa-no-so-ra)上の空

Kare wa kesshite kiite inai, kare wa **uwanosora** desu.

He never listens, he is **absent-minded**.

彼は決して聞いていない、彼は上の空です

1043.

Want – Iru (i-ru)いる

Sore wa **iri**masen.

I don't **want** it.

それはいりません

1044.

Take Out – Dasu (da-su)だす

Ryōshin ga ie ni kaeru mae ni gomi o **dashite** kudasai.

Take out the rubbish before your parents are home.

両親が家に帰る前にごみを出してください

1045.
Broken – Kowareteiru (ko-wa-re-tei-ru)壊れている
Isu ni suwatte wa ikemasen, **kowarete** iru.
Don't sit on the chair, its **broken**.
椅子に座ってはいけません、壊れている

1046.
I'm ...Watashi wa...desu (wa-ta-shiwa...de-su)私は・・・です
Watashi wa sensei **desu**.
I'm a teacher.
私は先生です

1047.
Itch – Kaku (ka-ku)かく
Kaku to akka shimasu.
If you **itch** it, it will become worse.
掻くと悪化します

1048.
Outstanding – Subarashī (su-ba-ra-shee)素晴らしい
Kanojo no engi wa **subarashi**katta.
Her performance was **outstanding**.
彼女の演技は素晴らしかった

1049.
Love – Aishiteru (ai-shi-te-ru)愛してる
Watashi wa anata o **aishiteru**.
I **love** you.
私はあなたを愛してる

1050.
Coin – Kōka (ko-ka)硬貨
Sono kikai wa**kōka**shika ukeiremasen.
The machine only accepts **coins**.
その機械は硬貨しかうけいれません

1051.

Facial Hair – Kao no ke (kao no ke)顔の毛
Watashi wa kare no **kao no ke**ga kiraidesu, kare ni sotte hoshī desu.
I hate his **facial hair**, I want him to shave.
私は彼の顔の毛が嫌いです彼にそってほしいです

1052.
Late – Chikoku (chi-ko-ku)遅刻
Chikoku shite sumimasen.
I am sorry for being **late**.
遅刻してすみません

1053.
Flower – Hana (ha-na)花
Kare wa kanojo ni kinenbi no**hana** o agemashita.
He gave her a **flower** for their anniversary.
彼は彼女に記念日の花をあげました

1054.
Minus – Mainasu (mai-na-su)マイナス
Soto wa **mainasu** Ju-do desu.
It's **minus** ten degrees outside.
外はマイナス十度です

1055.
Hang – Kakeru (ka-ke-ru)かける
Kōto o yōfuku dansu ni **kakemasu**.
Hang your coat in the wardrobe.
コートを洋服ダンスにかけます

1056.
Go On A Trip - Ryokō ni ikimasu (ryo-ko ni iki-ma-su)旅行に行きます
Raigetsu Amerika e **ryokō ni ikimasu**.
We will **go a trip** to America next month.
来月アメリカへ旅行に行きます

1057.
Umbrella – Kasa (ka-sa)傘

Ame ga futte imasu, **kasa** o motte kudasai.
It's raining, take your **umbrella**.
雨が降っています、傘をもってください

1058.
Rock – Iwa (i-wa)岩
Kare wa mizūmi ni **iwa** o nageta.
He threw a **rock** into the lake.
彼は湖に岩を投げた

1059.
Give Me – Kudasai (ku-da-sai)ください
Hanmā o **kudasai**.
Give me the hammer.
ハンマーをください

1060.
From – Shusshin (shu-sshin)出身
Watashitachi no atarashī sensei wa Furansu **shusshin** desu.
Our new teacher is **from** France.
私たちの新しい先生はフランス出身です

1061.
Repeat – Kurikaesu (ku-ri-kae-su)繰り返す
Sore o kurikaeshite kuremasen ka?
Can you **repeat** that?
それを繰り返してくれませんか

1062.
Rose – Bara (ba-ra)バラ
Watashinohaha wa akai **bara** ga suki desu.
My mother likes red **roses**.
私の母は赤いバラが好きです

1063.
Turn off – Dengen o kiru (den-gen o ki-ru)電源を切る

Terebi no **dengen o kiri**nasai, anata wa benkyō suru hitsuyō ga arimasu.
Turn off the TV, you need to study.
テレビの電源を切りなさい、あなたは勉強する必要があります

1064.
Don't Like – Kirai (ki-ra-i)嫌い
Watashi wa sakana no nioi ga **kirai** desu.
I don't like the smell of fish.
私は魚のにおいが嫌いです

1065.
Every Day – Mainichi (mai-ni-chi)毎日
Ryūchō ni naritainara, **Mainichi** renshū shinakereba narimasen.
If you want to be fluent, you must practise **every day**.
流暢になりたいなら、毎日練習しなければなりません

1066.
Wind – Kaze (ka-ze)風
Kaze ga watashi no bōshi o fukitobashita.
The **wind** is blew my hat off.
風が私の帽子を吹き飛ばした

1067.
Sick – Kibun ga warui (ki-bun ga wa-ru-i)気分が悪い
Watashi wa hikō-go **kibun ga waruku** natta.
I felt **sick** after the flight.
私は飛行後気分が悪くなった

1068.
Fill Out – Kinyū (ki-nyu)記入
Mōshikomi yōshi ni **kinyū** shite watashi ni watashite kudasai.
Fill out the form and hand it back to me.
申込用紙に記入して私にわたしてください

1069.
Remove – Torihazusu (to-ri-ha-zu-su)とりはずす

Watashi wa kare ni sono e o **torihazushite** moraitai.
I want him to **remove** that picture.
私は彼にその絵をとりはずしてもらいたい

1070.
Something – …nakoto (na-ko-to)・・なこと
Kare wa watashi ni totemo jūyō**na koto** o itta.
He told me **something** very important.
彼は私にとても重要なことを言った

1071.
Truth – Hontō no koto (hon-to n -ko-to)本当のこと
Hontōno koto o oshietekudasai, naniga okottano desu ka?
Tell me the **truth**, what happened?
本当のことを教えてください、何がおこったのですか

1072.
Station – Eki (e-ki)駅
Watashitachi wa **eki** ni modotte densha ni notta.
We walked back to the **station** and caught the train.
私たちは駅に戻って電車に乗った

1073.
Other – Hokano (ho-ka-no)ほかの
Watashi no kamera wa **hokano** kaban ni haitte imasu.
My camera is in the **other** bag.
私のカメラはほかの鞄に入っています

1074.
I'm sorry – Gomen'nasai (go-men na-sai)ごめんなさい
Sakende **gomen nasai**.
I'm sorry for shouting at you.
叫んでごめんなさい

1075.
Joke – Jōdan (jo-dan)冗談

Sore wa **jōdan** deshita ga, kanojo wa omoshiroi to omowanakatta.
It was a **joke** but she did not find it funny.
それは冗談でしたが彼女はおもしろいと思わなかった

1076.
What Time Is It? – Nanji desu ka? (nan-ji de-su ka)何時ですか
Tokei o nakushimashite, **nanji desu ka**?
I've lost my watch, **what time is it**?
時計をなくしまして、何時ですか

1077.
Correct – Tadashī (ta-da-shee)正しい
Anata no kotae wa **tadashī** desu, arigatō.
Your answer is **correct**, thank you.
あなたの答えは正しいです、ありがとう

1078.
Hammer – Hanmā (han-ma)ハンマー
Kono kugi ni wa ōkina **hanmā** ga hitsuyō desu.
I need a big **hammer** for this nail.
この釘には大きなハンマーが必要です

1079.
Mat – Matto (ma-tto)マット
Yūbin haitatsuin wa doa no **matto** no ue ni nimotsu o oita.
The postman left the package on the door **mat**.
郵便配達員はドアのマットの上に荷物を置いた

1080.
King – Ō (ou)王
Ō wa nan-sai desu ka?
How old is the **king?**
王は何歳ですか

1081.
Sometimes – Tokidoki (to-ki-do-ki)時々

Tokidoki kanojo wa arukōru o nomimasu.
Sometimes she drinks alcohol.
時々彼女はアルコールを飲みます

1082.
Ruler – Jōgi (jo-gi)定規
Jōgi o kashite moraemasu ka?
Can I borrow a **ruler**?
定規を貸してもらえますか

1083.
Perfect – Kanpeki (kan-pe-ki)完璧
Kanojo no egao wa **kanpeki**dato omoimasu.
I think her smile is **perfect**.
彼女の笑顔は完璧だと思います

1084.
Run Out – Tarinai (ta-ri-nai)たりない
Gyūnyū ga **tarinaku** narimashita.
We have **run out** of milk.
牛乳がたりなくなりました

1085.
That Way – Sochira desu (so-chi-ra de-su)そちらです
Toire wa **sochira desu**.
The toilets are **that way**.
トイレはそちらです

1086.
Just – Bakari (ba-ka-ri)ばかり
Watashi wa ima suwatta **bakari** desu, atode sore o shimasu
I have **just** sat down, I will do it later.
私は今座ったばかりです、あとでそれをします

1087.
Meaning – Imi (i-mi)意味

Kono uta no **imi** wa nani desu ka?
What is the **meaning** of this song?
この歌の意味はなにですか

1088.
Prince – Ōji (o-ji)王子
Ōji wa totemo hansamudaga, amari atama ga yokunai.
The **prince** is very handsome but not very smart.
王子はとてもハンサムだが、あまり頭がよくない

1089.
Sex – Sekkusu (sek-ku-su)セックス
Sekkusu ni tsuite hanasu to kanojo wa kinchō suru.
She gets nervous when we talk about **sex**.
セックスにういて話すと彼女は緊張する

1090.
Coming – Kiteiru (ki-tei-ru)きている
Kono inu wa maiasa watashitachi no ie ni **kite imasu**.
This dog keeps **coming** to our house every morning.
この犬は毎朝私たちの家にきています

1091.
Now – Ima (i-ma)今
Watashi wa **ima** sukoshi isogashī desu, atode denwa shite kudasai.
I'm a bit busy **now**, call me later.
私は今少し忙しです、後で電話してください

1092.
Name – Namae (na-ma-e)名前
Kanojo no **namae** wa nan desu ka?
What is her **name**?
彼女の名前はなんですか

1093.
Saliva – Daeki (dae-ki)唾液
Inu no kuchi kara **daeki** ga shitatari ochita.

Saliva dripped from the dogs mouth.
犬の口から唾液がしたたりおちた

1094.

Newspaper – Shinbun (shin-bun)新聞
Sono otoko wa densha no naka de **shinbun** o yonde imashita.
The man was reading the **newspaper** on the train.
その男は電車の中で新聞を読んでいました

1095.

Tooth – Ha (ha)歯
Haisha wa kare no ushiro no **ha** o nuita.
The dentist removed his back **tooth**.
いた
歯医者は彼の後ろの歯を抜いた

1096.

Same – Onaji (o-na-ji)同じ
Watashitachiha **onaji**doshi desu.
We are the **same** age.
私たちは同じ年です

1097.

Show – Miseru (mi-se-ru)見せる
Shashin o **misete** kudasai.
Show me the picture.
写真を見せてください

1098.

Children – Kodomotachi (ko-do-mo-ta-chi)こどもたち
Watashi no **kodomotachi** wa watashi o shiawaseni shimasu.
My **children** make me happy.
私の子供たちは私を幸せにします

1099.

Ceiling – Tenjō (ten-jo)天井

Naze kare wa **tenjō** o kiiro ni nutta no desu ka?
Why did he paint the **ceiling** yellow?
なぜ彼は天井を黄色に塗ったのですか

1100.

Can – Kan (kan)かん
Kan ni wa mada tōmorokoshi ga arimasu.
There is still some corn in the **can**.
缶にはまだトウモロコシがあります

1101.

Difference – Chigai (chi-gai)違い
Kōhī to kōcha no **chigai** wa nan desu ka?
What is the **difference** between coffee and tea?
コーヒーと紅茶の違いはなんですか

1102.

Bored – Taikutsu (tai-kut-su)退屈
Anata ga **taikutsu** shiteiru nonaraba, hon o yonde kudasai.
If your **bored**, read a book.
あなたが退屈しているのならば、本を読んでください

1103.

Please Forgive Me – Yurushite kudasai (yu-ru-shi-te ku-da-sai)許してください
Yurushitekudasai, watashi wa mada anata o aishiteimasu.
Please forgive me, I still love you.
許してください、私はまだあなたを愛しています

1104.

This – Kono (ko-no)この
Kono sukāfu wa yawarakai desu ga, kubi ga kayuku narimasu.
This scarf is soft but it makes my neck itchy.
このスカーフは柔らかいですが、首がかゆくなります

1105.

Tired – Tsukareru (tsu-ka-re-ru)疲れる
Watashi no neko wa itsumo **tsukarete** iru.
My cat is always **tired**.
私の猫はいつも疲れている

1106.
Place – Basho (ba-sho)場所
Kono **basho** wa chīsakute shizuka desu.
This **place** is small and quiet.
この場所は小さくて静かです

1107.
Complicated – Fukuzatsu (fu-ku-zat-su)複雑
Sore wa **fukuzatsuna** mondai desu, tasuke ga hitsuyō desu.
It's a **complicated** issue, I need help.
それは複雑な問題です、助けが必要です

1108.
Funny – Omoshiroi (o-mo-shi-roi)面白い
Kare no tomodachi wa **omoshiroi**, kare wa min'na o warawaseru.
His friend is **funny**, he makes everyone laugh.
彼の友達は面白い彼はみんなを笑わせる

1109.
Bike – Jitensha (ji-ten-sha)自転車
Shako ni aru anata no **jitensha** o dashite kudasai.
Out your **bike** in the garage.
車庫にあるあなたの自転車をだしてください

1110.
Area – Atari (a-ta-ri)あたり
Kono **atari** de kekkō desu, takushī o tomete kudasai.
This **area** is fine, please stop the taxi.
このあたりでけっこうです、タクシーをとめてください

1111.

Address – Jūsho (ju-sho)住所
Anata no **jūsho** wa nan desu ka?
What is your **address**?
あなたの住所はなんですか

1112.

Break – Kowasu (ko-wa-su)壊す
Kiotsukete, **kowa**sanaide kudasai.
Be careful, don't **break** it.
気を付けて　壊さないでください

1113.

Depends – Kakaru (ka-ka-ru)かかる
Anata no seikō wa anata no doryoku ni **kakatte** imasu.
Your success **depends** on your effort.
あなたの成功はあなたの努力にかかっています

1114.

Spoon – Supūn (su-pun)スプーン
Anata wa sūpu o taberu tame ni **supūn** ga hitsuyō desu.
You need a **spoon** to eat soup.
あなたはスープを食べるためにスプーンが必要です

1115.

Seat – Seki (se-ki)席
Kare wa sono rō fujin ni jibun no **seki** o yuzutta.
He gave the old lady his **seat**.
彼はその老婦人に自分の席を譲った

1116.

What Floor? – Nan-kai? (nan-kai)何階
Anata no apāto no**nan-kai** desu ka?
What floor is your apartment on?
あなたのアパートの何階ですか

1117.

Taxi – Takushī (ta-ku-shi)タクシー
Takushī to yonde mo ī desu ka?
Can you call us a **taxi**?
タクシーと呼んでもいいですか

1118.
Ugly – Minikui (mi-ni-kui)醜い
Kanojo wa jibun ga **minikui** to omotte imasuga, utsukushī desu.
She thinks she's **ugly**, but she is beautiful.
彼女は自分が醜いと思っていますが美しいです

1119.
Take Off – Nugu (nu-gu)脱ぐ
Ie ni hairu mae ni kutsu o **nuide** kudasai.
Take off your shoes before entering the house.
家に入る前に靴を脱いでください

1120.
Farm – Nōjō (no-jo)農場
Kare no oji wa ōkina **nōjō** o shoyū shite imasu.
His uncle owns a big **farm**.
彼の叔父は大きな農場を所有しています

1121.
Teach – Oshieru (o-shi-e-ru)教える
Rirī wa gakkō de furansugo o **oshiete** imasu.
Lily **teaches** French at the school.
リリーは学校でフランス語を教えています

1122.
Ready – Junbi (jun-bi)準備
Tabi no **junbi** wa dekite imasu ka?
Are you **ready** for the trip?
旅の準備はできていますか

1123.

Crawl – Hau (ha-u)はう
Sono akachan wa yuka o yokogitte **hatta**.
The baby **crawled** across the floor.
その赤ちゃんは床を横切ってはった

1124.

Steal – Nusumu (nu-su-mu)ぬすむ
Kare wa nidoto **nusum**anai to itta.
He said that he would never **steal** again.
彼は二度と盗まないといった

1125.

Man – Otoko (o-to-ko)男
Otoko wa kanojo no tame ni tobira o aketa.
The **man** opened the door for her.
男あ彼女のためにとびらをあけた

1126.

Feel – Kibun (ki-bun)気分
Kyō no **kibun**wa dō desu ka?
How do you **feel** today?
今日の気分はどうですか

1127.

Nobody – Daremo (da-re-mo)誰も
Neko ga doko ni itta no ka **daremo**shiranai.
Nobody knows where the cat went.
猫がどこにいったのか誰もしらない

1128.

Mad – Okoru (oko-ru)おこる
Okoranaide, Jōdan desu.
Don't be **mad**, it's a joke.
怒らないで、冗談です

1129.

Every Month – Maitsuki (mait-su-ki)毎月
Kanojo wa **maitsuki** ani o tazuneru.
She visits her brother **every month**.
彼女は毎月兄を訪ねる

1130.

Try On – Shichaku (shi-cha-ku)試着
Sore ga auka kono shatsu o **shichaku** mite kudasai.
Try on this shirt to see if it fits.
それが合うかこのシャツを試着してみてください

1131.

Patient – Gaman (ga-man)がまん
Gaman shite kudasai, watashitachi no junban wa tsugi desu.
Be **patient**, we are next in the Que.
我慢してください、私たちの順番は次です

1132.

Famous – Yūmei (yu-mei)有名
Wattopō wa **yūmei**na jiin desu.
Wat pho is a **famous** temle.
ワットポーは有名な寺院です

1133.

Child – Kodomo (ko-do-mo)子供
Kore wa anata no **kodomo** desu ka, Nan-sai desu ka?
Is this your **child**, how old is he?
これはあなたの子供ですか、何歳ですか

1134.

Other People's Children - Tanin no kodomotachi (ta-nin no ko-do-mo-tachi)他人のこどもたち
Tanin no kodomotachi ga watashi o nayama semasu.
Other people's children annoy me.
他人の子供たちが私を悩ませます

1135.

These – Korera (ko-re-ra)これら
Korera no kutsu wa kitsu sugiru.
These shoes are too tight.
これらの靴はきつすぎる

1136.

Everywhere – Itarutokoro (i-ta-ru-to-ko-ro)いたるところ
Watashi wa kono machi no **itarutokoro** ni ikimashita.
I've been **everywhere** in this city.
私はこの町のいたるところに行きました

1137.

Tree – Ki (ki)木
Watashi no inu wa kono **ki** ga suki desu.
My dog likes this **tree**.
私の犬はこの木が好きです

1138.

Someone – Dareka (da-re-ka)だれか
Darekaga kinō watashi ni denwa shita.
Someone called me yesterday.
誰かが昨日私に電話した

1139.

Stomach ache – Onaka ga itai (o-na-ka ga itai)お腹が痛い
Sōtai shite mo ī desu ka? **Onaka ga itai** desu.
Can I go home early? I have a **stomach ache**.
早退してもいいですかお腹が痛いです

1140.

Toilet – Toire (toi-re) トイレ
Toire wa ittu-kai ni arimasu.
The **toilet** is downstairs on the ground floor.
トイレは一階にあります

1141.

Dizzy – Memai (me-mai)めまい
Watashi wa sukoshi**memai** o kanjimasu, suwaru hitsuyō ga arimasu.
I feel a bit **dizzy**, I need to sit down.
私は少しめまいを感じます、座る必要があります

1142.
Outside – Soto ni deru (so-to ni de-ru)外にでる
Soto ni detemimashou. Utsukushī hi desu.
Let's go **outside**. It's a beautiful day.
外にでて見ましょう　美しい日です

1143.
Shame – Hajiru (ha-ji-ru)恥じる
Kanojo wa jibun ga shita koto ni **hajiru** koto wa arimasen.
She doesn't have any **shame** after what she's done.
彼女は自分がしたことに恥じることはありません

1144.
Please – Kudasai (ku-da-sai)ください
Ju-punkan musuko o mitete **kudasai**.
Please, look after my son for 10 minutes.
１０分間息子をみててください

1145.
Fool – Baka (ba-ka)ばか
Kare wa **baka** mitai ni furumau.
He acts like a **fool**.
彼は馬鹿みたいにふるまう

1146.
Favourite – Okiniiri (o-ki-ni-iri)お気に入り
Kōhī wa watashino **okiniiri** no nomimono desu.
Coffee is my **favourite** drink.
コーヒーは私のお気に入りの飲み物です

1147.

Those – Sorerano (so-re-ra-no)それらの
Sorerano utsukushī hana o mite kudasai.
Look at **those** beautiful flowers!
それらの美しい花を見てください

1148.

Hate – Kirai (ki-ra-i)嫌い
Watashi wa karai tabemono ga **kirai** desu.
I **hate** spicy food.
私は辛い食べ物が嫌いです

1149.

Glasses – Megane (me-ga-ne)めがね
Sūjī wa akai **megane** o kakete imashita.
Suzy was wearing red **glasses**.
スージーは赤いめがねをかけていました

1150.

With – Issho ni (i-sho ni)一緒に
Kon'ya wa birī to **issho ni** ikimasu ka?
Are you going **with** Billy tonight?
今夜はビリーと一緒に行きますか

1151.

Because – Nanode (na-no-de)なので
Herushī**nanode** sarada o tabemasu.
I eat salad **because** it is healthy.
ヘルシーなのでサラダを食べます

1152.

None – Daremo (da-re-mo)だれも
Seito wa **daremo**shiken no junbi o shite inakatta.
None of the students were prepared for the exam.
生徒は誰も試験の準備をしていなかった

1153.

Entrance – Iriguchi (i-ri-gu-chi)入口
Kurabu no **iriguchi** ni gādo ga imashita.
There was a guard at the club **entrance**.
クラブの入口にガードがいました

1154.
What's Your Phone Number -
Anata no denwabangō wa nan ban desu ka?
(a-na-ta no denwa-bango wa nan ban de-su ka)
Anata wa kawaī desu ne.あなたの電話番号は何番ですか
Anata no denwabangō wa nan ban desu ka?
You are pretty. **What's your phone number**?
あなたの電話番号は何番ですか

1155.
End – Owari (o-wa-ri)終わり
Kore de kare no kyaria no **owari** desu.
This is the **end** of his career.
これで彼のキャリアの終わりです

1156.
Pick Up – Dakiageta (da-kia-ge-ta) 抱き上げた
Kare wa sono akachan o **dakiageta**.
He **picked up** the baby.
彼はその赤ちゃんを抱きあげた

1157.
Backpack – Ryukku (ryu-kku)リュック
Watashi wa itsumo **ryukku**o seotte ryokō shimasu.
I always travel with my **backpack**.
私はいつもリュックを背負って旅行します

1158.
Take a Picture – Shashin o toru (sha-shin o to-ru)写真をとる
Watashitachi no **shashin o totte** moraemasu ka?
Can you **take a picture** of us, please?
私たちの写真をとってもらえますか

1159.

Together – Issho ni (issho-ni)一緒に
Watashitachiha **issho ni** jimu ni ikimashita.
We went to the gym **together**.
私たちは一緒にジムに行きました

1160.

Before – Izen (i-zen)以前
Watashi wa kono on'nanoko ni **izen** atta koto ga aru to omou.
I think I've met this girl **before**.
私はおの女の子に以前あったことがあると思う

1161.

Painful – Itai (i-tai)痛い
Watashi wa yubi o kitteshimatta, itai desu.
I cut my finger, it is **painful**.
私は指を切ってしまった、痛いです

1162.

Interested – Kyōmi (kyo-mi)興味
Mōshiwakearimasenga, kono ibento ni wa **kyōmi** ga arimasen.
Sorry, I am not **interested** in this event.
申し訳ありませんがこのイベントには興味がありません

1163.

Flu – Infuruenza (in-furu-enza)インフルエンザ
Infuruenza ni kakatte irunara, beddoni ite kudasai.
Stay in bed if you have the **flu**.
インフルエンザにかかっているなら、ベッドにいてください

1164.

So – Dakara (da-ka-ra)だから
Dakara kyō wa ikemasen.
So that's why I can't go today.
だから今日は行けません

1165.

New – Atarashī (ata-ra-shee)新しい
Watashi no ani wa **atarashī** terebi o kaimashita.
My brother bought a **new** tv.
私の兄は新しいテレビを買いました

1166.

Busy – Isogashī (iso-ga-shee)忙しい
Watashi wa totemo **isogashī** desu, ima wa hanasemasen.
I am very **busy**, I cannot speak now.
私はとても忙しいです、今は話せません

1167.

Writing – Hikki (hi-kki)筆記
Hikki shiken wa mottomo kon'nan'na bubun deshita.
The **writing** test was the most difficult part.
筆記試験は最も困難な部分でした

1168.

Keep The Change – Otsuri wa irimasen (o-tsu-ri wa i-ri-ma-sen)おつりはいりません
Tabemono wa oishi. **Otsuri wa irimasen**.
The food is tasty,**keep the change**.
食べ物は美味しい　おつりはいりません

1169.

Saw – Mita (mi-ta)見た
Sakuya, watashitachi no sensei o naitokurabu de **mita**.
I **saw** our teacher at a nightclub last night.
昨夜、私たちの先生をナイトクラブで見た

1170.

Next – Jikai (ji-kai)次回
Jikai wa issho ni ikimasu.
Next time we will go together.

次回は一緒に行きます

1171.

Crying – Naku (na-ku)泣く
Riyū mo nanoni **naku** no o yamero.
Stop **crying** for no reason.
理由もないのに泣くのをやめろ

1172.

Queen – Joō (jo-o)女王
Subete no josei wa **joō** desu.
Every woman is a **queen**.
すべての女性は女王です

1173.

Injury – Kega (ke-ga)怪我
Untenshu wa **kega** de ayauku shinu tokoro deshita.
The driver almost died because of the **injury**.
運転手は怪我で危うく死ぬところでした

1174.

Street – Tori (to-ri)通り
Dono **tori**?
Which **street**?
どの通り

1175.

Excited – Kōfun (ko-fun)興奮
Kodomo-tachi wa tanjōbi pātī ni **kōfun** shite imashita.
The kids were **excited** about the birthday party.
子供たちは誕生日パーティに興奮していました

1176.

Passport – Pasupōto (pa-su-po-to)パスポート
Pasupōto o funshitsu shita to omoimasu.
I think I have lost my **passport**.

パスポートを紛失したと思います

1177.

Pinkie – Koyubi (ko-yu-bi)小指
Koyubi wa ichiban chīsana yubi desu.
Pinkie is the smallest finger.
小指は一番小さな指です

1178.

Car – Kuruma (ku-ru-ma)車
Watashi wa ju-hachi-sai no toki ni saisho no **kuruma** o katta.
I got my first **car** when I was 18.
私は１８歳のときに最初の車を買った

1179.

Bitter – Nigai (ni-ga-i)苦い
Dākuchokorēto wa **nigai** desu.
Dark chocolate is **bitter**.
ダークチョコレートは苦いです

1180.

Excuse Me – Sumimasen (su-mi-ma-sen)すみません
Sumimasen, okanjo o moraemasu ka?
Excuse me, can I get the bill?
すみません、お勘定をもらえますか

1181.

Neither – Dochiramo (do-chi-ra-mo)どちらも
Dochiramo eigo ga hanasemasen.
Neither of them can speak English.
どちらも英語が話せません

1182.

Bad Luck – Fuun (fu-un)不運
Watashi wa **fuun** o shinjite imasen.
I don't believe in **bad luck**.

私は不運を信じていません

1183.

Drunk – Yopparau (yo-ppa-rau)酔っぱらう
Yopparatteru no?
Are you **drunk**?
酔っぱらってるの

1184.

To Call Someone – Denwa o suru (den-wa o su-ru)電話をする
WaAnata wa kare ni **denwa o suru** koto ga dekimasu?
Can you **call** him?
あなたは彼に電話をすることができますか

1185.

Tourist – Kankōkyaku (kan-kok-ya-ku)観光客
Machi no kono eria ni wa ōku no **kankōkyaku** ga imasu.
There are many **tourists** in this part of the town.
町のこのエリアには多くの観光客がいます

1186.

Life – Jinsei (jin-sei)人生
Anata ni attekara watashino**jinsei** wa yoku natta.
My **life** got better when I met you.
あなたに会ってから私の人生は良くなった

1187.

Danger - Kiken ni sarasarete iru (ki-ken ni sa-ra-sa-re-tei-ru)危険にさらされている
Samu wa **kiken ni sarasarete iru**.
Sam is in **danger**.
サムは

1188.

Fall – Korogeru (ko-ro ge-ru)転げる
Korogeu kara, hashiranai.
Don’t run, you will **fall**.

転げるから走らない

1189.

Me – Watashi (wa-ta-shi)私
Doa o akete kudasai,**watashi** desu.
Open the door, it's **me**.
ドアを開けてください、私です

1190.

Bad – Warui (wa-ru-i)悪い
Subete no **warui** tabemono o sutemasu.
Throw away all the **bad** food.
すべての悪い食べ物を捨てます

1191.

Parents – Ryōshin (ryo-shin)両親
Ryōshin o tsuneni sonkei shite kudasai.
Always respect your **parents**.
両親お常に尊敬してください

1192.

Last – Saigo (sai-go)最後
Watashi ga **saigo** ni kanojo ni atta no wa ju-nen mae desu.
The **last** time I saw her was 10 years ago.
私が最後に彼女に会ったのは十年前です

1193.

Jealous – Shittobukai (shi-tto-bu-kai)嫉妬深い
Kanojo no otto wa totemo **shittobukai** hito desu.
Her husband is very **jealous** man.
彼女の夫はとても嫉妬深い人です

1194.

Only – Dake (da-ke)だけ
Watashi wa Bankoku ni itta koto ga aru **dake** desu.
I have **only**been to Bangkok.

私はバンコクに行ったことがあるだけです

1195.

Sleeping – Nemutte (ne-mu-tte)眠って
Mearī wa saikin amari yoku **nemutte** imasen.
Mary is not **sleeping** very well these days.
メアリーは最近あまりよく眠っていません

1196.

See – Miseru (mi-se-ru)見せる
Mibun-shō o **misete** itadakemasu ka?
Can I **see** your ID please?
身分証を見せていただけますか

1197.

Stop – …naide (nai-de)・・ないで
Hito o mitsume**naide** kudasai.
Stop staring at people.
人をみつめないでください

1198.

Finish – Oeru (o-e-ru)終える
Anata wa mazu shukudai o **oenakereba** narimasen.
You must **finish** your homework first.
あなたはまず宿題を終えなければなりません

1199.

Shut Up – Damare (da-ma-re)黙れ
Damatte watashi no iu koto o kiki nasai.
Shut up and listen to me.
黙って私の言うことを聞きなさい

1200.

Free Time – Hima na toki (hi-ma na to-ki)暇なとき
Anata ga **hima na toki** ni watashi ni denwa shite kudasai.
Call me when you have **free time**.

あなたが暇なときに私に電話してください

1201.

Wall – Kabe (ka-be)壁

Kono **kabe** o nurubeki desu.

We should paint this **wall**.

この壁を塗るべきです

1202.

Say – Iu (i-u)言う

Nani mo kangaezu ni bakanakoto o **iu** hito mo imasu.

Some people **say** stupid things without thinking.

何も考えずにばかなことを言うひともいます

1203.

Camera – Kamera (ka-me-ra)カメラ

Kare wa kōkana **kamera** o nakushita

He lost his expensive **camera**.

彼は高価なカメラをなくした

1204.

Gun – Kenjū (ken-ju)拳銃

Kenjū wa omocha dewa arimasen.

A **gun** is not a toy.

拳銃はおもちゃではありません

1205.

Let's Go – Ikimasho (iki-ma-sho)行きましょう

Sanpo ni **ikimashou**.

Let's go for a walk.

散歩に行きましょう

1206.

Hurt – Itameru (ita-me-ru)傷める

Watashi wa shigoto de senaka **o itame**ta.

I **hurt** my back at work.

私は仕事で背中を傷めた

1207.

Pregnant – Ninshin chū (ni-shin chu)妊娠中
Ninshin chū no josei wa totemo utsukushī desu.
Pregnant women are very beautiful.
妊娠中の女性はとても美しいです

1208.

Again – Mōichido (mo-ichi-do)もう一度
Mōichidoittekudasai?
Can you say that **again** please?
もう一度言ってください

1209.

Noise – Sōon (so-on)騒音
Kono hitotachi wa takusan no **sōon** o dashite imasu.
These people are making lots of **noise**.
この人たちは沢山の騒音をだしています

1210.

What Is It? – Na desu ka? (nan de-su ka)何ですか
Sagashimono wa **nan desu ka**?
What is it you're looking for?
探しものは何ですか

1211.

Middle Finger – Nakayubi (na-ka yu-bi)中指
Rūshī wa kanojo no **nakayubi** ni yubiwa o hamete iru.
Lucy wears a ring on her **middle finger**.
ルーシーは彼女の中指に指輪をはめている

1212.

Win – Katsu (kat-su)勝つ
Chanpion wa tsuneni **kachi**masu.
Champions always **win**.

チャンピョンは常に勝ちます

1213.

Crazy People – Kurutta hitobito (ku-ru-tta hi-to-bi-to)狂った人々
Kurutta hitobito kara hanarete kudasai
Stay away from **crazy people**.
狂った人々から離れてください

1214.

Relaxed – Rirakkusu (ri-ra-kku-su)リラックス
Yoga wa watashi o **rirakkusu** sa semasu.
Yoga makes me feel **relaxed**.
ヨガは私をリラックスさせます

1215.

Good Evening – Konbanwa (kon-ban-wa)こんばんは
Konbanwa, soshite watashinoie e yōkoso.
Good evening and welcome to my house.
こんばんは　そして私の家へようこそ

1216.

Worst – Saiaku (sai-aku)最悪
Getsuyōbi wa shūno **saiaku** no hi desu.
Monday is the **worst** day of the week.
月曜日は週の最悪の日です

1217.

Every time - ...tabi ni (ta-bi-ni)・・・たびに
Watashi wa anata ni au **tabi ni** hohoemimasu.
I smile **every time** I see you.
私はあなたに会うたびに微笑みます

1218.

Night Time – Yakan (ya-kan)夜間
Tokidoki, karera wa **yakan** ni hatarakanakereba narimasen.
Sometimes, they have to work at **night time**.

時々、彼らは夜間に働かなければなりません

1219.

Turn – Magaru (ma-ga-ru)曲がる
Kono tōri e hidari ni **magatte** kudasai.
Turn left to this street.
この通りへ左に曲がってください

1220.

Think That – To omoimasu (to o-moi-ma-su)と思います
Kare wa kono shigoto ni pittarida **to omoimasu.**
I **think that** he is perfect for this job.
彼はこの仕事にぴったりだと思います

1221.

Often – Yoku (yo-ku)よく
Watashi wa **yoku** haha o tazunemasu.
I **often** visit my mother.
私はよく母を訪ねます

1222.

Main – Shu (shu)主
Kono eiga no **shu**jinkō wa dare desu ka?
Who is the **main** character of this movie?
この映画の主人公は誰ですか

1223.

Lesson – Jugyō (ju-gyo)授業
Watashi wa riyū mo naku **jugyō** o minogasu koto wa nakatta.
I never missed a **lesson** without a reason.
私は理由もなく授業を見逃すことはなかった

1224.

After - …no ato (no-a-to)・・のあと
Shigoto **no ato** ni aimashou!
See you **after** work!

仕事の後に会いましょう！

1225.

Looks Like – Niru (ni-ru)似る
Kono otokonoko wa chichioya ni **nite**iru.
This boy **looks like** his father.
この男の子は父親に似ている

1226.

Screw – Neji (ne-ji)ねじ
Kono **neji** wa suchīrusei desu.
This **screw** is made of steel.
このねじはスチール製です

1227.

Bus – Basu (ba-su)バス
Watashi wa **basu** de shigoto ni ikimasu.
I go to work by **bus**.
私はバスで仕事に行きます

1228.

Moment – Shibaraku (shi-ba-ra-ku)しばらく
Shibaraku shite akachan ga naki hajimemashita.
A **moment** later the baby started crying.
しばらくして赤ちゃんが泣き始めました

1229.

Trap – Wana (wa-na)罠
Chūi shite kudasai, soreha **wana** desu.
Be careful, it's a **trap**.
注意してください、それは罠です

1230.

Afraid – Kowai (ko-wai)怖い
Watashi no neko wa inu ga **kowai**.
My cat is **afraid** of dogs.

私の猫は犬が怖い

1231.

Agree – Dōi (doi)同意
Kanzen ni anata ni**dōi** shimasu.
I totally **agree** with you.
完全にあなたに同意します

1232.

Anybody – Daredemo (da-re-de-mo)誰でも
Daredemo machigai o okasu kanōsei ga aru.
Anybody can make a mistake.
誰も間違いをおかす可能性がある

1233.

Weird – Henjin (hen-jin)変人
Daremo **henjin** ga suki dewa arimasen.
Nobody likes **weird** people.
誰も変人が好きではありません

1234.

Fart – Onara (o-na-ra)おなら
Hitomae de **onara**o shinaide kudasai
Please don’t **fart** in public.
人前でおならしないでください

1235.

Train – Ressha (re-sha)列車
Watashitachi wa mada **ressha** ni noru made go-fun arimasu.
We still have five minutes to catch the **train**.
私たちはまだ列車に乗るまで五分あります

1236.

Television – Terebi (te-re-bi)テレビ
Terebi wa jūyōna jōhōgen desu.
Television is an important source of information.

テレビあ重要な情報源です

1237.

Stuck – Hamaru (ha-ma-ru)はまる
Karera wa maiasa kōtsū jūtai **ni hamari**masu.
They get **stuck** in traffic every morning.
彼らは毎朝交通渋滞にはまります

1238.

Which way – Dochira (do-chi-ra)どちら
Dochira ni ikeba ī desu ka.
Which way should I go now?
どちらに行けばいいですか

1239.

Wish – Yokattanoni (yo-katta-no-ni)よかったのに
Watashi wa haha no yō ni kashikokereba **yokattanon**i.
I **wish** I was as smart as my mother.
私は母のように賢ければよかったのに

1240.

Document – Shiryō (shi-ryo)資料
Kono **shiryō** taisha made ni motte kite kudasai.
Bring me this **document** by the end of the day.
この資料退社までにもってきてください

1241.

Subway – Chikatetsu (chi-ka-tet-su)地下鉄
Watashi wa **chikatetsu** o hotondo no baai tsukaimasu.
I use **subway** most of the time.
私は地下鉄をほとんどの場合つかいます

1242.

Pay – Harau (ha-rau)払う
Yūshoku no daikin o **harawa** sete kudasai.
Let me **pay** for your dinner.

夕食の代金を払わせてください

1243.

Angry – Okoru (o-ko-ru)怒る
Watashi wa **okotte** imasen, tsukarete imasu.
I am not **angry**, I am tired.
私は怒っていません、疲れています

1244.

Happy – Manzoku (man-zo-ku)満足
Anata wa atarashī shigoto ni **manzoku** shite imasu ka?
Are you **happy** with a new job?
あなたは新しい仕事に満足していますか

1245.

Fight – Kenka (ken-ka)喧嘩
Otokonoko wa itsumo**kenka** shimasu.
Boys always **fight** with each other.
男の子はいつも喧嘩します

1246.

Slowly – Yukkuri (yuk-ku-ri)ゆっくり
Suberi yasuinode **yukkuri** arukimashou.
Walk **slowly** because it's slippery.
すべりやすいのでゆっくり歩きましょう

1247.

Half – Hanbun (han-bun)半分
Hanbun dake agete kudasai.
Give me **half** only.
半分だけあげてください

1248.

Decision – Ketsudan (ket-su-dan)決断
Watashitachiha issho ni kono **ketsudan** o kudashimasu.
We make this **decision** together.

私たちは一緒にこの決断をくだします

1249.

Wrist – Tekubi (te-ku-bi)手首
Kanojo no **tekubi** niwa utsukushī buresuretto ga arimashita.
There was a beautiful bracelet on her **wrist**.
彼女の手首には美しいブレスレットがありました

1250.

Lie – Yoko ni naru (yo-ko ni na-ru)横になる
Yoko ni natte shibaraku rirakkusu shite kudasai.
Lie down and relax for a while.
横になってしばらくリラックスしてください

1251.

Gold – Kin (kin)金
Kono ringu wa **kin** de dekite imasu.
This ring is made of **gold**.
このリングは金でできています

1252.

Should - ...bekidesu (be-ki-de-su)・・・べきです
Anata wa watashi ga itte iru koto ni mimiwokatamukeru**bekidesu**.
You **should** listen to what I am saying.
あなたは私の言っていることに耳を傾けるべきです

1253.

Building – Tatemono (tate-mo-no)建物
Kare no kazoku wa senshū betsu no **tatemono** ni hikkoshita.
His family moved to another **building** last week.
彼の家族は先週別の建物に引っ越した

1254.

Window – Mado (ma-do)窓
Karera wa kūki o tōsu tame ni **mado** o aketa.
They opened the **window** to let air pass through.

彼らは空気を通すために窓を開けた

1255.

Maybe – Tabun (ta-bun)多分

Tabun rainen wa motto yoi ichinen o okuru koto ga dekiru deshou.

Maybe we will have a better life next year.

多分来年はもっと良い一年を送ることができるでしょう

1256.

Grammar – Bunpo (bun-po)文法

Bunpō wa muzukashī koto ga arimasu.

Grammar can be difficult.

文法は難しいことがあります

1257.

Learn – Narau (na-ra-u)習う

Kanojo wa mōsugu eigo o **narai**tai desu.

She would like to **learn** English soon.

彼女あもうすぐ英語を習いたいです

1258.

How Much – ikura (iku-ra)いくら

Chūko-sha ni **ikura** haraimasu ka?

How much are you willing to pay for a second hand car?

中古車にくら払いますか

1259.

Dead – Shibō (shi-bou)死亡

Sumimasen, anata no inu wa **shinde** imasu

I'm sorry, you dog is **dead**.

すみません、あなたの犬は死んでいます

1260.

Door – Doa (do-a)ドア

Doawo shimeru.

Close the **door.**

ドアを閉める

1261.

Talk – Hanashi (ha-na-shi)話
Watashi wa karera no jōshi to **hanashi** o shitai no desu ga.
I would like to **talk** to their manager.
私は彼らの上司と話をしたいのですが

1262.

Bring – Motte iku (mo-tte iku)もっていく
Anata ni onsen e essensharuoiru o **motte itte** hoshī desu.
I want you to **bring** the essential oils for the spa.
あなたに温泉へエッセンシャルオイルをもっていってほしいです

1263.

Dream – Yume miru (yu-me mi-ru)夢見る
Watashi wa seikō suru koto o **yumemite** imasu.
I **dream** of being successful.
私は成功することを夢見ています

1264.

Idiot – Baka (ba-ka)馬鹿
Kare wa jibun ga **baka** dato omoi tsuzuketa.
He kept on thinking that he is an **idiot**.
彼は自分が馬鹿だと思い続けた

1265.

Slipper – Surippa (su-rippa)スリッパ
Kanojo no hokano **surippa** wa sunahama de nakunatta.
Her other **slipper** was lost at the beach.
彼女の他のスリッパは砂浜でなくなった

1266.

Stand – Tatsu (tat-su)立つ
Stand straight – Chokuritsu (cho-ku-ri-tsu)直立
Yoi shisei o tamotsu tame ni wa, **chokuritsu** suru hitsuyō ga arimasu.

I need to **stand straight** regularly to have good posture.
良い姿勢を保つためには直立する必要があります

1267.
Brush – Migaku (mi-ga-ku)磨く
Karera wa yuka nikōtaku deru made **migaku** deshou.
They will **brush** the floor until it is shiny.
彼らは床に光沢でるまで磨くでしょう

1268.
Bill – Seikyū sho (sei-kyusho)請求書
Seikyū showa okurete todoita.
The **bill** arrived late.
請求書は遅れて届いた

1269.
Lights – Akari (a-ka-ri)灯り
Subete no **akari**ga kieta.
All the **lights** were turned off.
すべての灯りが消えた

1270.
Defecate – Haiben (hai-ben)排便
Watashi wa **haiben** suru hitsuyō ga arimasu
I need to **defecate**.
私は排便する必要があります

1271.
Book – Hon (hon)本
Watashi wa ryokō suru toki wa itsumo **hon** o motteikimasu.
I always bring a **book** with me when I travel.
私は旅行するときはいつも本を持っていきます

1272.
Pot – Nabe (na-be)なべ
Kitchindana no nakani wa ōkina **nabe** ga arimasu.

There is a huge **pot** inside the kitchen cabinet.
キッチン棚のなかには大きな鍋があります

1273.

University – Daigaku (dai-ga-ku)大学
Daigaku wa watashi no kenkyū ni yosan o dashimashita.
The **University** gave a budget for my research.
大学は私の研究に予算を出しました

1274.

Who Is That – Dare desu ka (da-re desu ka)誰ですか
Ichinichijū anata to issho ni iru hito wa **dare desu ka?**
Who is that person with you all day?
一日中あなたと一緒にいる人は誰ですか

1275.

Town – Machi (ma-chi)町
Machi ni matsuri ga arimasu**.**
There is a festival in **town.**
町に祭りがあります

1276.

Picture – Shashin (sha-shin)写真
Watashitachi no kurasu **shashin** wa kōtei de totta mono desu.
Our class **picture** was taken at the schoolyard.
私たちのクラス写真は校庭でとったものです

1277.

Beautiful – Utsukushī (ut-su-ku-shee)美しい
Kanojo no egao wa totemo utsukushī.
Her smile is so beautiful.
彼女の笑顔はとても美しい

1278.

Dust – Hokori (ho-ko-ri)埃

Heya wa hokori-darake
The room is full of **dust**.
部屋は埃だらけ

1279.
Sad – Kanashī (ka-na-shee)悲しい
Watashi wa hijō ni kanashī desu
I feel very sad.
私は非常に悲しいです

1280.
Scissors – Hasami (ha-sa-mi)はさみ
Watashi no **hasami** wa mō nanimo kiru koto ga dekimasen deshita.
My **scissors** could not cut things anymore.
私のはさみはもうなにも切ることができませんでした

1281.
Blood – Chi (chi)血
Kizu kara **chi** ga detekimasu.
There is **blood** coming out from the wound.
傷から血が出てきます

1282.
Country – Kuni (ku-ni)国
Sono **kuni** wa genzai kaigenreika ni oka rete iru.
The **country** is now placed under martial law.
その国は現在戒厳令下におかれている

1283.
Customer – Kokyaku (kok-ya-ku)顧客
Kokyaku wa watashi ni shiharai o watashita.
The **customer** handed me her payment.
顧客は私に支払いを渡した

1284.
Try – Tamesu (ta-me-su)試す

Watashi wa jinsei no naka de atarashī koto o **tamesu** hitsuyō ga arimasu.
I need to **try** new things in my life.
私は人生のなかで新しいことを試す必要があります

1285.

Kill – Korosu (ko-ro-su)殺す
Watashi wa shōdōbutsu o **korosu** hōhō o shitte imasu.
I know how to **kill** small animals.
私は小動物を殺す方法を知っています

1286.

Enough – Jūbun (ju-bun)十分
Tabemono wa jūbun desu ka?
Is the food enough?
食べ物は十分ですか

1287.

Too much – …sugairu (su-gai-ru)・・・過ぎる
Kōshinryō ga ō sugiru
Too much spice.
香辛料が多すぎる

1288.

Sleep – Nemuru (ne-mu-ru)眠る
Motto nemuru hitsuyō ga aru
I need to **sleep** more.
もっと眠る必要がある

1289.

Next Time – Jikai (ji-kai)次回
Watashi wa **jikai** machigai o shinai yō ni motto ki o tsukemasu.
I will be more careful not to make mistakes **next time**.
私は次回間違いをしないようにもっと気をつけます

1290.

City – Machi (ma-chi)町

Kono **machi** ni wa takusan no omise ga arimasu.
There are so many shops in this **city**.
この町には沢山のお店があります

1291.

Traffic – Kōtsū ryō (kot-suryo)交通量
Shinai no **kōtsū ryō** wa taerarenai.
The **traffic** in the city is almost unbearable.
市内の交通量は耐えられない

1292.

Wedding – Kekkonshiki (kek-kon-shi-ki)結婚式
Kekkonshiki wa itsu desu ka?
When is the **wedding**?
結婚式はいつですか

1293.

Language – Kotoba (ko-to-ba)言葉
Futari no hōmon-sha no aida niwa **kotoba** no kabe ga arimasu.
There is a **language** barrier between the two visitors.
二人の訪問者の間には言葉の壁があります

1294.

Telephone – Denwa (den-wa) 電話
Karera wa **denwa** o tsukatte byōin ni tsuita.
They used a **telephone** to reach the hospital.
彼らは電話を使って病院についた

1295.

Both – Ryōhō (ryo-ho)両方
Watashitachi **ryōhō**tomo raigetsu kaigai ni iku yotei desu.
Both of us are going abroad next month.
私たち両方とも来月海外に行く予定です

1296.

Here – Kokoni (ko-ko-ni)ここに

Watashi wa megane o **kokoni** oite itta.
I left the glasses over **here**.
私はめがねをここに置いていった

1297.

Very – Hijo/totemo (hi-jo/to-te-mo)非常/とても
Kyō wa totemo atsui.
it is very hot today.
今日はとても暑い

1298.

Almost – Hotondo (ho-ton-do)ほとんど
Watashi wa hotondo haha no tanjōbi o wasurete imashita
I **almost** forgot mom's birthday.
私はほとんど母の誕生日を忘れていました

1299.

Keep – Tamotsu (ta-mot-su)保つ
Atama o massugu ni tamotsu.
Keep your head straight.
頭をまっすぐに保つ

1300.

But – Desu ga (de-su-ga)ですが
Gaishutsu shitai no **desu ga**, okane o tsukaitaku wa arimasen.
I want to go out **but** I don't want to spend money.
外出したいのですが、お金を使いたくはありません

1301.

Free – Muryō (mu-ryo)無料
Watashi wa gakkou no fea de **muryō** no shinamono o te ni iremashita.
I got **free** items at the school fair.
私は学校のフェアで無料の品物を手にいれました

1302.

For – Tameni (ta-me-ni)ために

Watashi wa shōrai no **tameni** takusan no gisei o haratte imasu.
I am doing a lot of sacrifices **for** my future.
私は将来のために沢山の犠牲を払っています

1303.

Should Not – Surubeki dewa nai (su-ru-be-ki de-wanai)するべきではない
Watashitachiha kantan ni tanin no handan **surubekide wa arimasen**.
We **should not** judge other people too easily.
私たちは簡単に他人を判断するべきではありません

1304.

Know – Shiru (shi-ru)知る
Anata wa kare o **shitte** imasu ka
Do you **know** him?
あなたは彼を知っていますか

1305.

Calm Down – Ochituite (o-chit-su-ite)落ち着いて
Ochitsuite mokuhyō ni shūchū suru hitsuyō ga arimasu.
I need to **calm down** and focus on my goal.
落ち着いて目標に集中する必要があります

1306.

Many – Ōku (o-ku)多く
Ōkunohitobito ga shin seifu ni nayande imasu.
Many people are bothered about the new government.
多くの人々が新政府に悩んでいます

1307.

Somebody – Darekaga (da-re-ka-ga)誰かが
Darekaga watashi no keikaku o tedasuke shite kurerudeshou.
Somebody will help me in my project.
誰かが私の計画を手助けしてくれるでしょう

1308.

Everything – Subete (su-be-te)すべて

Watashi wa jibun de **subete** o manabimashita.
I learned **everything** on my own.
私は自分ですべてを学びました

1309.
Wood – Ki (ki)木
Karera wa kyanpufaiyā no tame ni **ki** o kitta
They chopped **wood** for the campfire.
彼らはキャンプファイヤーのために木を切った

1310.
Don't Want - …takunai (ta-ku-nai)・・たくない
Karera wa nayami**takunai**.
They **don't want** to get in trouble.
彼らは悩みたくない

1311.
Important – Jūyō (ju-yo)重要
Tomodachi ni tsutaeru tame no **jūyō**na messēji ga arimasu.
I have an **important**message to tell to my friends.
友達に伝えるための重要なメッセージがあります

1312.
Annoying – Meiwaku (mei-wa-ku)迷惑
Kono-ko wa totemo **meiwaku** desu
This child is so **annoying**.
この子はとても迷惑です

1313.
Like – Suki (su-ki)好き
Watashi wa akarui iro no akusesarī o tsukeru no ga **suki** desu.
I **like** wearing bright coloured accessories.
私は明るい色のアクセサリーをつけるのが好きです

1314.
Did – Mashita ka? (ma-shi-ta ka)ましたか

Anata wa sono mise ni iki**mashita ka**?
Did you go to the shop?
あなたはその店に行きましたか

1315.

Good – Yoku (yo-ku)よく
Daremoga **yoku** naru yō ni tsutomerubeki desu.
Everybody should try to be **good**.
誰もがよくなるように努めるべきです

1316.

Comb – Kushi (ku-shi)くし
Surudoi **kushi** wa kanojo no atama o kizutsukete imasu.
The sharp **comb** is hurting her head.
鋭いくしは彼女の頭を傷つけています

1317.

Its Okay – Daijōbu desu (dai-jo-bude-su)大丈夫です
Tokini machigai o okashite mo **daijōbu desu.**
It's okay to make mistakes sometimes.
時に間違いをおかしても大丈夫です

1318.

Voice – Koe (ko-e)声
Kanojo no **koe** wa ochitsuite anshin saseru.
Her **voice** is calming and soothing.
彼女の声は落ち着いて安心させる

1319.

Eye – Me (meh)目
Hidari**me** ga itai.
I hurt my left **eye**.
左目が痛い

1320.

Needle – Hari (ha-ri)針

Kare wa itsumo **hari** o osorete ita.
He has always been afraid of **needles**.
彼はいつも針を恐れていた

1321.
Want To - …tai (tai)・・たい
Watashi wa doresu o kai**tai** desu.
I **want to** buy a dress.
私はドレスを着たいです

1322.
Am - …desu (de-su)・・です
Watashi wa kyōshi **desu**.
I **am** a Teacher.
私は教師です

1323.
Good Morning – Ohayōgozaimasu (o-ha-yo-go-zai-ma-su)おはようございます
Sensei ni au tabi ni **ohayōgozaimasu** to iimasu.
Every time I see my teacher I say **good morning**.
先生に会うたびにおはようございますと言います

1324.
Ghost – Yūrei (yu-rei)幽霊
Anata wa **yūrei** o osorete imasu ka?
Are you afraid of **ghosts**?
あなたは幽霊を恐れていますか

1325.
To Have – Motsu (mot-su)持つ
Ōkina ie o **mochi**tai desu.
I want **to have** a big house.
大きな家を持ちたいです

1326.

Return – Henkyaku (hen-kya-ku)返却
Hon o kyō toshokan ni **henkyaku** shinakereba narimasen.
I have to **return** the books to the library today.
本を今日図書館に返却しなければなりません

1327.

Job – shokugyō (sho-ku-gyo)職業
Anata no **shokugyō** wa nan desu ka?
What is your **job**?
あなたの職業はなんですか

1328.

Holiday – kyūjitsu (kyu-ji-tsu)休日
Ashita wa **kyūjitsu**nanode, shigoto ni iku hitsuyō wa arimasen.
It's a **holiday** tomorrow, I don't have to go work.
明日は休日なので仕事に行く必要はありません

1329.

Kiss – Kisu (ki-su)キス
Watashi wa kare ni **kisu** o shitai desu.
I want to **kiss** him.
私は彼にキスをしたいです

1330.

Ship – Fune (fu-ne)船
Watashitachi no **fune** wa mō minato ni arimasu.
Our **ship** is in the harbour already.
私たちの船はもう港にあります

1331.

Sand – Suna (su-na)砂
Sunahama ni itta ato watashi no kaban wa**suna** de ippai desu.
My bag is full of **sand** after the beach.
砂浜に行ったあと私の鞄は砂でいっぱいです

1332.

Brick – Renga (ren-ga)れんが
Dōro wa kiiroi **renga** de dekite imasu.
The road is made of yellow **bricks**.
道路は黄色いレンガでできています

1333.

Place Of Birth – Shusshōchi (shi-sshin-chi)出身地
Watashi wa maitoshi watashi no **shusshōchi** o otozuremasu.
I visit my **place of birth** every year.
私は毎年私の出身地を訪れます

1334.

News – Shirase (shi-ra-se)知らせ
Watashitachiha byōin kara yoi **shirase** o emashita.
We've got good **news** from the hospital.
私たちは病院から良い知らせをえました

1335.

Advice – Jogen (jo-gen)助言
Shiseikatsu ni tsuite no **jogen** wa hitsuyō arimasen.
I don't need **advice** for my private life.
私生活についての助言は必要ありません

1336.

About – Tsuite (tsu-ite)ついて
Jibun ni **tsuite** mottooshiete kudasai.
Tell me more **about** yourself.
自分についてもっと教えてください

1337.

Nearby – Chikaku (chi-ka-ku)近く
Chikaku ni sunde imasu, anata o mukaeni iku koto ga dekimasu.
I live **nearby**, I can pick you up.
近くに住んでいます、あなたを迎えに行くことができます

1338.

Punch – Naguru (na-gu-ru)殴る

Bokusā wa otagai ni takusan **naguri** masu.
Boxers **punch** each other a lot.
ボクサーはお互いに沢山殴ります

1339.

Appointment – Yoyaku (yo-ya-ku)予約
Watashi wa ju-ji ni **yoyaku** o shite imasu.
I have an **appointment** at 10 o'clock.
私は十時に予約をしています

1340.

Any – Itsudemo (itsu-de-mo)いつでも
Itsudemo watashi ni denwa suru koto ga dekimasu.
You can call me at any **moment.**
いつでも私に電話することができます

Conclusion

And there you have it, you've reached the end of this great list of essential words in Japanese. Congratulations, if you have studied these words correctly, your vocabulary in Japanese should have sky rocketed, not to mention your confidence too. Just think how far you've come.

That's amazing progress.

Now you have a solid foundation of grammar and vocabulary which you can build on. All you need to do is combine this with some practice and tutoring lessons, then before you know it your fluency will shoot through the roof.

I am happy to have helped you along your journey in Japanese and hope we'll talk again soon, definitely in another book.

Remember, never give up on your language goals, with the right resources fluency is right around the corner.

Can I ask a quick favor? Would you be kind enough to leave a small review for this book on Amazon? I love hearing feedback from you guys.

Thanks for reading our content. Good luck with your Japanese studies. We'll speak again soon!

Languages World

www.ingramcontent.com/pod-product-compliance
Lightning Source LLC
LaVergne TN
LVHW081054100425
808240LV00004B/346
* 9 7 8 1 9 1 3 4 8 8 0 5 5 *